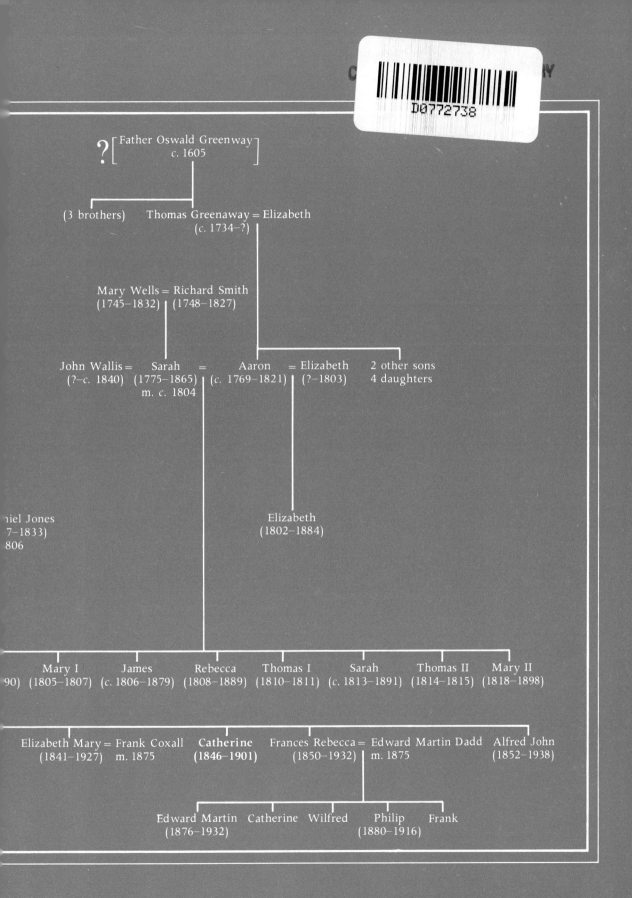

? ⎡Father Oswald Greenway⎤
  ⎣   c. 1605   ⎦

(3 brothers)   Thomas Greenaway = Elizabeth
                     (c. 1734–?)

Mary Wells = Richard Smith
(1745–1832) (1748–1827)

John Wallis =   Sarah   =   Aaron   = Elizabeth   2 other sons
(?–c. 1840) (1775–1865) (c. 1769–1821) (?–1803)   4 daughters
             m. c. 1804

                                Elizabeth
                               (1802–1884)

niel Jones
7–1833)
806

Mary I   James   Rebecca   Thomas I   Sarah   Thomas II   Mary II
90) (1805–1807) (c. 1806–1879) (1808–1889) (1810–1811) (c. 1813–1891) (1814–1815) (1818–1898)

Elizabeth Mary = Frank Coxall   **Catherine**   Frances Rebecca = Edward Martin Dadd   Alfred John
(1841–1927) m. 1875   **(1846–1901)**   (1850–1932) m. 1875   (1852–1938)

        Edward Martin Catherine Wilfred   Philip   Frank
        (1876–1932)   (1880–1916)

KATE GREENAWAY

A Biography

To my Parents

First published by Schocken Books 1981
10 9 8 7 6 5 4 3 2 1   81 82 83 84

Library of Congress Cataloging in Publication Data

Engen, Rodney K
  Kate Greenaway, a biography.
  Includes index.
  1. Greenaway, Kate, 1846-1901. 2. Water-colorists—
England—Biography. 3. Illustrators—England—Biography.
ND1942.G8E54   759.2   80—14850   AACR1

Manufactured in the United States of America

ISBN 0—8052—3775—5

KATE GREENAWAY

A Biography

RODNEY ENGEN

SCHOCKEN BOOKS · NEW YORK

ACKNOWLEDGMENTS

This new biography of Kate Greenaway, the first for over seventy-five years, has been made possible by the kindness of Mr Francis Carpenter, who deposited the surviving Greenaway papers with me, and Mr Aidan Chambers, who generously turned over his preliminary researches to me. I can only hope my book has done justice to the wealth of material that was willingly sent to me during the past six years by the following individuals and institutions, both here in England, and abroad. To them all I wish to record my grateful thanks.

Those individuals offering invaluable help were first of all Bill and Nicola Sandal, with their interest and the enthusiasm of keen Greenaway collectors; and the following: Mrs F. K. Airy, Patricia Allderidge, William Blatherwick, R. A. Brimmell, Leslie F. Brown, Christopher Brunel, G. E. Camm, Charles Chadwyck-Healey, Dr. Wilfrid and Mrs Peggy Coltart, Mrs John Donnelly, Mrs Dora Duncan, John Greenaway, Samuel Gurney, Mr and Mrs Bernard Hammond, Dorothy Hay, Mrs I. A. F. Hayes, Michael Heseltine, Robert Hewison, Michael Hutchins, Robert Inglis, Joyce Jones, Lynton Lamb, E. H. S. Longhurst, Mary Lutyens, Jane Madden, Jeremy Maas, Angela Murphy, Mr and Mrs Peter Opie, E. T. N. Pease-Watkin, Audrey Peter, Eric Quayle, Dorothy W. Raleigh, Katherine Rantzen, Kenneth Rendell, Andrew Saint, Justin Schiller, Arthur Searle, Mrs John Sloan, Miss E. J. Smith, Mrs H. M. Stancomb, the late Sir Charles Tennyson, A. Hessell Tiltman, Mrs Lilian Utting, Dr. H. G. Viljoen, Miss D. E. Houstonne, Ina Ward, Miss E. E. Webb, Dr. Jerry Wood.

Those British institutions that have allowed access to materials include: Allen and Unwin, publishers, Antiquarian Book Review Monthly, Ashmolean Museum, Oxford, Bodleian Library (John Johnson collection), Oxford, Bolton Art Gallery, British Museum and British Library, London Borough of Camden, Christie's, Fine Art Society, Guildhall Library, London Borough of Hackney, Heatherley's School of Art, Islington Library, University of London Library, Manchester City Art Gallery, Mid-Sussex District Council, Nottinghamshire County Council, Phillips, Royal Academy of Arts Library, Ruskin Galleries, Bembridge, Isle of Wight, Slade School, Sotheby's, Tate Gallery, Victoria and Albert Museum Library and Print Room, Witt Library, Cortauld Institute.

Those institutions abroad include: the Baltimore County Library, Boston Public Library, Detroit Public Library, Free Library of Philadelphia, Hunt Institute, Carnegie-Mellon University, Pittsburgh, New York Public Library, Osborne Collection, Toronto Public Library, Pierpont Morgan Library, and the University of Southern Mississippi.

Finally on the production side, I wish to thank my editors Felix Brenner, Caroline Taggart, Jock Curle, my photographer Graham Bush, and my agent Juliet Burton. But most importantly the dedication of my assistant and proofreader Shaun Hammond must not go unacknowledged, for without his help the book could never have been completed.
R. K. E.
London 1980

ILLUSTRATIONS

The author and publishers wish to thank the following for supplying the photographs on the pages listed:

Bodleian Library (John Johnson Collection), Oxford, 103; British Library, London, 10, 45, 54, 88, 89, 124, 125, 130, 140, 143, 206, 209; Camden Borough Library, London, 169; Christie's, London, facing 67, 114, facing 201; Courtauld Institute (Witt Library), London, 80 left, 172; Detroit Public Library, 94; Doris Frohnsdorff, Washington, 8; Greenaway Estate, 74 left, 74 right, 168 foot (3), facing 198 top left, facing 198 top right, facing 198 centre, 220; Hunt Institute, Pittsburgh, 79; Henry E. Huntington Library and Art Gallery, San Marino, California, 43 right; Islington Borough Library, London, 28 top, 28 foot, 35; Lady Lever Art Gallery, Port Sunlight, 170; Archive of Liberty's, London, 218 foot left, 218 foot right; National Portrait Gallery, London, 68; Private Collections, 6, 17, 104 left, 104 right, 105, 156 right, facing 164, 176, 181, 182, 191; Sotheby's, London, 48, 53, 57, 92, 159, 161, 188 left, 188 right; Spielmann and Layard, 18 left, 18 right, 19 left, 19 right, 20, 33 top left, 36 left, 36 right, 39, 47 left, 63, 111, 120 right, 121, 149 left, 183, 196, 202, 204, 217; Victoria and Albert Museum, London, 33 top right, 33 foot left, 33 foot right, 42 left, 42 right, 43 left, 47 right, 50 left, 50 right, 51 left, 51 right, 60, opposite 64 foot, opposite 64 top, 69, 75, 77, 83, 91, 97, opposite 98 top, opposite 98 foot left, opposite 98 foot right, opposite 101 top, opposite 101 foot, 106, 120 left, 127, 129, 132, 133, 134, 146, 147, 149 right, 153, 156 left, 160, 162 left, 162 right, opposite 167, 185, opposite 198 foot, 213, 218 top.

All other photographs are taken from the author's collection.

Contents

John Greenaway, from an old photograph.

1   The Little Lunnoner
1846–1852

Oh, I'll stay in the country, and make a daisy chain
And never go back to London again.

MARIGOLD GARDEN

On 17 March 1846 John and Elizabeth Greenaway's second child was born in a small house in Cavendish Street, Hoxton, London. While it was intended that she should be named Kate, 'as a result of a blunder' she was registered Catherine Greenaway. This birth, with its additional demands on the family's resources, marked a turning point in the lives of the Greenaway parents.

In many respects John and Elizabeth were a well-matched couple. Each had been born into a large working-class family, riddled with domestic turmoil. They had both had to endure the instability of irresponsible parents and relatives, and had both developed into strong-willed, principled adults, determined to make more of their lives than their parents had done.

John Greenaway's struggles began at an early age. Born on 20 September 1816 in Mint Street, Southwark, south of the Thames, he was the son of Aaron Greenaway, owner of a successful second-hand furniture business, established sometime in the late eighteenth century, when his family had moved to London from the Sheerness dockyards. Aaron married twice, fathered nine children and died at the age of fifty-one, five years after John was born. Shortly after his death, his widow, Sarah, sixteen years his junior, made a disastrous second marriage to John Wallis, a Welsh journeyman tailor, who terrorized his new family, drank excessively and squandered all his wife's inheritance of about £450. On more than one occasion young John was called upon to shield his mother or one of the four surviving sisters and two brothers from Wallis's brutal attacks. Eventually, when the boy was fifteen, Wallis was able to free himself from John – a constant threat to his supposed role as head of the family – by apprenticing him for seven years to the London engraver Robert Brandard. Moreover, John was forced to leave home and took lodgings not far away at 15 William Street. There, at some indeterminate time, he began to learn wood-engraving, a skill for which, he perceptively realized, there was an increasing demand. The number of illustrated periodicals published in London had risen astronomically and, according to the London Post Office Directory, in the next twenty years the number of wood-engraving firms would double, from twenty-four at the time of John's apprenticeship to forty-seven in 1852.

About 1840 John Greenaway was introduced to one of the giants of this new profession, Ebenezer Landells. He had served his apprenticeship under Thomas Bewick and by good fortune was searching for eager new talent, when he asked twenty-four-year-old John Greenaway to join his rapidly growing establishment. John immediately agreed, for about this time Wallis's sudden death left Sarah and her children destitute. The need to support his family spurred young Greenaway on and he quickly progressed up the firm's hierarchy to become Landells's assistant. But Landells was (according to the Dalziel brothers) 'a man

The Chappells' cottage kitchen, Rolleston. Pencil sketch by Kate Greenaway.

brimful of ideas and full of energy. One hardly ever met him [but] that he had some new project which was certain to be a fortune – a fortune that never came to him.'[1] For young, impressionable John Greenaway, this relentless optimism was to prove a dangerous example.

Not long after John joined Landells he met Elizabeth Jones, the daughter of Nathaniel Jones, a Welsh-born butcher who worked in Shoreditch with his wife, Rebecca, the daughter of a wealthy Dagenham farmer. Of the Jones family's six children Elizabeth was the second of four girls. At Elizabeth's coming-of-age party in 1833 her father had shocked the family by announcing he would not live out the year. He died shortly after, leaving his wife and children to fend for themselves. The family soon dispersed: the eldest daughter, Sarah, was adopted by an aunt and moved to Rolleston, Nottinghamshire, where she married into a wealthy local family in 1838; the two troublesome brothers, John and James, both emigrated to Canada, where one soon begged Elizabeth to send his mistress and illegitimate child to him.

The break-up of her family must have influenced Elizabeth in her decision to accept John Greenaway's proposal of marriage. Moreover, unlike her brothers, John was a hard worker, with a thoroughly amiable nature; on several occasions he had even made her laugh – a considerable feat, for Elizabeth rarely appreciated frivolity. She had inherited her mother's stern, religious nature, and, above all else, she was resolved to do what was, in her view, morally right. When John asked her to be his wife she was twenty-seven, three years his senior, and must have seen his proposal as an opportunity to escape the threat of lifelong spinsterhood; yet she was certainly fond enough of her fiancé to write him love letters: in later years Kate planned to begin her autobiography with the carefully preserved text from one such letter, written in her mother's hand.

Elizabeth married John Greenaway on 10 May 1840, in the thirteenth-century Lady Chapel of the parish church of St Saviour (now Southwark Cathedral). The ceremony was witnessed by her sister Mary Ann and Mary Ann's fiancé (and John Greenaway's close friend), Joshua Thorne. The newly weds moved to 43 Southampton Street (now Calshot Street), not far from Landells's new offices in Barnsbury. A year later their first child, Elizabeth Mary ('Lizzie') was born. Five years later, after they had moved to Hoxton, to be nearer Elizabeth's mother in Britannia Street (now Britannia Walk), their second child, Kate, was born.[2]

By this time John Greenaway was hoping for a chance to strike out on his own. Shortly after Kate was born, the opportunity arose when a London publisher, Edmund Appleyard, proposed the publication of a series of pictorial inserts to accompany the novels of Charles Dickens. The first of this projected series was a collection of illustrations to a new edition of *Pickwick Papers*, to consist of thirty-two pictures after the drawings of John Gilbert, and to be sold in eight twopenny monthly parts of four full-page engravings each. When John Greenaway was offered the job of engraving these plates and subsequent numbers in the series, he could not refuse. He left Landells and entered into a partnership with a slight acquaintance, William Wright, selecting an office just south of Fleet Street, not far from Appleyard's premises in Farringdon Street.

Soon the demands on John Greenaway's time were so great that if he wanted to see his family at all he had to take work home with him. Then the crowded conditions at Cavendish Street hindered him; the children's room was too small to be used as both nursery and workroom. On the strength of what looked like a secure future, John decided to move to a larger house with a garden, and leased 28 Napier Street (later renumbered 52, now Napier Grove), Hoxton, one of the many newly-built three-storey terraced artisan houses in the immediate neighbourhood.

Shortly after the family moved, John decided it would be best if he could have a period of absolute freedom to devote to his work and to complete the first of the Dickens commissions undisturbed by his family. Elizabeth reluctantly agreed to a separation and suggested a brief stay with relatives in Rolleston, where in November 1846, she, five-year-old Lizzie and eight-month-old Kate went to stay with her aunt, Sarah Wise. It was a long, tiring journey, taking over six hours and costing more than a pound by either rail or coach. In addition, railway passengers to Rolleston in 1846 had to accomplish a complicated series of manoeuvres, changing trains twice, then taking either a coach or a canal boat from Nottingham to Rolleston village, there being no railway link with the village until the following year. Elizabeth Greenaway arrived exhausted and was immediately taken seriously ill, probably due to the severe influenza epidemic that was to rage in the area for over a year. She was so ill that she had to put the infant Kate out to nurse with a local family. This separation, following so soon after her parting from her husband, came as yet another severe blow to Elizabeth's morale. Yet she accepted her misfortune with

Ebenezer Landells.

characteristic stoicism, for the situation was, after all, only temporary. Meanwhile she patiently waited for news that her husband's projects were going well enough for her to return to London.

It was nearly two years before such news finally arrived. In that time John had completed both the *Pickwick Papers* commission and begun the illustrations for *Nicholas Nickleby*. Appleyard had advertised the first number of *Nickleby* to be on sale by October 1847, again 'engraved in the best style'. Having found himself in continual employment since October 1846, and encouraged by his employer's public display of confidence in his work, John eagerly waived his family home in September 1848. He had given up a good job with Landells' firm, he had accumulated a pile of printers' bills and had not seen his family for months – all in the hope of a secure future. But, for all his optimism, he had not received one penny in payment. Even when he heard about the disappointingly low sales figures of the *Nickleby* number, he did not immediately despair. Sales continued to wane, and Appleyard repeatedly refused to recognize John's anxious demands for payment. The pressure mounted until finally, late in 1848, John received the news he feared: Appleyard was bankrupt, and Greenaway and Wright were left without a penny or a hope of recovering their considerable losses.

The consequences of this disaster made themselves felt immediately. For the next two years John was forced to accept whatever engraving commissions he could find, however small or time-consuming. In an attempt to remain solvent, he moved to smaller offices at 4a Wine Office Court, north of his previous premises and still off Fleet Street; but, even in new surroundings, his business future appeared very bleak indeed.

The situation grew worse. Two years after Appleyard's bankruptcy John vacated Napier Street and moved his family nearer Rebecca Jones, to a house, washhouse and garden at 60 Britannia Street, previously owned by a Greenaway relative. There, in 1850 Elizabeth gave birth to a third daughter,

Frances Rebecca ('Fanny'); this further strain on John's financial resources, meant he had to increase his work load and he engraved for such periodicals as the *Illustrated London News*, and began to work on illustrated children's books, starting with the popular *A Treasury of Pleasure Rhymes for Children*, engraved after the much-admired animal drawings of Harrison Weir and J. Absolon. This led to further commissions until John achieved a small reputation as an interpreter of the designs of these two artists.[3] But such work was time-consuming, and not sufficiently well paid to support a family of five. Each day John returned in the evening, his pockets filled with half-finished woodblocks to be completed over-night, and each night his wife watched her husband's dedication to his arduous, often soul-destroying job. As he sat bent over, assiduously carving minute lines on the hard boxwood lying in a pool of concentrated light in an otherwise dark room, she saw his jovial nature deteriorate and desperately wanted to help; but her hands were tied by the needs of three young children whom she refused to let grow up unattended.

The new move meant that the Greenaways were among 60,000 struggling residents of Hoxton New Town, crammed into street after street of uniform three-storey brick terraces that by 1850 had replaced the fields and market gardens of eighteenth-century rural Hoxton. Theirs was the westernmost section of the new development, built to accommodate the rush of immigrant and artisan families into London. Although part of Shoreditch (where the over-all population nearly doubled between 1830 and 1860), the Greenaways' neighbourhood had its own distinct boundaries: the Regent's Canal to the north, Shepherdess Walk directly west, and on the east and south the dense traffic and deafening noise of carts, horses, waggons and omnibuses thundering up the commercial arteries of the New North Road and the busy City Road. In these depressing and restricted surroundings Elizabeth zealously watched over her children's activities; on those rare occasions when Kate and her sisters were allowed out, they were always chaperoned, either by Elizabeth herself or by a helpful relative.

An account of one of these early outings gives a first picture of young Kate. Although she was then only four years old, the event made such a deep impression that late in life Kate clearly recalled her ecstatic delight at the sights and sounds of her strange neighbourhood. It began one evening, when she and Lizzie were taken by an aunt down Britannia Street, south towards the City Road. They passed house after uniform house inhabited by master craftsmen and their families, each dedicated to a life preparing 'those little things necessary for civilized life'; they suddenly emerged from the dark, narrow street into the open clearing of the City Road, and its attractions left them mesmerized: there were tall red and blue bottles in the chemist's shop window, glowing in the semi-darkness; there were the stars overhead, twinkling in a rare glimpse out of the fog and dust of the evening sky. So entranced were they by these sights that they tumbled into a nearby street gutter, and emerged 'muddy and disgraced'. The shock of this disaster remained with Kate, but her delight in the escape from the dullness of her home surroundings could not be diminished even by the scolding her mother gave her when she and her sister returned home muddy, dishevelled and ashamed.

From this early age Kate was an introspective, extremely shy child who tended to keep her feelings to herself. However, she had shown signs of determination and precociousness when, at the age of eight months, she stubbornly refused to allow anyone to help her learn to walk; later, when just beginning to speak, she criticized her sister Lizzie for what seemed to her obvious mispronunciations, – a characteristic act of single-mindedness.

As the family income grew increasingly irregular, Elizabeth decided to open a millinery shop, despite the risk of failure of another family business. After careful consideration, she decided that a shop selling children's dresses as well as fancy goods – those flowers, buttons and lace trimmings which at the time were so essential to the well-dressed woman – would have a moderate chance of success. She seems to have turned to her mother for the necessary backing, for Rebecca Jones not only owned her Britannia Street house but also collected rent on four cottages in Dagenham; this made her the most prosperous member of both families. Elizabeth calculated she would need between £300 and £400 to open a shop in the nearby prime commercial area of Upper Street, Islington, a district known for its milliners' and drapers' establishments, and late in 1851 arrangements were completed for the Greenaway family to move into a flat at 96–7 Upper Street in Commerce Row, opposite the parish church of St Mary. Here Elizabeth, pregnant again, opened her shop in the central portion of what had been an Elizabethan country house, flanked on either side by adjoining wings. The Greenaways shared the house with two other families: the ironmonger Thomas Hartrup and his family, whom Kate recalled as 'unpleasant people who were a great annoyance'; and J. Tompion, a brush manufacturer and his family, 'quiet folk with a number of sheds in the back garden smelling and all yellow with sulphur'. Working in one wing were a stay-maker, a trunk-maker and a piano-maker, while in the other a confectioner, a tobacconist, a butcher and a fruiterer; each added his distinctive talents to the diversity of the area. This made Upper Street a considerable change from the dreary back streets of Hoxton. Here, too, patches of rural life remained: a dairy with cows and, to the north, pockets of pastureland over which sheep still grazed. By the early 1850s, however, Islington was rapidly being transformed from a quiet rural village famous for its inns into a busy suburban shopping centre second only to the west end of London.

Above Elizabeth's shop the family had a flat with large windows overlooking bustling Upper Street; Kate used to spend hours at these windows, watching her neighbours and the shoppers strolling below. The flat consisted of a large sitting room, bedrooms, and numerous corridors which threaded the upper floors, leading into derelict rooms, dusty and dark. These passageways fed the imagination of the five-year-old, who believed some were haunted, some led off to a magical garden in the sky, while others led 'dreadfully to nowhere'. One of her favourite rooms was called the 'floorcloth room', because of its abandoned appearance; she regarded it with a devotion second only to the attachment she formed to the large back garden, which soon became 'Kate's domain', despite the fact that it had to be shared with the other two families. To the uninitiated this small patch of ground was little more than a series of long-neglected flower beds bordering a few rather makeshift, paint-smeared sheds. But to Kate the garden represented something she had longed for, an open expanse of sheer space, that led into a country lane and a field filled with idly grazing sheep. Here, in a rural retreat behind the busy Islington streets, Kate's imagination had space to form and grow into a fascination with fields and gardens that would comfort her throughout her life.

Years later this garden remained an important part of her childhood memories, the source of her vision of what a perfect flower garden should be like, as she then remarked in a letter to a friend:

> I often think just for the pleasure of thinking, that a little door leads out of the garden wall into a real old flowering garden, full of deep shades and deep colours. Did you always plan out delightful places just close and unexpected, when you were young? I did. My bedroom window used to look out over red roofs and chimney pots, and I made steps up into a lovely garden up there with nasturtiums growing and brilliant flowers so near to the sky. There were some old houses joined ours at the sides, and I made a secret door into long lines of old rooms, all so delightful, leading into an old garden. I imagined it so often that I knew its look so well, it got to be very real.[4]

By the time Kate's brother, Alfred John ('Johnnie'), was born in July 1852, Elizabeth's shop was realizing a profit on which the family could live. This was fortunate, for John Greenaway had come home one evening to announce that his partner, William Wright, had abandoned him to struggle on alone with his business and his debts. John Greenaway's name subsequently disappeared from the Post Office Directory for two years. Meanwhile, Elizabeth exploited her initial success and in 1853 moved yet again, a short distance further up the street, to a shop with house behind at 119 Upper Street (now renumbered 147). The new home lay at the corner of a dark, but blissfully quiet, forecourt of a Georgian house. It was the same forecourt, Terrett's Court, which had previously so impressed Dickens that he described it in *Martin Chuzzlewit*. Elizabeth's shop faced the main road and the family reached their home through a narrow passage-way which they shared with five other residents, including W. Dawe and Sons, a bedding warehouse, Miss Hare, a stay- and dressmaker, and, at number three, the occupant of the Georgian house itself, the portrait sculptor Charles Rivers. The new house was considerably larger, lighter and more pleasant than the passages and damp, dark rooms of number 96. But, comfortable as it was, it could never satisfy Kate's longing for fantasy; in its enclosed courtyard setting it lacked the single essential feature, a garden.

Nevertheless, this was the house and neighbourhood where Kate spent the formative years of her childhood. There she learned the principles of middle-class morality, and to recognize and accept that most important of middle-class virtues, respectability. Shortly after the move, Elizabeth Greenaway changed the sign of her shop from simple 'milliner' to the more impressive 'ladies' outfitter', suggesting subtle, but very important changes in her shop's clientele. Fortunately Elizabeth's judgement was sound, and the shop grew in scope and reputation, despite the fact that within easy reach ten other milliners provided keen competition. But the business was well placed, with neighbouring shopkeepers specializing in such luxuries as jewellery, looking glasses and picture frames. Within weeks, Elizabeth's clientele noticeably 'smartened up' to include women dressed in the height of fashion who arrived with their pampered children to replenish their already bulging wardrobes.

After the move Kate rarely saw her mother leave her shop. Elizabeth worked long hours (on weekdays 8 a.m. to 8 p.m. and on Saturdays to 11 p.m.), which left her no time for child-minding, and this became a serious problem, now that they had moved too far away from Rebecca Jones to consider her help. Elizabeth had to leave the younger ones in the care of twelve-year-old Lizzie, with firm instructions that they were to go no further afield than the house-lined streets behind their home – all else was out of bounds. Nearby was a playground made especially safe by the bordering Church Missionary College green to the north and Milner Square green to the west. There, despite its limitations, Kate came to regard her neighbourhood with wide-eyed delight.

Wellington Street, like many parts of Islington, frequently turned into a child's dream-world come true; a circus of wonder brimming with acrobats, jugglers and showmen anxious to sell a peep at their remarkable talents for a few pennies. Here anyone with pretensions to being an entertainer could set up a pitch and 'earn a few coppers' from the local children and their parents. Kate, on her walks with Lizzie and Fanny, often saw the many characters who became household names; people such as the great Fantoccini, a street magician 'of the highest order', who put on his act equipped with a toy Mother Goose, her milk pails filled with toy children which leapt in and out of their containers; or a toy skeleton that Kate remembered miraculously coming apart and snapping together again with the flick of Fantoccini's wrist. Once she came upon a sailor with a wooden leg, pathetically appealing for coins by displaying, as explanation of his crippled condition, a large and luridly painted picture of a shipwreck caused by a whale. Best of all there was the familiar screech and drumming of the Punch and Judy show. Kate, her sisters and all the neighbourhood children would then drop what they were doing and race to the source of the noise to watch with open-mouthed eagerness the progress of a story they knew so well, yet never tired of hearing. Often the show was cut short, when the assembled audience proved too poor to pay the actors, and Kate and her sisters were left heartbroken and disappointed.

The longer Kate explored her new surroundings the more she revelled in their unexpected attractions. Upper Street was a seemingly unending row of shop fronts that transformed the area into 'one long fanciful emporium'. Here she could freely 'gaze and gaze for ever' at the picture books and puzzle maps in glass cases – until she was driven away by an irate shop-owner who realized she had no money. Above all, she longed for 'a little chalk house with coloured gelatine windows' that glowed in candle light, and 'a little cardboard village covered in snow', but both these were too expensive. Wealth fascinated her, and she and Fanny devised a game they called 'Pretence', in which they tried to mimic the mannerisms of those strange, wealthy shoppers and their children who invaded the street and Mrs Greenaway's shop. Could anyone be more grand or mysterious, Kate wondered? 'Two there were in particular,' she later wrote, 'had their homes in the sky, descending to earth daily for their morning's exercise.' For years this fascination remained, and her impressions of those affected were eventually incorporated into *Under the Window*, accompanied by the verse:

> *Yes, that's the girl that struts about,*
> *She's very proud – so very proud!*
> *Her bow-wow's quite so proud as she;*
> *They both are very wrong to be.*

The surprises and inequalities Kate encountered on the streets drove her into her own thoughts and daydreams where she happily created a world of her own. This explains why, years later, she quite categorically claimed, 'I had such a very happy time when I was a child, and curiously, was so very much happier than my brother and sisters, with exactly the same surroundings.'

Nevertheless, the disappointments and disturbances Kate experienced in childhood affected her deeply. From an early age she was at the mercy of her feelings, allowing them to sweep her along to emotional heights which sometimes ended in deep depressions that lasted for days. 'I had days of gloom – sometimes – but I believe even those were so strong as to be a satisfaction to me,' she wrote later to a friend. For example, she was once told of a children's party to be given in the near future. As the day approached she became unduly anxious and over-excited. She began to imagine how much cake she would eat, how much lemonade she would drink, how beautiful her fellow guests would be in their party dresses. When the day arrived she surrendered to the moment and danced and laughed like the rest of the guests; but such momentary enjoyment was followed by an irrational depression: why did the party only come once a year? Why couldn't there be cake and lemonade every day?

She suffered from this alternation of high spirits and deep despair all her life; yet at this early age she was determined to correct the condition. One day at the breakfast table she announced that she would neither speak nor smile for the entire day; this was by way of preparation for a party she was going to in the afternoon. Her family, long accustomed to such determined outbursts, only laughed and accepted her announcement as merely 'Kate's way'. Then, despite her pledge, she was carried away by the gaiety of the event and a short time later the depression returned, not for a few hours but for several days. When she was old enough to write in her carefully formed handwriting, she recorded in a childhood notebook two attempts to understand her confusion: 'Sudden joy kills sooner than excessive grief . . . Joy surfeited turns to sorrow.' But this gave little comfort.

Kate was fortunate in that she was left alone to cultivate her fantasies. She discovered one sure way to escape safely into a world of her own creation was through her doll collection which continued to be important to her well into her adult life, when she replaced the tattered, childhood dolls with painted, china ones elaborately dressed in clothes she designed and sewed herself. Her doll collection became a source of great pride and joy; even in its early stages its size and scope impressed those friends and relations who were allowed to see it.

Had she really managed to forego sweets and save a farthing every week for twenty-four weeks just to buy a tiny toy piano for her dolls' house? one relative asked. The variety of her collection was equally impressive. There were half a dozen Dutch mannikin dolls, all small enough to fit in one hand; there were wax dolls with varying coloured hair and the much-loved wooden dolls, some missing an arm or a leg, dressed only in paint or rags tied together with string. Of these Kate's favourite was one she appropriately named 'One-eye'. Then there was the royal family grouping: Prince Albert and Queen Victoria, each costing a halfpenny and reigning from the top shelf of her dolls' house-cum-cupboard, while their princes and princesses, carefully dressed in scraps discarded from Mrs Greenaway's shop, were dutifully arranged on the shelves below, and studied to learn about the lives of the real royal family.

Kate gives a clear picture of herself as a strong-willed child in a description of a children's party about this time. 'It [the party] was some way off; even now I remember the shivery feeling of the drive in the cab, and the fear that always beset me that we might have gone on the wrong day.' When they arrived she characteristically took a place at the back of the room, from which she could safely survey the scene, while running no risk of encountering the unexpected. As she gazed into the crowd of young guests her eyes focused on one girl, who was in her view 'an ideal of perfect beauty'. This creature held Kate spellbound. She was (in Kate's words) 'one big tomboy of a girl, with beautiful blue eyes and tangled fair hair . . . This girl I loved and admired intensely, and never spoke to . . . in my life, she had merry ways and laughing looks and I adored her.'[5] Such fair-haired girls were later to become the models for many of her admired 'Greenaway children', but it was characteristic now that she should make no attempt to speak to her child-vision. She would always assume the position of the spectator, the passive guest who preferred her own version of life to that which in reality might prove unpleasant. In this instance the mere sight of the girl was enough to provide her with material for daydreaming; to approach her would have been to risk shattering her image of perfect beauty.

There were other occasions during her childhood when fantasy played an important role. One in particular became the most influential in driving her visual sense out of London and into an idyllic countryside. It usually began early in the summer, whenever the Greenaways had enough money for the journey. Then Kate, her two sisters and, when he was old enough, her brother were sent off to stay with their relatives at Rolleston. Although Kate returned to Rolleston quite often – until the early 1870s, when she was well into her twenties – it was these visits during the 1850s, when she was only five or six, that left the most lasting impressions and proved to be the most stimulating to her imagination. It was then she sensed the escape from the claustrophobic streets of Islington to the open expanses of a blossom-filled Nottinghamshire countryside. Rolleston represented a release from anxiety and she willingly retreated there whenever city life became too unpleasant.

Rolleston was an impressive little village 130 miles north-west from London, in the valley of the River Trent, five miles from Newark to the east, two and a half miles from the cathedral town of Southwell to the west. It boasted a mention in the Domesday book and a long history as a market town; a Saxon

Rolleston primroses. Watercolour by Kate Greenaway.

church and a village green marked by an old cross and stocks 'for the punishment of evil doers' remained intact in Kate's time. Around this green were nestled a number of thatched and red-tile-roofed cottages. Down the road, past the cottage where Kate stayed, lay the parish 'pinfold' or 'strayard' – an enclosed grassy space used by the villagers since the sixteenth century for penning cattle. The surrounding fields of maize, corn and wild flowers, market gardens and a village railway station built in the 1850s complete the picture of Victorian Rolleston.

But there was more to the charm of the village than fields and ancient buildings. Its inhabitants fascinated young Kate, for they were people who, like so many of their rural neighbours, had preserved links with their eighteenth-century ancestors and still wore old-fashioned clothes. The men working in the fields wore embroidered smocks dyed blue; on Sundays their wives appeared at the village church in frilly dresses and large poke bonnets ('charity bobs'). These curious outfits immediately struck young Kate, and she soon came to regard the villagers, their enchanting clothes, and their unusual personalities with the utmost respect. They, in their turn, opened their hearts to this stranger, and willingly shared their leisure hours with their 'little Lunnoner'.

Some of the villagers remained firmly fixed in Kate's mind years later, when she attempted to write her autobiography. William Crowder was the village shopkeeper who, in addition, served as village cobbler, cow-doctor and rat-catcher. On Sundays he was also to be found ringing the four bells in the church tower, fortified by a 'large jar of ale' that his brother John Crowder, the village organ-blower, had cautiously placed at his feet. John Miller was, according to village legend, its most important citizen; he had served as chef to George IV, William IV and Queen Victoria, then moved to Rolleston where he played out his retirement in the church orchestra. There was John Parnham, who ran the Sunday school that occupied the front room of the village pub. Here, when they were old enough to understand such things, Kate and her sisters were sent to endure Parnham's lessons from the Bible. These were administered in a typically eccentric way, in which everyone in attendance was forced to read aloud. Meaning was apparently not as essential as rhythmic, flowing speech, and a reader would fight his way through a particularly tortuous passage, filled with unpronounceable words, until Parnham irritably waved him on with a curt 'Hard word go on!' The vicar, Drummond Hay, was another Sunday affliction. When, perched on one of the village church's painfully hard wooden pews, Kate was forced to sit through one of his interminable sermons, her only slight relief was to watch the vicar's extremely long 'Dundreary whiskers' wave mysteriously through the air.

When she was in Rolleston, Kate always stayed at the farm of Thomas and Mary Chappell. Mary Chappell's sister, Ann Barnsdale, and Kate's own great-aunt, Sarah Wise, lived with them. This was the household that had taken her in 1846, when Elizabeth Greenaway put her out to nurse, and from that time onwards each member of the household left a distinct impression on the child. When she was old enough to talk she gave each of them a name: Thomas became her 'Dadad', Mary her 'Mamam', and Ann, who was often occupied with the task of teaching her about the farm, became her 'Nanan'.

Left: Mary Chappell seated by the kitchen fender and *right*: Mrs Neale preparing for market. Both early sketches by Kate Greenaway.

Mary Chappell in particular occupied a prominent place in Kate's childhood world. Years later Mary remained 'the kindest, most generous, most charitable, the cheerfulest and most careful woman' Kate had ever known. 'In all things she was highest and best,' she recalled, her remark influenced by the fact that Mary had instilled in her the importance of 'being in love with cheerfulness'. From Kate's recollection we get the impression that she and Mary Chappell were inseparable, one always there to delight the other. Mary was the fount of country folklore and superstition, always ready with a relevant proverb or a fantastic story to help pass the time or emphasize a lesson. One proverb deeply impressed Kate, for it heralded a bizarre farmyard incident. Mary was accustomed to whistling while she worked, a habit often interrupted by the blood-curdling crow of the most offensive of her farmyard animals – a hen known to dominate the entire yard, attack intruders on sight and terrorize its fellow inhabitants. When this happened, Mary would lift her head and angrily sputter 'a whistling woman and a crowing hen, are neither good for God nor men,' and send Kate off to the safety of a nearby corner. There she watched in amazement as Mary attacked the hen with a broom, scattering dust and animals alike, 'breathing dreadful threats' and running 'nigh out of her life'. Almost breathless from exhaustion, she would finally fall in a heap at Kate's feet, but would quickly recover from what she called her 'dither'. Back on her feet, she warily awaited the hen's return, and the entire ritual would be repeated. Mary was stubbornly convinced that the hen's interruptions were a 'monstrous breach of nature'; one that could only signal an impending disaster, when 'some terrible thing would be sure to happen.'

Left: Thomas Chappell in familiar pose and *right*: the Chappell kitchen appears as background. Both early watercolours by Kate Greenaway.

The Chappell kitchen, a watercolour by Kate Greenaway.

Mary's husband, Thomas, was of a completely different disposition. He had long suffered from poor health, and Mary used to describe him as the 'poor creature'. Thomas came to accept his wife's evaluation, and even believed that it gave him an added distinction in the village. He was known as the invalid farmer at the end of the road, and visitors always found him ready for a long chat as he rested in his favourite position, seated on a rush-bottomed chair before the kitchen fire. Here he held court, dressed in a thick shepherd's smock, his work-gnarled hands idly folded over his ever-present walking stick. Kate took her guardian's idleness for granted, and laughed at his eccentricities, especially his market day behaviour. This was so peculiar that she never forgot how Thomas duly stationed himself outside the farm-house, leaned against the gate that led into the main road, and watched the steady stream of farm carts loaded with livestock and provisions for the nearby Southwell and Newark markets. From time to time, to relieve the boredom, he would lure an unsuspecting farmer into his own farmyard under the pretext that he was looking for new livestock to augment his herd. The farmer would proudly parade his animals before Thomas, who would gleefully turn his victim away, dismissing the stock as being of too poor a quality to measure up to his own rigorous standards. Insulted and angry at this waste of time, the farmer would hurry away, swearing, as old Thomas returned to his gate, 'blandly smiling, placid and undisturbed'.

Mary Chappell's sister, Ann Barnsdale, was a tall, angular woman in her forties, illiterate but often witty; a woman Kate loved for her 'clumping awkwardness'. Previously in service with Sarah Wise, she had accompanied her employer to the Chappells' after the sale of the Wise farm. She looked after Kate's elderly great-aunt, and tended the family's milk cows, from which her sister made the much admired butter and cheeses that were sold in the local market. Kate loved to accompany 'Nanan' in the early morning ritual of herding the cows back to the farm for milking. On those wonderful mornings, after Ann had jostled Kate out of bed, they would go together to the village pinfold to collect the cows. When they had reached the field, Ann would yell, 'Get along ye bad 'uns,' and slap the beasts' sides with a flat stick that filled the dawn silence with a resounding crack, sending shivers up Kate's spine.

Kate's great-aunt, Sarah Wise, left an equally important impression. A widow in her seventies, she retained her striking appearance and formidable manner until her death in 1857. 'Aunt Sarah' appeared in the pages of *Under the Window* and *Little Ann* as Kate remembered seeing her, seated at the window of the Chappells' front room, 'a grand-looking old lady with a pink complexion, wearing always a black silk dress with a finely embroidered white collar round her neck, a muslin and lace cap on her head'.

Kate's life at the Chappells' was often enlivened by excursions into the surrounding countryside. Here she was excited by the sight of a road edged with primroses or a field filled with poppies and singing haymakers. There were memorable visits to the Neales, the new owners of the Wise farm. Thomas Neale, whom Kate recalled as 'an easy-going, idle person,' smoked and drank and allowed his farm and butcher's business to 'slip through his fingers'. With his wife, Mary Ann, he lived in a spacious farmhouse called The House, surrounded by a large farm, vast storage bins for grain and an immense garden. To Kate, the Neales' garden was 'my loved one of all the gardens I have ever known', and she vividly recalled its seasonal changes in her autobiography. The Greenaways were regular visitors, and enjoyed the cowslip wine and sponge cakes which were so often a part of their welcome.

It was, however, with severe reservations that Kate approached calling upon her nearest relatives – her mother's sister, Sarah, and her wealthy husband, Thomas Aldridge, who lived on a sprawling 190-acre farm complete with a large house they called Odd House. Sarah was an extremely snobbish woman. She had married into the much-respected Aldridge family, with its eighteenth-century origins in Southwell and wealth accumulated from property owned in the East Indies. She now took every opportunity to remind Kate and other members of her family of her good fortune and her superior standing. In Kate's view Sarah Aldridge was a 'dark and good-looking woman' spoiled by a 'dreadfully untidy appearance and a mean disposition'. Since Sarah had lost two of her four children at an early age, this tragedy had turned her into a callous and mean-spirited woman who seemed to display the fiery tips of her temper whenever Kate was around. On very select occasions Sarah took her young niece to Newark on market day, where she was given tea at the imposing Saracen's Head Inn and had her first glimpse of 'really polite society'. But, on the whole, Kate was uncomfortable and shied away from her aunt and her blatant snobbishness. She even suggested to Mary Chappell that the hen that terrorized her farmyard should be called 'Sarah Aldridge', since the parallels were unmistakably clear: both her aunt and the hen possessed 'thoroughly bad characters', while each enjoyed 'a charmed and wholly undeserved existence' of one capable of taking 'the biggest share of everything'. On the other hand Kate remembered Thomas Aldridge as a man 'full of fun and jokes, and very fond of children', the man who delighted her by stealing apples from the orchard his wife kept locked against intruders; but she also did not forget her keen disappointment when he denigrated her beloved Chappell family, as he often did.

Besides studying the characters of Rolleston's inhabitants, Kate developed a deep interest in its countryside. She was taken for walks to nearby Fiskerton Mill, a perilous trek for a six- or eight-year-old, along a raised pathway with a dark, deep stream threatening on one side, a long drop into a ditch and field on the other. She longed to repeat this walk, which led into a deep, shady plantation, then to the mill itself, with its dusty sacks of white flour stacked near the rushing stream. There she learned the names of wild flowers and watched as apples on overhanging trees dropped into the water and bobbed to the surface. On other outings she walked to Greet Close, a nearby hayfield, where she experienced her first hay-making, 'the great Happiness – the joy and love of it all'. The Wednesday ride to Newark market, when Kate helped Mary Chappell deliver her dairy produce, also ranked among her favourite excursions. On the long ride in a green cart pulled by her favourite pony, Fanny, Kate was given a seat behind her guardian, a place she shared with baskets of plums, apples, pears, sage cheeses, and sometimes, much to her horror, live chickens and ducks which flopped and squawked helplessly at her feet. She told herself they would never be sold for slaughter, but be bought by some kind soul who would 'put them to live in a nice place where they could be happy'. This was the beginning of a lifelong abhorrence of cruelty towards animals. On other days Kate accompanied Thomas Chappell in his cart to Southwell for a delivery of malt; then the sensation of jogging along tree-lined roads into the market town with its huge cathedral was one she always cherished: 'I didn't mind how long it took, it was all a pleasure.'

From her brief, unfinished autobiography one clear fact emerges: at an early age Kate was enchanted by the sights, sounds, smells, flora, fauna, the

Detail of 'From Market' and detail of 'The Daisies' from *Marigold Garden*.

Above: Detail of 'Hide and Seek' from *Kate Greenaway's Book of Games*.

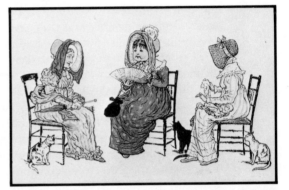

Middle right: Elderly woman modelled after Aunt Sarah Wise, *left*: detail of 'Heigh-Ho' and *above*: the Rolleston Floor, all from *Under the Window*.

workaday world of Rolleston. 'In those early days all the farm things were of endless interest to me,' she later recorded. Aware of this, the Chappells encouraged her to share in their life and bought her 'a tiny hayfork, a little kit to carry milk in, and a little washing tub, all exactly like the real ones, only small'. These Kate learned to use in imitation of her elders. As a result, her earliest childhood summers were spent immersed in a romanticized rural setting, far from the realities of the farmers' bitter efforts to survive; her later account is innocent of what agricultural life was really like in the 1850s, free of the boredom of tedious, mundane jobs, oblivious of the annual struggle to harvest enough crops to live on during the winter. By her own admission, this very personal, stilted image of country life was formed when 'the golden spectacles were very big'. It was with that vision in mind that she later expressed her shock and surprise at the harsh conditions farmers in other parts of the country were forced to endure, their lives in her estimation 'little more than labourers'. Her romantic memories of those early days in Rolleston provided an escape from the unpleasantness of adult life. 'I suppose I went to it very young before I could really remember and that is why I have such a wild delight in cowslips and apple blossoms,' she wrote to a friend years later. 'They always give me the strange feeling of trying *to remember*, as if I had known them in a former world.'

In other instances Kate's impressions of Rolleston remained remarkably clear. One picture in particular involved a vision of herself as a little girl of five or six, waiting at the Chappell farm gate for her promised walk to Fiskerton Mill. There she stood, in a shady lane bordered by high hedges 'all hawthorns blossoming', with wide, grassy patches of speedwell, stitchwort, and daisies; there she could look through gates into fields full of buttercups until the whole scene was filled with sunlight. 'Now you see my little picture,' she wrote, 'and me a little dark girl in a pink frock and hat, looking at things a good deal, and thoughts filled up with such wonderful things – everything seeming wonderful, and life to go on for ever just as it was. What a beautiful long time a day was! Filled with time . . .'[6] The image was one she used in *Under the Window* and also, to some extent, to justify remaining a lifelong child: if life was wonderful and seemed 'to go on for ever just as it was' when she was a child, then a child she wished to remain.

This early innocent approach was not, and could not be, altered, even after it was darkened by the reality involved in two village disasters. Both she clearly described in her autobiography as having an impact on her, but the influence was quite the reverse of what might be expected. Instead of being frightened of the natural elements involved, Kate was fascinated by the way in which they transformed Rolleston into a unified community concerned with the welfare of each member.

The first was a large-scale village fire: 'It was a blazing hot day in August, in the morning, about 11 o'clock, when suddenly there were loud shrieks of "Fire!" and I saw Ann rushing to the gate shouting out "Fire!" at the top of her voice, quite unconscious of what she was doing,' Kate began. Then followed a vivid description of the village mobilizing into action; the rush of workmen and servants racing to the site on the Neales' farm; their forming a line to pass water buckets to extinguish the blaze. Eventually the fire was put out, and to celebrate the villagers broke open the wine barrels salvaged from the house. 'Some of the men behaved disgracefully,' Kate remembered, her remark no doubt influenced by the Chappells' disgusted reactions, as she ended her account: 'I shall never forget my terror and fright of this day, and to 'Mamam' it was as the end of all things.'[7]

The second disaster struck in November 1852, when Kate was six and she and her sisters had returned to Rolleston to allow her mother a rest following Johnnie's birth. While the villagers dismissed it as yet another instance of 'the waters being out', the local newspapers were more sensational: in their opinion it was 'the greatest flood since 1795'. The Trent and Greet rivers raced over their banks; the Trent, rising fourteen feet nine inches above its average level, flooded the village green and the lower floors of houses, and drowned a great many animals. 'The people used to wait at the end of the street where the water rushed over, and people who were passing in carts would drive them through the water, and boys crossed over in washing tubs.' Kate found the experience so inspiring that she later used the tub-floating incident in *Under the Window*. 'After some days the floods began to subside and you could begin to get about. After the water had all gone the country was horrible, covered with mud and dead worms, and it smelt dreadfully.' However, the water-drenched landscape miraculously 'returned pretty much to its old look again', and her impression of idyllic Rolleston was restored.[8]

Leaving Rolleston was always a painful experience for, try as she might, she could never reconcile herself to the injustice she felt she suffered by being sent back to the noisy streets of Islington. There a brick-lined 'prison' replaced the freedom of seeing birds and dragonflies in an open field. A later verse, written for *Marigold Garden*, describes her sense of loss:

> *I live in a London street, then I long and long*
> *To be the whole day the sweet Flowers among*
> *Instead of tall chimney-pots up in the sky,*
> *The joy of seeing Birds and Dragon Flies go by.*
> *At home I lie in bed, and cannot go to sleep,*
> *For the sound of cart-wheels upon the hard street.*
> *But my eyes close up to no sound of anything*
> *Except it is to hear the nightingales sing.*

But gradually, after sleepless nights and angry outbursts demanding to return to Rolleston, she would accept her fate – at least until the next summer's visit. And, when asked, she would always insist that her true home was in the countryside, whatever her parents had planned for her.

2   The Way to Somewhere Town
1853–1873

Which is the way to Somewhere Town?
Oh, up in the morning early;
Over the tiles and the chimney-pots,
That is the way, quite clearly.

UNDER THE WINDOW

The transition from child to grown-up was for Kate a painful process. She relished her childhood happiness and always recalled how: 'I hated to be grown-up, and cried when I had my first long dress.' But her mother insisted that she must have a proper training and relentlessly planned Kate's education, despite her objections to classroom humiliations, 'impossible lessons', and her fear of her teachers, that turned Rolleston's wide-eyed, happy 'little Lunnoner' into a shy, inward-looking, unassuming young woman.

Kate's lessons began at Mrs Allaman's infant school, run by an elderly, inoffensive woman she remembered as always wearing a large, frilly cap, a scarf wrapped round her shoulders, a long apron filled with sewing equipment round her waist. She taught Kate her 'letters', and the proper use of needle and cotton, of which Kate remembered one incident: her desperate attempt to thread a needle while Mrs Allaman watched impatiently from behind, tapping her on the head with a silver thimble until she succeeded. Kate quickly poked the cotton through the needle, and thrust it over her head for approval, catching her instructor's finger in the process. For this she was severely scolded and disgraced before her fellow students.

She was subsequently enrolled in a series of private dame schools, each progressively more intimidating and difficult. The first was Miss Jackson's school, situated half a mile from home, in Halliford Street, and chosen as meeting Mrs Greenaway's requirements of convenience and reasonable price. There Kate was overwhelmed by 'impossible lessons', and after frantic pleading with her mother she was removed after 'only a few days'. Miss Varley's school in south Pentonville was a second choice, but here again Kate found her lessons too much of a strain, and, according to her mother, became mysteriously ill. After a short recovery period she was sent to the Misses Fiveash Ladies' School, Barnsbury, where a fresh and even greater threat greeted her in the shape of the headmistress, Miss Anne Fiveash, who suffered from 'cross eye', a dreadful handicap which induced in young Kate trembling fits that 'lasted for days'. Not surprisingly, Kate suffered from a second attack of her mysterious illness, and she was promptly removed.

In this way Kate managed temporarily to avoid the strain of school. With her extreme sensitivity she was easy prey to classroom fears and the discomforts endured by most children. But they seem to have made a considerably greater impact on her, so that throughout her life she associated true happiness only with the days before lessons and school bells.

What she could not avoid, however, was the stern, private religious training instigated by her mother and her grandmother, Rebecca Jones. According to a relative, the Greenaways were well known among their friends as 'very religious, strictly puritanical people', and this attitude influenced Kate from an early age. She accepted the constant church-going, the Bible reading and religious maxims impressed on her by her mother, even recording several in a childhood notebook. The most telling of these perhaps was 'God cometh with leaden feet but striketh with iron hands'; it heralded a period of religious doubts or (according to her autobiography) 'my religious fit', when she tried to consider the 'yes or nos' of her thoughts and actions, and the possibility of falling from God's grace.

Mrs Greenaway was determined to provide her daughters with a proper training in at least one or two useful skills, and she was willing to work extra hours in her shop to provide the necessary money. Her eldest daughter, Lizzie, for example, had early expressed an interest in the piano, and she was given a long series of expensive lessons to enable her to play proficiently and to study at the Royal College of Music. Despite Kate's past failures, she was given a second chance to prove her abilities, this time outside the classroom. A woman tutor was engaged to teach Kate French and the piano privately on two or three afternoons a week, and she remained in this capacity until Kate was sufficiently confident to return to the Fiveash school for a final session.

It was only while struggling over her private lessons that Kate eventually convinced her parents she could succeed at a task if allowed to approach it at her own pace. 'I was never told I was tiresome when I was young, but I was constantly told I was *odd*,' she recalled later. She used her new freedom from the classroom to master the piano, although she found the physical dexterity necessary to keep 'one's hands so flat a penny would not fall off while playing' a difficult task for her short, stubby fingers and awkward hands. Stumbling through the scales and chords, she learned to play from memory the popular song 'Gauraca', and played it with sufficient skill to please her tutor and her parents. Mrs Greenaway was thrilled with Kate's success, and rewarded her with a gigantic doll, nearly four feet tall. Kate named it Gauraca, dressed it in Johnnie's cast-offs, including full-size baby shoes, and dragged it about the house until she found it too awkward and heavy to lift.

Moreover, when left to her own devices Kate took a keen interest in the books, pictures and magazines her father left lying about the house. By studying the illustrations in periodicals, children's books and newspapers, she built up a keen awareness of visual detail. Only when a story failed to emerge through its illustrations did she ask about or read the text. She maintained this purely visual approach to books throughout her life: a story was 'clever' if it had convincing illustrations; a book was a disappointment if she could not picture its settings.

She was encouraged to read on Sunday evenings when her parents, brother and sisters gathered in the sitting room to read and listen to Lizzie play the piano. Kate long remembered one Sunday when Lizzie sang and played 'Hear Me Norma' while her brother and sisters laughed, danced round the room, and overturned the sofa. On more sedate Sundays she pored over her father's

Above: Early Victorian street scene near Hoxton, *c.*1841.

Left: Terrett's Place, with Greenaway house on right.

Below: Islington, *c.*1843.

collection of engravings: his copies of the *Illustrated London News*, a cherished scrapbook of coloured and uncoloured engravings, and a selection of older volumes of the magazines he kept locked in a special cupboard. She loved the illustrated poems of Tennyson and Wordsworth in one number of the *Illustrated Family Journal*, and learned to identify the drawings of John Leech, John Gilbert and Kenny Meadows, all acknowledged masters of black and white illustration who had a considerable influence on her first published work. Kenny Meadows's delicate fairies and imaginative figures had the greatest appeal, particularly his illustrations to an edition of Shakespeare's plays. From these Kate learned the basic plot of each play, which she remembered as the culmination of her attempt to learn exclusively from pictures: 'It is curious how much pictures tell you − like the plays without words,' she wrote years later. 'I suppose I asked a good deal about them [Shakespeare's plays] and was told, and read little bits anyhow. I never remember the time I didn't know what each play was about.'[1]

With the plots firmly in mind, Kate was taken by her father to the theatre. Despite her mother's objections that this was not a respectable place for young girls, Kate learned to share her father's enthusiasm for the stage, and she was seven when she saw her first Sadler's Wells production, *Henry V*, followed the same year by *Henry IV (Part 2)*. Both starred the widely acclaimed Shakespearean actor Samuel Phelps, whose later innovative production of *A Midsummer Night's Dream* ('with its green gauze curtains instead of the then popular glitter') left Kate longing for more romances and dramas, with themes and characters of visual beauty. On another occasion she attended one of Charles Dickens' readings of *A Christmas Carol* and was enchanted by the spell Dickens had over the audience. ('His delivery was *so quiet*.')

Drama, romance and beauty became essential ingredients in her adolescent reading. Of all the children's books read to her by her parents, her favourites were 'those wonderful little books they used to sell in coloured covers a penny and halfpenny each − they were condensed and dramatic.' And yet romances with happy endings were most important: 'I never cared so much for Jack the Giantkiller, or Jack and the Beanstalk, or Tom Thumb, as I did for The Sleeping Beauty in the Wood, Cinderella, and Beauty and the Beast. I did not like Puss in Boots as well either. Of course they were all fascinating, but the three pretty ones I liked the best,' she later wrote to a friend.[2]

The early-nineteenth-century children's writers Jane and Ann Taylor were her favourite authors; their verses about child beggars, cripples, 'The Vulgar Little Lady' and 'The Gaudy Little Flower' were clear descriptions of the life Kate found outside her Islington window. In the case of her favourite Taylor poem, which she called the 'daisy poem', she was captivated by its simple plea, made by a daisy to warn insensitive humans:

> *Little lady, as you pass*
> *Lightly o'er the tender grass*
> *Step about but do not tread*
> *On my meek and lowly head.*

As she read more, however, Kate began to be fascinated by the bizarre, the brutal and the bloodthirsty. They reinforced her awareness of the differences between the beauty and romance she associated with the world of her daydreams and fantasies, and the pain, brutality and fear she found so startlingly evident in what she called the real world. 'I used to be thrilled by *Uncle Tom's Cabin*,' she once remembered. The bloodthirsty characters in Bluebeard filled her with 'delicious excitement'. She read and reread the tantalizing story, until she decided it was 'a very real thing mixed up with great reality'. She never tired of hearing her father reading it aloud in the agonized voice of Bluebeard's wife, and, as he built up to the climax, Kate could hardly breathe with expectation. The brutal murder story of Pepper and Salt was also 'most enjoyable and afflictive', particularly the part when the wicked stepmother was haunted by her murdered victim's spirit, chanting:

> *She drank my blood and picked my bones*
> *And buried me under the marble stones.*

Grandmother Jones, whom Kate loved 'best of all', was an ever-flowing source of tales and bizarre events not found in books at home. She was a bright, clever woman in her seventies with remarkable spirits and strange ways. When Kate had learned to write, she copied into a notebook several 'shrewd sayings' of her grandmother's. These ranged from superstitious warnings ('You must spit over your shoulder when meeting a hare') to the correct approach to romance ('If you sneeze on Sunday before breakfast, you will see your true love before a week's past') and, finally, in a section Kate marked 'Charms, etc.' a reassuring prayer for one obsessed with stories of evil:

> *From witches and wizzards,*
> *And longtail Buzzards*
> *And things that run at the bottom of the hedge,*
> *Good Lord, deliver us.*

Kate learned all this on long, self-indulgent Sunday afternoon visits to Britannia Street, where she stuffed herself with Coburg loaves and rounds of toast spread with raspberry jam or honey, then settled down to listen to her grandmother's stories. Particular favourites were the stories Rebecca told (in a 'brisk tone and alert manner') about her mysterious husband, Nathaniel. Everything about the grandfather Kate never knew seemed tantalizingly vague: how Nathaniel was born somewhere in Wales, and 'belonged to people who were called Bulldicks because they were big men and great fighters, and they used as children to slide down the mountains on three-legged milking-stools'.

When Rebecca Jones died late in 1856, the loss of her favourite relative meant that Kate had to turn elsewhere for Sunday teas, inspiring stories and useful advice. Her father's mother and two spinster sisters had moved from Southwark to rooms at 4 Evelyn Street (now Evelyn Walk), Hoxton New Town, where, much to Elizabeth Greenaway's dismay, John Greenaway agreed to support them. On her visits there, Kate discovered that her grandmother Sarah was a strangely apathetic person who rarely went out or paid visits; her aunt

Teatime in the Greenaway house, from a plate used in *Little Ann*, with Mrs Greenaway, Lizzie, Kate, Fanny and Johnnie.

Rebecca worked as a bookbinder when her brother gave her work; and her aunt Mary worked as a wood-engraver. It was this aunt Mary who was adopted as Kate's new mentor; Mary always had time for a walk and treats for tea, followed by readings from *The Pilgrim's Progress, John Gilpin,* or *Why the Sea Became Salt.* She also loved poetry, and the verses she read to her niece were the origin of Kate's love of poetry, an essential part of both their lives.

In mid-1856 John Greenaway was commissioned by the *Illustrated London News* to illustrate aspects of the sensational murder trial of William Palmer, the 'Prince of Poisoners', an event which left a great impression on Kate. Palmer had committed a series of ghastly poisonings in the Staffordshire town of Rugeley, and John Greenaway was sent there during the trial to capture the atmosphere of an event that outraged the nation. His drawings of Rugeley streets appeared in May issues and heightened Kate's fascination in the proceedings, which she later recalled as being of supreme interest and importance: 'I was an avid follower of current events and used to take an immense interest in the talk I heard going on.'

A year later the sensational news of the Indian Mutiny shocked the country. The *Illustrated London News* offered vivid, first-hand accounts of the slaughtering of innocent women, nurses and children by Sepoy rebels, and Kate studied each new instalment with growing concern. She was horrified by the engravings of the bloodthirsty Sikhs with dark, leering faces and bands of knives wrapped round their waists, and deeply moved by the fates of their many innocent victims. The 10 October 1857 issue contained a soldier's account of the massacre of Cawnpore, written after a survey of the wreckage, in all its horrifying detail: 'I have seen the fearful slaughter-houses . . . The quantity of dresses, clogged thickly with blood, children's frocks, frills and ladies' underclothing of all kinds . . . bonnets all bloody and one or two shoes,' the soldier began. With the fates of the Mutiny victims firmly lodged in her mind, Kate began to draw the escaping women and children on a small slate and became obsessed with their safety. She struggled to depict 'the Highland woman who heard the bagpipes' – a moving rescue by Scottish Highlanders, and, in trying to imagine the terror of pursuit, the horror of dying at the hands of Sepoy rebels, Kate worked herself into an emotional state that brought vivid nightmares. 'I could sit and think of the Sepoys till I could be wild with terror, and I used sometimes to dream of them,' she recalled later. 'But I was always drawing the ladies, nurses, and children escaping. Mine always escaped and were never taken.'[3]

Such displays of emotion and sensitivity were commonplace to most of Kate's family, but they did embarrass her older sister. One evening John Greenaway took Kate and Lizzie to Astley's equestrian theatre to see *The Storming and Capture of Delhi*, a theatrical tribute to General Havelock, the hero of the Mutiny. Staged with the aid of picturesque scenery of mountain passes, open country and rebel Sepoy camps, the production was a convincing re-enactment of the important Mutiny battles. During the 'Relief of Lucknow' scene, when an actor on a white stallion appeared as Havelock, Kate was so overwhelmed that she burst into tears and sobbed long and loud, refusing to stop when her sister told her she was being silly. Only her father understood his younger daughter's feelings. It was several years before Kate actually tried to describe those emotions; then, recalling her impressions on meeting Lord Roberts, she wrote, 'They are a brave and noble lot – to think how people can be like that, going to certain death – to the suffering of anguish. It feels to me too much to take – too much to accept – but it's beautiful.'[4]

One Sunday evening, while searching through the pages of her father's engraving scrapbook, Kate was impressed by Cruikshank's picture of Edward Underhill being burnt at the stake on Tower Green – an illustration for Ainsworth's *Tower of London*. Underhill was convincingly depicted, 'losing self-command in his horrible sufferings, and in agony plunged his hands into his face', before a crowd of eager spectators. The picture brought to mind Kate's despair over the murdered Mutiny victims and she became profoundly depressed. She hid the engraving, but was impelled to bring it out again to renew her impression and try to comprehend her grief. A short time later, gazing into a local printseller's window, she came upon an even more graphic portrayal of death and ultimate destruction, in a coloured mezzotint of John Martin's painting *The Great Day of His Wrath*. There, in the minutest detail, were bodies writhing and tumbling into a fiery abyss, with mountains crumbling and lightning striking as the end of the world drew near. Kate was amazed by this accurate picture of what she had always been taught the end of the world would be like. On her way home, her dread of man's fate was increased by meeting a ragged prophet of doom, dressed in animal skins and blowing his trumpet to announce that the end of the world was near. This warning and the series of events leading up to it plunged Kate into an even

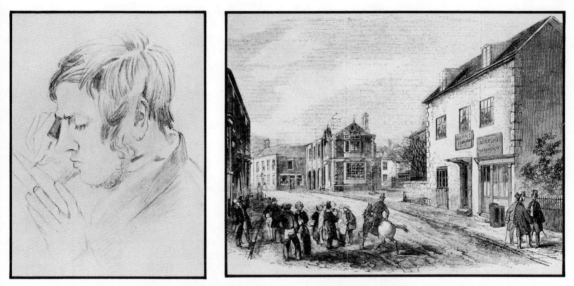

Left: John Greenaway at work. Pencil drawing by his colleague, Birket Foster.

Above right: Detail of street scene, Rugeley, Staffordshire, drawn and engraved by John Greenaway for the *Illustrated London News*, May, 1856.

Below: Two plates engraved by John Greenaway after Harrison Weir's animal drawings, published in *Trottie's Story Book* (c.1878).

'Which is the way to Somewhere Town?' Detail of a plate from *Under the Window* using recollections of childhood in London.

deeper depression, one that lasted for months and drove her 'almost frantic with terror at the thought of worlds afloat in space as dark as night'. Unable to imagine the purpose of life or what was behind it all, she became convinced that death was followed by 'a blank wall of nothingness'.[5]

Years later she clearly remembered the dreams of uncertainty and apprehension that plagued her childhood. As a child, she often dreamed of falling through water, with the relaxed comfort of passing green weeds and the pause before reaching the bottom and awakening. She dreamed of a chase and that, just as her capture was imminent, up she would soar over her pursuers' heads, above a steep staircase, out of one window, into another, when she awoke in ecstasy yearning to repeat the experience. She dreamed of an old wood where she knocked at a cottage door, to be answered by the ugliest old woman imaginable, with a face so terrible it jolted her awake, frightened and trembling. There were some early fears she could not understand, like the fear of water-taps that remained a life-long threat: these she mentioned but failed to explain in her autobiography.[6]

Although her mother generally confided family secrets and problems to young Kate ('I used to feel sometimes "Oh – why me?" she later confessed), during her moments of greatest distress, Kate turned to her father for comfort. He always seemed to understand, called her his favourite, nicknamed her 'Knocker' (because when she cried her face looked like the one on their door-knocker), made her laugh, and, most importantly, encouraged her in her drawing. On especially troubled, sleepless nights he allowed her to creep out of bed and watch him engrave; then she returned to her bed until the early morning, when she would prepare his breakfast and give her opinion of the finished woodblock. Sometimes he invited her to his offices on the first floor of an old house off Fleet Street, and there he soon appreciated her genuine interest in his work, her sharp eye for detail and keen desire to learn; and he did what he could to promote them.

About 1857 Kate's Aunt Thorne decided to emigrate to Canada, and her eldest daughter, Marion, remained behind, to be trained by John Greenaway as his engraver-assistant. Marion moved into the Greenaway household and stayed for several years; an arrangement Kate much disliked. She found her cousin too much like her aunt ('a most disagreeable person'), a demanding girl who complained when she failed to get her way, and seldom if ever appeared friendly. Part of Marion's training involved evening classes at the Finsbury School of Art, then about a mile away in William Street, Wilmington Square (off the present Claremont Square), and too great a distance for Marion to travel alone at night. Kate was persuaded to accompany her cousin each evening, and, while Marion grew bored and abandoned her lessons after a short time, Kate showed a serious interest in the school. She persuaded her mother (who had just inherited £100 from Rebecca Jones) to pay the threepence a lesson fee for her to attend evening classes twice a week, two hours each night. There she was taught to make accurate copies of geometric shapes and architectural ornaments. When she showed her work to her father he detected what he thought were undoubted signs of ability and believed he had found the answer to his daughter's future.

As a result, a year later, at the age of twelve, Kate was enrolled as a full-time student at the school, which had moved to Canonbury House. This was a large, impressive, Elizabethan mansion Kate called her 'ancient palace', with original

Canonbury Tower, site of Kate's early art school training.

35

Left: Kate Greenaway in 1862, aged 16, from an original photograph. *Right*: One of a set of six award-winning tile designs by Kate Greenaway to fulfil the National Art Training scheme, Stage 22c – 'Elementary Ornaments', for which she was awarded a national medallion in 1864.

moulded ceilings, stucco and carved oak chimney-pieces still intact. There for the next four years she continued her studies, and when, in 1862, the school moved again, to St George's Hall, Barnsbury, she followed it and studied for a further two years. During this time she became known as a dedicated, conscientious student who impressed her instructors, Miss Sarah Doidge and W.S. Hipwood. They in turn encouraged her to persevere and complete the formidable National Course of Art Instruction.

This early art training, with its emphasis on geometry, linear outline and decorative design, had a considerable influence on the development of the Greenaway style. The course was initiated by Henry Cole to create a nation of designer craftsmen, men and women capable of altering the quality and standards of public taste in Britain. Graduates of the National Course were awarded numerous certificates and medals to prove they had mastered the design principles Cole thought essential for creating the carpets, wallpapers and manufactured bric-à-brac essential to the mid-Victorian home. His students were meant to leave their local schools prepared to become ornamental designers in industry, where they would propagate Cole's principles of good taste.

The Finsbury School of Art was one of the largest and (according to the number of medals awarded) most successful of Cole's local branch schools. It was geared, like the other branches, to teach uniformity in technique and design principles. Its instructors enforced those lessons supplied by the central school established at South Kensington; they arranged competitions between other local schools (judged by central school officials), and submitted student work to annual national competitions at South Kensington. Students progressed along four carefully composed courses: Drawing, Painting, Modelling and Elementary Design, each completed using official supplies and publications originated at the central school.

Kate attended classes for four hours a week and began by copying a series of printed geometric outlines (*Dyce's Outlines*) and shading elaborate copies of printed architectural ornaments 'from the flat', graduated to drawing plaster casts 'from the round', and finally analytical botanical specimens for design motifs applicable to tiles and wallpapers. The underlying intention of the course was to rid students of the desire to make pretty pictures; those students with fine art aspirations, hoping to become painters or sculptors, soon abandoned their ambitions under the weight of an exhaustive series of lessons which, according to critics of the scheme, 'killed all joy in art work save the finishing of it'. The first stages of the Drawing Course were intended to teach perseverance and the importance of accurate detail. One student felt the strain of lessons he described as 'three months at the Egg Plant – and two and a half months at the Pilasters', and it was not uncommon for others to take as long as a year to complete the first stages of the course. Some found this useless; as one explained, 'we poor girls used to waste the precious hours labelled "Drawing" in slavish copying of the design of a vase, or a fancy scroll, printed on card. The only trouble was to get both sides exactly alike. It was "corrected", rubbed out, improved, and finally "clear-lined", that is firmly and fiercely drawn over with a fresh sharpened pencil. It may take two hours to complete one of these horrors; then you turned a new page and were given another.'[7]

Kate, however, found even these early lessons stimulating, and she attacked each one with unusual confidence. She had no doubt learned from her past attempts in drawing outline figures on her slate, so her persistence and performance during the ten stages of the Drawing Course were most impressive: she completed the five Ornamental stages within a year and received a local medal for a shaded chalk drawing of a sculpted column (Stage 4b) in 1858. She passed on to stages 6 to 10, flower and figure drawing, copied the required printed reproductions, and received a local bronze medal for an outline flower drawing (Stage 10a), and a local medal for a shaded flower drawing (Stage 10b).

She went on to the seven stages of the Painting Course, and learned the technical skills she was to employ all her professional life. The course required painted copies, in watercolour, tempera or oil, of architectural ornaments, plaster casts, and natural objects such as sea-shells and stuffed animals. Completing these, she quickly moved on to the Modelling Course, devised to teach the technical expertise required to create models for manufacturers of bric-à-brac. In order to complete the course students had to produce clay copies of architectural ornaments, plaster blackberry sprigs, flowers and classical statuary, and although Kate certainly had to struggle with her lumps of clay, she eventually completed the requirements and passed.

The final stage of her local training was Stage 22, the Elementary Design Course, which represented a considerable challenge. The instructions were to devise an ornate floral pattern that was to be incorporated into a prescribed geometric shape, the shape being changed each year to ensure a variety of results. While completing this final stage, Kate received her first national award: a bronze medal for her six tile designs in tempera, done so proficiently that the central school purchased them for future study aids. This award was a double triumph: it not only marked the end of her six-year local art training, but was also the first national prize awarded her school in more than four years.

The most obvious place for her to continue her studies was at the Central or National Art Training School, in South Kensington, where she could continue to follow Henry Cole's design precepts. About 1865 Kate enrolled in its Female School of Art, and she remained there for at least six years. Sessions ran from January to July, October to Christmas, and the high point of the year was the National Art Competition in mid-May, when a student saw his work in competition with that of other central and branch school colleagues. The school's atmosphere proved quite a change from Finsbury, with classrooms on the upper floor of a newly built wing to the South Kensington Museum, opposite the present Victoria and Albert Museum lecture theatre (it is now occupied by the Royal College of Art). Classrooms were kept strictly separate from the nearby male school and surprised many with their spartan décor, huge studio windows that reached to the roof, and movable partitions to alter the size of each classroom. Beyond the studios were the galleries housing the renowned Sheepshanks collection of Landseers, Mulreadys and Websters, as well as rows of ceramics, casts and important collections of objects left over from the Great Exhibition of 1851. All prospective students were required to undergo a rigorous interview with the eccentric headmaster, Richard Burchett. He would assess the applicant's potential and, as a minor painter in the Pre-Raphaelite style himself, he would look for inclinations in that direction. It was an intimidating experience, as Kate's future classmate, Elizabeth Thompson, recalled how she approached the 'bearded, velvet-skull-capped and cold-searching-eyed' Burchett in his office, seated behind a huge desk, then waited for 'The Presence' to speak. He asked to see her work, and when she spread it before him he scrutinized it with 'that Eye', mercilessly attacking weaknesses and suggesting reasons why further study was needed. Kate herself was nervous during her interview, but eventually Burchett warmed toward her and was impressed by her determination to succeed.

A whole new exhilarating world now opened before her. The behaviour of the school's students was a welcome contrast to Burchett's icy-cold manner, and each day they took their places amid 'much twining of arms and *darling-ing*' as they greeted old friends. According to Elizabeth Thompson, friendships were based upon making a good first impression: one girl, with short hair brushed back from her high forehead and double eye-glasses on a long out-thrust nose, was 'a capital hit'; another, 'a dear little girl with a pretty head and large eyes', laboured pathetically over her rendering of *The Fighting Gladiator* cast and received encouragement for her daunting task. On the whole, the female students came from middle-class families and were respectable young women who wished to emancipate themselves by training as artisans and decorative designers. In such company Kate immediately felt isolated: she had never found making friends an easy task, and here her plain, unobtrusive appearance proved a definite obstacle. A photograph taken when she was

Kate Greenaway, aged 21, a photograph taken in 1867, while enrolled at South Kensington.

twenty-one, two years after her enrolment, gives a hint as to why many of her fellow students scarcely noticed her: her hair was now brushed back from her forehead and fell down her back in a long, single, stringy curl; her face was plain, quite full, with deep dark eyes and a melancholy expression; she wore a loose-fitting, plain dress with a high collar and a thick chain and cross round her neck. Surrounded by vivacious 'well-spoken' young girls wearing bright, fashionable dresses, Kate preferred to avoid close contact. At one point, she filled a student notebook with apt sayings which reveal her feelings of inferiority and her attempts to rationalize her plain appearance: 'Beauty is but skin deep'; 'Beauty unadorned, adorned the most'; and 'Fair faces need no paint', appear among others on a similar theme.

One of the few students Kate considered her friends was the vivacious and extremely personable Elizabeth Thompson (afterwards Lady Butler, the famous genre and military painter). After only three months in Kate's class, Elizabeth confidently claimed, 'I am now a friend of more girls than I can individualise, and they all seem to like me.' However, even here Kate's natural shyness made their friendship a limited one. When, years later, she was asked about Kate, Elizabeth dismissed the relationship as incidental, 'She was a very quiet student, so it is difficult to find anything to say of her. Indeed so quiet and peaceable a student was necessarily liked and she never, to my knowledge, gave trouble or offence to anyone in the schools.' The two women were often seen working side by side, commenting on each other's work, but Kate made no effort to extend the relationship into her private life. Elizabeth believed that this was because Kate's shyness prevented easy conversation on topics other than art.[8] It was to become a lifelong problem for one so dedicated to her work.

Immediately after her enrolment, Kate became a member of the school's Sketching Club, and forgot her reserve when competing with her 'kindred spirits', as members chose to be called. She loved this organization, the regular meetings, the obligatory red cross badge used to sign one's work, the motto 'Thorough', often used to suggest Burchett's omnipresent influence, and, of course, the competitions based on students' interpretations of a literary or artistic theme. The awards were equally worthwhile, as Kate discovered during her first year when she won a copy of Tennyson's *Idylls of the King* as first prize.

However, the training Kate received at South Kensington was not very different from that at Finsbury, since she merely chose one of the National Course stages she had previously undertaken, and tried to improve on her past performance. The challenges came when learning to draw elaborately shaded studies of plaster casts in the soul-destroying 'South Kensington manner' – measuring with string, outlining, shading, stippling and stumping with paper cones and chalk until she had achieved a precise, lifeless copy just like every other student's. Eventually she passed into the coveted Life Room, where drawings were made from a fully clothed model, often costumed as a classical or historical figure. Kate was dedicated in her attempts to learn from Burchett and his assistants and even worked overtime; after hours she and Elizabeth Thompson shared a studio to pursue their studies. During the summer holidays, when Kate and her family returned to Rolleston, she took sketchbooks, paper, pencils and watercolours and applied her Kensington-acquired skills to the Nottinghamshire countryside. There she drew her favourite flowers, made several watercolours of the Chappells' kitchen, a portrait of Thomas Chappell seated at the kitchen hob and numerous pencil and chalk drawings of local plants and trees.

In 1867 Kate's first book illustration was published – the frontispiece to *Infant Amusements, or How to Make a Nursery Happy*, a parent's guide to furnishing the nursery. Kate's full-page black and white drawing, with crude contemporary figures grouped into boxes surrounded by plant borders, was heavily influenced by John Leech and John Gilbert illustrations. The work is only important in that it suggests that by 1867 Kate was considering work as a book illustrator; her decision probably influenced by her father, who worked for the book's publishers, Griffith and Farran.

The following year Kate exhibited publicly for the first time, sending her drawings to the Dudley Gallery, Egyptian Hall, Piccadilly. The Dudley was unusual in giving amateur artists and struggling art students the opportunity to exhibit their works, regardless of past performances. It was there, in the spring watercolour shows and later Black and White exhibitions, that the early works of Walter Crane and Randolph Caldecott were shown, as well as the pictures of such important illustrators as Leech and Gilbert. For her first appearance Kate chose six drawings on wood of fairies and gnomes, and she continued to exhibit at the Dudley throughout her student days.

In 1869 Kate began an important illustration commission – six watercolour designs for *Diamonds and Toads*, a children's toybook published by Frederick Warne. She used her eighteen-year-old sister Fanny as a model, and took over a year to complete her most ambitious project to date. That spring her first painting to be publicly exhibited, *The Fairies of the 'Caldon Low'*, was shown at the Dudley Gallery. Based upon a fairy theme, it demonstrates how far her skills in drawing from the imagination, as well as from models, were developing outside the classroom.

After four years at South Kensington, Kate received national recognition for her work. In 1869, among the total enrolment of 767 students (470 men, 297 women), she was awarded one of the two silver medals given to female students. The presentation was made early in 1870, at an impressive ceremony attended, according to the *Art Journal*, by 'a distinguished and numerous audience', and presided over by the Prince of Teck. After a brief lecture by Richard Burchett, Kate mounted the speaker's platform and received her medal, and a few days later her name appeared in the national papers.[9] This was a significant development: her medal was given for a watercolour of a young boy's head 'from life' (Stage 17), which suggested that if she concentrated more on study from models and less on the decorative, ornamental aspects of her training, she would have even greater success.

In fact Kate was not satisfied with the Kensington life class, with its bored models dressed in suits of armour or elaborate costumes that made figure study more a lesson in copying details than a study of the human form. She recognized the importance of study from the nude, but only the fine art students enrolled at the Royal Academy schools were allowed such study, and then only after hours spent on studies of classical sculpture. The problem was vexing to many art educators of the period. 'Here in our schools every difficulty would seem to be put in the way of study from life,' protested the neoclassical painter Edward Poynter, an early campaigner for life study. In his view an art student first needed to know 'something of the construction of the human body from the living model' before 'the idealised forms of Greek sculpture' could be understood. The chances for women students to study 'from life' were even more limited, and only those willing to augment their formal training by enrolling in a private school could hope to develop their figure drawing.

One popular venue for figure study from the nude model for male and female students was Heatherley's School of Art, the only school of its kind in London, where artists could simply pay their fees and study from the nude, undeterred by prerequisites or entrance requirements. Edward Poynter, Burne-Jones and Walter Crane had all attended Heatherley's; and Kate now followed suit and enrolled in evening classes while she was still a day student at South Kensington. From the start, however, she found the new school's atmosphere and approach quite unlike anything she had previously experienced, and she became bewildered and confused. Thomas Heatherley, the school's director, was himself an enigma, an artistic character totally dedicated to his school and his students, with an uncanny ability to impress everyone he met. He roamed the school looking like a biblical ghost, an intense expression on his gaunt face. 'You took to him at once,' one student recalled, 'he had a high forehead, a straight nose, deep-set eyes, hollow cheeks, long hair and beard, almost colourless, like his complexion, and a quiet voice. He used to pace up and down the school in slippers, clad only in a black velvet gown, which reached to his heels, and softly humming to himself.'[10]

41

When Kate entered Heatherley's it was filled with students intent on studying from the live model, draped or nude. Even more surprising, men and women worked in the same classroom, the nude class separated only by a brief screen and curtain from the rest of the classes. On the walls hung rows of familiar plaster casts and the occasional surprise, like the death mask of Thomas Lawrence, 'on which some of his whiskers were to be seen', which was a great favourite among students.

Kate soon discovered that her Kensington certificates and medals meant nothing at Heatherley's, and her confidence changed to a sense of inadequacy as Heatherley stressed a more adventurous, individual approach to figure study. She was told that her technical skills needed to be loosened until she developed her own style. 'Mr Heatherley will not countenance carelessness of any kind. But at the same time he does not concentrate on technique. In fact, we are allowed – I should say encouraged – to develop our own style,' one student recalled.[11] This was a bewildering challenge which Kate worked three hours each night to master, until it became intolerably frustrating. Heatherley's emphasis on individuality lacked the rigidity, the regimented discipline forced on her under the National Course training scheme. She needed to know the boundaries, the guidelines of her lessons, and eventually had to turn elsewhere to find them.

During 1870 and 1871, in addition to her studies at Kensington and Heatherley's, Kate was also preparing more book illustrations. She earned £36 from the colour printer, Kronheim, for her watercolour designs for *Diamonds and Toads*; and she finished a new series of watercolours to illustrate nine of Madame D'Aulnoy's fairy tales published by Gall and Inglis, as well as black and white drawings for a new Griffith and Farran commission, *My School Days in Paris*. As a result, by the end of 1871 she had earned over £70, and future commissions were assured.

A short time later Kate left Heatherley's and enrolled in the Slade School of Art, which had been established in 1868 to give equal opportunities to male and female students. From 1871 it was directed by Edward Poynter, whose objective was to remove the restrictions placed on art education by Henry Cole and the National Course scheme. He developed the Slade into a school with a

Left: Elizabeth Thompson (Lady Butler) and *right*: Edward Poynter.

 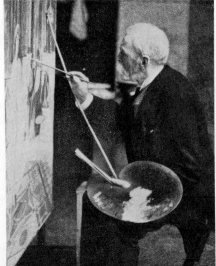

Left: The Life Class, Slade School, 1883 and *right*: self-portrait watercolour.

reputation rivalled only by that of the Royal Academy schools. Kate met Poynter at the obligatory student interview, the only requirement for enrolment. She was placed in one of three life classes, where she found Poynter a stern taskmaster, who demanded absolute obedience to his principles. 'Do not copy, express form,' he bellowed until it became a student catch-phrase. 'Breadth and freedom come first and detail will follow.' Here again was the conflict between Kate's early copyist training and the freer style advocated at Heatherley's. Again she made an honest attempt, but when she settled down to measure, then outline a model's pose, Poynter changed the pose before her first lines were down, forcing a rigorous, exhausting pace among his students until they produced 'an intelligent representation of the model . . . with special reference to action, light, shade, tone and general correctness of drawing'.

It is not known how long Kate remained at the Slade, although its influence is apparent in the watercolours and figure studies she exhibited in the early 1870s, especially the two children's portraits exhibited at the Dudley in 1872 and four the following year at the Royal Society of British Artists. These watercolours contain the earliest known examples of Greenaway children, painted from local models, some in Islington street settings, and posed in dresses of Kate's own design and making. The most notable watercolour is *A Fern Gatherer*, of a single young girl posed in an old hat and dotted, bright turqoise smock, a bundle of ferns hanging from a string over her shoulder. The pose itself reveals Kate's attempt to present the body as naturally as possible, but, as in most of her pictures of this period, the figure remains stiff and awkward, the arms suspended, the viewer's interest invariably drawn to the meticulous detail of background, face or costume.

Despite her struggles with figure drawings, by 1873, in addition to her modest success in the galleries, Kate was accepting sufficient offers to illustrate books and magazines for her to feel it was safe to leave art school to pursue a career as artist, illustrator and, if she worked hard enough, an author.

3   The Amazing Reward
1873–1879

Above the world now, above its good and ill,
I ventured on a new and lovely life –
'Sesame!' had been said and I passed in,
My soul and body no more waged in strife.

KATE GREENAWAY

During the next six years Kate tried to reward her mother's sacrifices by taking on a growing number of commissions. Her letters, the great amount of card, book and periodical work, and the little evidence of any private life at this time suggest that she worked extremely hard to achieve her goal, and did very little else.

The first encouraging signs appeared when Kate began to design greeting cards. By the early 1870s the greeting card industry had experienced a phenomenal growth, and the Belfast-based firm of Marcus Ward and Company was among the most influential. With a London office established in 1867, and a staff of imaginative designers, the firm flooded stationers', drapers' and milliners' shop windows with striking, well designed, colour lithographed cards. As a result of sales in America and on the Continent, their reputation spread quickly and the *Art Journal* (1870) claimed enthusiastically: '. . . their merest trifles are sound Art-teachers, and they circulate nothing that endangers a true and pure taste for what is excellent in art.' Kate was introduced to the London branch manager, William Hardcastle Ward, a shrewd judge of talent who eventually employed over thirty designers, including Walter Crane, his brother, Thomas Crane (the firm's artistic director) and Henry Stacy Marks. She arrived for her interview carrying a rough watercolour sketch for a Valentine, which failed to impress him, but did indicate her abilities as an ornamental designer. He accepted the design and had it altered by his staff artists. To his astonishment, when it was published sales reached 25,000 copies in a few weeks. For this Kate received about £3 and Ward's assurance that she now had a future with his firm.

Although the exact number of Kate's designs for Ward is not known (neither kept a complete record or set of cards), those that do survive indicate that she was under pressure to find her own saleable design formula. She began by filling cards with flowers; then added tiny fairies and children posed among the foliage; on other occasions she told a story, as in her extremely successful series 'The Story of Little Red Riding Hood's Christmas'. These were issued in sets of from two to eight cards each, folded, some sewn-bound, and sold with ornate envelopes. Ward had seen the meticulously worked watercolour portraits of young children Kate exhibited at the Dudley and he recognized from them that 'her special talent was in the direction of costume figures and dainty colours'. At his instigation, Kate designed a series of cards showing children dressed in historical costume, placed against plain backgrounds, with ornate coloured and gold-trimmed borders. With their romantic poses and evocative verses, these became the highly successful Greenaway cards that made her reputation as a Ward designer. Her formula had been established only after months of painstaking struggle and frustration, for despite Kate's art school training, choosing colours suitable for lithographic reproduction proved a major stumbling block. As a result, many of her watercolour designs were at first gaudy and unusable. She made frequent studies of colour schemes in favourite paintings at the National Gallery, and practised the elaborate lessons outlined in Redgrave's *An Elementary Manual of Colour*. Then, armed with a number of new designs, she would approach William Ward, occasionally including examples of her own verses with her watercolours. But Ward was a hard taskmaster and merciless in his judgement of his artists' work. When he decided her designs were too crude or her figures too detailed for the lithographer's stone, Kate willingly destroyed them and started again. And yet, when he attacked her verses as 'rubbish and without poetic feeling', she only stopped showing them, continuing to write in private, and returned to her saleable design work. Her notebooks and letters of this period show her as a determined career woman, hard at work despite serious disappointments and setbacks. 'Fatigue promises reward, perseverance gets the prize,' appeared on one notebook page; on another she planned 'outlines for Christmas cards in colours or gold outline, long lines and two or three pretty quaint figures in plain gold and white, pale salmon border or duck's egg colour', or the more evocative card with 'a little angel gathering flowers in a field of white flowers, a rosy sunset, sky, moon and one star – or sunlight'.

At the same time as she was producing her greeting card designs, Kate undertook commissions for black and white illustrations of various children's books. Two men were responsible for most of these: her father, and her new patron, the Reverend William Loftie. William Loftie had bought her drawings on wood at the Dudley Gallery in 1868, and in 1873, as the newly appointed

The 'Little Red Riding Hood' set with envelope, 1868, designed by Kate Greenaway. One of her earliest card designs.

45

editor of *People's Magazine*, he decided to publish them. A short time before publication he invited Kate to his office to explain her bewildering drawings of fairies and flower-pot gnomes. At that first meeting, despite the differences in their backgrounds, she made a lasting impression on her new patron. Loftie was a refined, cultured man in his early thirties, with a house in Upper Berkeley Street, a talented, sympathetic wife and a long list of literary and journalistic accomplishments to his credit. In addition to editing *People's Magazine*, he served as assistant chaplain at the Chapel Royal, Savoy, was a staff member of the *Guardian*, an indomitable antiquarian and later author of several tourist guides and twenty art books. With his personable manner and obvious concern, he quickly made Kate feel at ease. He, in his turn, was impressed by the subtleties of her character, and later described her at their first meeting as: 'very small, very dark, and seemed clever and sensible, with a certain impressive expression in her dark eyes that struck everyone'. Following their amiable discussion Loftie published five of her six drawings and adopted her as his protégée, securing future book commissions and directing her card work for their mutual acquaintance, William Ward. He also introduced Kate to his wife, invited her to their home, and in later years relished his position as her first real patron. This led the *Dictionary of National Biography* to conclude that 'It was on his advice that Kate Greenaway devoted her energies solely to the illustration of children's books.'

This claim was not entirely valid, for Kate's father had by far the most immediate influence over her early career. John Greenaway knew all too well the trials and anxieties involved in establishing oneself as an illustrator, and he was determined to help his daughter whenever he could. Their working relationship strengthened with each new book or periodical commission he engraved from her drawings, and John Greenaway's influence remained a guiding force throughout the 1870s, when he introduced Kate to the unfamiliar regions of the publishing world. Had it not been for his encouragement and advice, Kate would scarcely have had the confidence to produce the large number of illustrations that appeared at this time. But the more he helped her, the more frustrating the situation became. From childhood Kate had been upset by her inability to reach beyond his smiles to understand his inner nature. Her quest had begun in a childhood dream that now characteristically recurred. In it she gazed into her father's face as it gradually transformed into a stranger's, until she awoke with a terrified start. She always feared losing him, and later clearly remembered her tortured reactions to the dream: how she woke 'in an agony of misery' each time a false face appeared, confused at being 'confronted with yet another and another but never his own'.[1]

By accepting the advice of her father, William Loftie and William Ward, Kate was carefully guided through the early stages of her professional career and her income quickly rose. At the end of 1874 she recorded a total of £120, earned from a full-page drawing for the *Illustrated London News*, a new black and white volume of stories, *Fairy Gifts*, for Griffith and Farran, and new card designs for William Ward.

In the middle of the following year the Greenaway household experienced a considerable upheaval, when Lizzie and Fanny both announced their engage-

The Elf Ring, detail of watercolour, compared with detail of Richard Dadd's *Puck*, engraved in the *Art Journal*, 1864.

ments and were married, leaving only Kate and her brother with their parents. Kate still occasionally turned to Johnnie for advice or his services as a model, but he was too engrossed in his new career as chemistry demonstrator at the Royal College of Chemistry, South Kensington, to be of much comfort. Johnnie had worked hard for this position. After a frustrating apprenticeship to his father, he had enrolled by his own wish at the Royal College, and, with characteristic Greenaway dedication, he now worked long hours to build up his reputation. The marriages of the Greenaway sisters were, in one sense, a mixed blessing, then – at least to Kate.

To the considerable relief of her mother, Lizzie Greenaway's turbulent romance with a Rolleston cousin several years her junior had come to an end, and she was safely married to Frank Coxall, a London businessman. But when Fanny married a distant cousin, Edward Martin Dadd, this marriage introduced a considerable amount of doubt and fear into the Greenaway household. Fanny's new husband came from the notorious Dadd family, which had a fearful legend attached to it. The family was well known to the Greenaways, and each of Fanny's five children lived under a cloud of apprehension and worry as to whether they would inherit the Dadd family strain of mental instability that had led their great-uncle Richard Dadd to kill his father and live out his life in a home for the criminally insane; another uncle, Stephen, and his sister Maria had suffered similar illnesses. According to the daughter of Edward Martin Dadd junior (Fanny's eldest child) this question was openly discussed among her family and the tragic story of Richard related when children were old enough to understand the problem, all in an attempt to warn future generations of the danger.

Although Kate never specifically mentioned the horrible fate of Richard Dadd, the clues she left behind in letters and notebooks suggest that she accepted his story with tolerance and understanding. It certainly seems highly likely that she would have found his work attractive, for Richard Dadd's fairies and gnomes, wood engraved and published in S.C. Hall's *Book of British Ballads* (1842), were in a style she had long admired. A Shakespeare enthusiast, Richard had painted pictures from the plays, such as his *Puck* (1841), which was subsequently engraved for the *Art Journal* (1864) at the time when Kate was a young art student searching through such periodicals for inspiration.

Detail of original watercolour for *Diamonds and Toads*, c.1870, using Fanny as a model.

Moreover, two years after Fanny's marriage into the Dadd family, there was still interest in Richard's work, despite his lengthy confinement. *The World* (26 December 1877) confidently claimed that he was still a potent force, for, although early 'shipwrecked', he 'never went actually to ruin. Art is thus his mistress still . . . it is to his beloved brush that he clings, and wills continuously, with that enthusiasm and unwearying ardour the true painter alone can know.'

It is interesting to consider Richard Dadd's influence on Kate's early work. For example, a comparison between Richard's 'Passion Series' watercolours of the mid-1850s and Kate's watercolour drawings for *Diamonds and Toads*, published fifteen years later, is quite revealing. There is a startling similarity of technique, as in the grotesque facial expressions and wide, frightening eyes emphasized by firm outlines. The work of both throughout this period is marked by the continual presence of witches and demonic gnomes. In addition, could Kate perhaps have had Richard in mind when she wrote the following maxims in a notebook found among her papers? 'Great wits to madness sure are near allied, of thin partitions do their bounds divide . . . Scandal will rub out like dirt when it is dry . . . There's a skeleton in every house.'

By the end of 1875 Kate's income had risen markedly. This was primarily the result of Marcus Ward and Company's reissuing her card designs in a new series of six elaborate gift volumes; her illustrations were used as coloured frontispieces tipped in to accompany new black and white pictures, or as coloured plates mounted into select volumes in their 'Chromograph' series. With the publication of these books, the public came to appreciate the wide range of Kate's skills: her tiny fairies cling to flowers in *A Cruise in the Acorn*; her Pre-Raphaelite-inspired lovers languish in misty landscapes in *Melcomb Manor*, and are epitomized in her Valentine masterpiece, *The Quiver of Love*.

As the number of her commissions increased, Kate decided she needed a studio where she could work undisturbed, free from her mother's threats to 'clear up' at the end of each working day. She found a small room in a three-storey terraced house a short distance away, at 1 College Place (now 25 College Cross), in a side street off the noisy Liverpool Road. This studio heralded a period of bright-eyed optimism in Kate's working life, as a friend later described her:

> She was then, as ever, gentle, patient, industrious, exquisitely sensitive, extraordinarily humorous, while under and over it all was an indomitable will. I always remember one little remark she made to me once when we were walking from her home in Islington to a little room she had taken as a studio (her first) in a side street. It was wet and miserable, the streets vulgar and sordid. 'Never mind,' she said, 'I shall soon be in the spring.' The first primrose she drew upon the sheet before her would place her in another world.'[2]

Kate worked in this small studio until 1879, painting the watercolour portraits of those young children she enticed off the street to pose in costumes of her own design and making. Some were placed against brick-lined back alleyways; others figured in imaginary flower-filled gardens. The most notable of these child portraits was *Little Miss Prim*, a large watercolour of her landlady's young daughter, Florence, portrayed with Rossetti-inspired frizzy red hair, seated in a visionary garden, dressed in mob cap and embroidered dress. When the picture failed to sell at the Dudley, Kate stored it away, until the news of her model's tragic death at the age of thirteen impelled her to give the picture to her landlady as a tribute to the beautiful child who had captured her heart. Stylistically, the painting gives a clear indication of Kate's development as a studio watercolourist: the garden foliage, dress and floral pattern show how much she still used her ornamental design training, while the stiffly posed child recalls her difficulties during life classes at Heatherley's and the Slade. The dress and mob cap are similar to her greeting card designs and suggest that the 'Greenaway child' formula was gaining in strength and purpose in Kate's mind.

At the end of 1876 Kate's income from book illustrations, cards and paintings came to £200, and her reputation as a black and white illustrator continued to grow. She concentrated on those books with immediate popular appeal: moralistic fairy tales and childhood reminiscences, stories written by prolific children's writers, and by amateur authors and society ladies. Most of these were published by Marcus Ward or Griffith and Farran, and indicate how heavily Kate relied on tried and true compositional themes and devices: Pre-Raphaelite-inspired maidens and children in long, flowing gowns, set in imaginary landscapes with castles and carefully trimmed gardens (see *Starlight Stories* and *The Quiver of Love*); or fairies and gnome-like creatures, often arranged in fairy rings. She even borrowed from Tenniel's illustrations in *Alice in Wonderland* to develop her own blonde girl confronted with a number of bizarre creatures. An early sketchbook (dated 1868) shows just how she went about her *Alice* studies, filling pages with crisp outlines to define her characters'

Left: a plate by Walter Crane from *The Quiver of Love*, 1876 and *right*: *Disdain*, a plate designed by Kate Greenaway from *The Quiver of Love*, 1876.

features. On other pages she made pen and ink costume studies using the heavy black outline and cross-hatching technique derived from Leech, Gilbert and other 'sixties school' illustrators.

A taxing black and white commission was offered by William Ward in 1877, when he proposed an illustrated edition of *Topo: a Tale about English Children in Italy* by Gertrude Brunefille (Lady Colin Campbell). It is odd that Kate was chosen to draw pictures of a country she had never visited, but she eagerly accepted the challenge. She arrived at Ward's office with sketch pad and pencil and, as he later remembered, 'almost as quickly as they could be talked about', she dashed off rapid sketches to fit each event in the story. Most of these she ruthlessly tore up herself or begged him to do so; then she returned to her studio to complete the forty-four drawings eventually published. These have a curious, uneven quality, her figures drawn with poorly defined legs and feet, set in vaguely Italianate backgrounds. The essential donkey in the story presented the greatest problem, and eventually, after at least a dozen attempts, she gave up and allowed one of Ward's draughtsmen to complete the drawing – a humiliating experience for her father, who had made his reputation drawing and engraving animals. Although the book went into a reprint, the poor production of the first edition raised doubts in Kate's mind about her future with its publisher. Many of her family and friends had warned that Ward was exploiting her by continually reissuing her card designs in books without consulting her. She asked Ward to return her original work so that she could control future publication, but he flatly refused. An argument ensued and Kate severed all ties with Ward and his firm. This meant that he could reissue only those card designs in his possession and that Kate had to consider taking on illustration work elsewhere. She accepted the rift (according to William Loftie)

Kate Greenaway's 'Dolly's Dream', engraved in *The Illustrated London News*, 15 December, 1875, compared with detail of Tenniel's *Alice in Wonderland*, 'Alice and the Dodo'.

'with remarkable good temper and moderation', which suggests that she was not then worried about her future. Indeed, the separation left her free to pursue a long-standing dream.

Kate had often hoped to have a book of her own designs and verses published, and she had spoken to her father about it. He advised her to be thankful for her ability to interpret other authors' works, and to forget about ambitions beyond the role of the everyday illustrator. This was an understandable reaction from one who had endured so rocky a career, but Kate remained determined. We know from her axiom-filled notebooks how strongly she yearned for recognition and greater creative independence: 'Desire of glory is the last garment that even wise men put off,' she wrote, very near, 'Fortune knocks once at least at every man's door.' Thus inspired, she started to fill a small notebook with verses and drawings of children in situations borrowed from her past: memories of Rolleston, bits of childhood rhymes and new verses worked round a favourite word. A number of these have a distinctly melancholy mood; for example, a forlorn Margery Brown waits at the top of a hill for a knight in shining armour; a pair of girls stand on a hill, overlooking the sea, bored and longing for excitement – 'Right sad were we to stand alone . . .'; a group of sad-faced children file out of their school house. According to Kate's own memories, these children should be laughing and happy to escape for another day; instead she gives them frowns and her verse asks 'Who can say what may not happen today?' There were even stronger reminders of her childhood fears: a witch luring children – 'Little boys and girls, will you come and ride with me on my broomstick – far and wide?'; or the Indian Mutiny-inspired goblin kidnapper with a defenceless boy in his clutches.

After filling nearly fifty pages, Kate showed her project to her father, and

51

impressed by her perseverance, he promised to mention it to an old friend and colleague at Landells', Edmund Evans, who now owned and ran a famous colour printing and engraving business. If anyone in London could advise Kate on publication of her project, John Greenaway believed Evans was the man.

By the 1870s Evans' firm had a high reputation. 'No firm in London could come near the result that Edmund Evans could get with as few, say, as three colour-blocks, so wonderful was his ingenuity, so great was his artistic taste and so accurate his eye.'[3] His firm printed most of the coloured children's toybooks in Britain, as well as covers for railway novels, fine art editions of poetry and prose, and colour plates for numerous periodicals. The 'mighty Evans' himself was an indomitable businessman, forever searching for new projects as his business grew. He filled the gaps between print runs by initiating his own series of children's toybooks, for which he secured the illustrations of Walter Crane and, from 1877, Randolph Caldecott, and which were distributed by the publisher George Routledge.

Unknown to Kate, Evans already admired her greeting card work – those 'very pretty quaint designs of little children, so cleverly lithographed' – and on the strength of these and her recent black and white illustrations to Cassell's *Little Folks* magazine, he agreed to meet her and discuss her book.

During the interview Evans warmed to his friend's daughter, and long afterwards remembered her book of 'odd drawings with nonsense verses written to them'. Attracted by its bold, spare compositions, the children often set amidst a sea of white space, the halting verses neatly pencilled underneath, he decided it would make 'a telling children's book'. He offered to buy it outright, and after due consideration Kate agreed to this and to the title – *Under the Window*, taken from one of the verses.

When Evans showed the manuscript to his associate, George Routledge's reaction was characteristically cool. The verses were too simple, too much nonsense verses, which he thought would fail to attract the book-buying public. But he agreed to distribute it if certain changes were made in the text. This decision, and Evans's obvious enthusiasm, meant that Kate's book had a good chance of success.

However, Kate's exploitation at the hands of William Ward made her approach her new business adviser with considerable caution. She was not a shrewd businesswoman, but in dealing with Evans she did manage to achieve considerable success. She had sold the copyright on her first drawings outright to Evans, and received a third of each book's profits. Later she asked Evans for a half share in the profits plus a £5 reproduction fee, for each drawing regardless of size; the original drawings were also to be returned to her. Such an arrangement was unlike any Evans had previously made, but on the strength of her first book's potential he agreed.

During the early months of 1878 Kate continued her career as a black and white illustrator and children's portrait artist. At the Dudley Gallery that year she exhibited three portraits, of which two were sold for a total of fifteen guineas and one was engraved as a full page in the *Illustrated London News*. In May at the Royal Academy she exhibited the full-length watercolour *Little Girl with Doll*; this was singled out by the *Athenaeum* for its 'extremely clever'

Original watercolour for *Hop o'my Thumb*, *c.*1871 in the Gall and Inglis Madame d'Aulnoy series (here, the arrival of Hop o'my Thumb with a message for the king).

drawing. She completed more illustrations for *Little Folks*, and began an association with a periodical based in New York, *St Nicholas, Scribners' Magazine for Girls and Boys*.

In the autumn Kate set to work preparing *Under the Window* for the engravers. Willing to accept advice from Evans or any of his associates, she received a letter from his latest protégé, Randolph Caldecott, who, in September 1878, wrote from his studio to recommend two professional models – 'One is a "Saxon boy" of six years old called A. Frost; the other is a "vivacious girl of an auburn colour" entitled Minnie Frost.'[4]

At the end of the month Kate met Caldecott on a weekend visit to Evans's country home in Witley, Surrey. There they discussed their careers and discovered that they had much in common: they were born the same year, loved the countryside, had begun their careers as black and white illustrators after lessons at the Slade and now shared employers and publishers. There may have even been a hint of romance in the air, for Caldecott was a strikingly handsome bachelor with a perpetual glint in his eye, a man of sparkling good humour and captivating charm. Kate, on the other hand, retained her shy, reserved manner. Caldecott insisted that his interest was only in her work, as he wrote to a friend

Edmund Evans in middle age.

shortly after his return to London: 'Many charming drawings – coloured – did I see on Sunday of children and child-life done on paper by Kate Greenaway, in whose company I passed the last weekend at Witley, near Godalming. We were staying in the same house, I mean. She had not a sunny smile; but the book which will contain the drawings – added to bits by herself – ought to be a success.'[5]

Evans had also shown Kate's work to his neighbour, George Eliot, who found the drawings 'quaint and pretty'; the verses left her 'unusually content'. When she heard that Kate and Caldecott were spending the weekend nearby, she urged them both to try their drawing skills on a pair of local twins. They agreed and, according to Caldecott, a Saturday afternoon sketching party was formed, when he and Kate 'produced sketch-books and made a grand pencil charge upon the village. A history of the twins was kindly given by the mother, how they lived together, ate together, slept together, walked together, did everything together. Interesting. My opinion was that they were 2 fat, ugly children who looked as though they laid down to their food and slobbered it up. We all thought them to be of the porcine genus.'[6]

Although *Under the Window* was planned for publication in late 1878, it was delayed by a year because of Routledge's insistence on changes in the verses. The publisher suggested that the popular poet of society verse, Frederick Locker, might be consulted, since his highly-praised first book of poems, *London Lyrics*, expressed many of the sophisticated, yet child-like, sentiments Kate had failed to convey in her verses. Evans agreed and sent Kate's manuscript to Locker, 'not to be rewritten', he later recalled, 'but to correct what they [Routledge] did not understand, the quaintness – quite in character with the illustrations, which were certainly original'.[7]

Locker was impressed by Kate's verses and drawings, and he showed them to his wife (herself the writer of children's stories and religious tracts), who was similarly taken by them. He quizzed Evans about the author, and, according to

Evans, was 'very much interested' in all he learned. Then, one day late in 1878, he boldly knocked at Kate's studio door, prepared to discuss her poetic technique. Kate opened the door to a fifty-seven-year-old gentleman, impeccably dressed in silk hat, dotted silk tie, his waistcoat and topcoat cut in the height of fashion. With kid gloves in his hand and a monocle in one eye, he must have seemed a curious intruder to the back streets of Islington. In fact he was a controversial figure: his friends called him a great dandy; his critics pronounced him affected, a retired civil servant turned fortune hunter, 'ignorant in the commonest concerns of life'. His first marriage, to a daughter of the Earl of Elgin, provided him with society connections; his second, to a wealthy heiress, assured him a life of leisure and dilettantism. He divided his time between collecting books and antiques and gracing the drawing rooms of London society, entertaining guests with stories of his artistic and literary friends, among them Tennyson, Browning, Ruskin, Burne-Jones and William Morris. He also had a particular penchant for struggling illustrators, had commissioned Cruikshank and Richard Doyle to prepare illustrations for him and, more recently, befriended young Caldecott.

With his store of charm and sophistication he immediately dazzled Kate. Like so many of his conquests, she had never known such a man: someone who (in Austin Dobson's words) 'had seen people of whom I had only heard he had visited places of which I had only read. He seemed to know everyone – to have the entrée everywhere . . . sketching them lightly with a deft, quick touch in which a native kindness was always tripping up a reluctant but very acute perception of anything like vulgarity or pretence.'[8] She considered his visit a great honour, and shortly afterwards she wrote to tell him so. However, despite his advice, she confessed to Evans that she did not like his alterations to her verses. 'She preferred her own in their ruggedness and quaintness,' he recalled, although her letter to Locker gave no hint of this: 'I am deeply obliged to you for taking so much trouble. I think them [her verses] much improved. Mr. Evans also is quite satisfied.' To emphasize her gratitude, she also promised to send three little cards and 'the rest of the set as soon as I get them', as well as the book's outline proofs.[9] Eight days later Evans also wrote to Locker, enclosing a complimentary book in thanks for 'the very generous way of treating us'.[10]

It was Kate's first letter that initiated a seventeen-year friendship with Locker. During this time he gained a position of considerable influence over her professional and private life, although the real reason for his ecstatic praises of her drawings and poems was at first unknown to her. They awoke in him the element of child-like innocence he had long tried to describe in his own verses. At the time of their first meeting, his poetic pen had all but dried up, and he could only reprimand himself for his inability to write. He recognized that the cause lay in his exhausting social life – his poetic muse 'strangled in his white ties' – which he nevertheless refused to abandon. In way of compensation, he determined to use his wealth and experience to guide not only Kate's literary skills but also her entry into the world of London society.

Early in 1879, with her previous year's earnings at £550 and the promised publication of *Under the Window*, Kate convinced her father that they could afford to move house. Despite reports of the worst economic depression to hit trade and business in years, Kate and her father pooled their resources and purchased a ninety-nine-year lease on a new and much larger house at 11 Pemberton Gardens. The house was one of several recently built in Holloway, transforming a vast meadow into a sedate suburb for respectable middle classs residents. It was, like most other houses in the street, a four-storey, semi-detached brick house with high front windows in Italianate plasterwork, a steep stair leading to a columned entry, and a long garden at the back. Beyond that lay the railway and the open expanses of Tufnell Park; to the north the still undeveloped land opposite rose toward the heights of Highgate, and to the west, the fields and country lanes of Hampstead. Pemberton Gardens remained for some years a prim, quiet (apart from the railway) and thoroughly respectable neighbourhood. Elizabeth Greenaway gave up her shop and regarded the move as a considerable social step up from Upper Street. Here she and her family conformed to the manners of their neighbours, while Kate was inspired by the peaceful setting and the large new studio in the house. The move to Pemberton Gardens signalled a greater optimism toward her work and her future as an artist.

Frederick Locker was the first to approve the move; he praised Kate's studio for its 'pretty studio view' overlooking the garden – a considerable improvement on the tiny room in College Place. Here respectability was very much in evidence, the Islington street urchins now replaced by the obedient, well dressed local children who passed the Greenaways' house on their way to the local church and school. Kate loved to watch these neighbourhood children from a window, and one Sunday she caught sight of three small girls, identically dressed in warm winter coats, muffs and bonnets, being ushered along the street by their proud mother. She recognized the woman as the schoolmaster's formidable, quite unapproachable wife; but in her excitement she rushed out of the door and after them. She politely implored the woman to let her children model for a periodical commission, but the horrified woman flatly refused. She would not have *her* children displayed on the cover of 'any popular magazine'! Angrily she stomped off, leading her daughters in front of her; while Kate rushed back to her studio. Determined not to be thwarted she prepared her drawing from memory. Then, when the magazine appeared with the picture of the three girls, the irate mother stared at it aghast, telling her daughters, 'She probably sketched you from her studio window!'

Such incidents helped Kate to bury herself in work while she waited anxiously for *Under the Window* to appear. She worked furiously to complete commissions for *St Nicholas* and *Little Folks*, and a coloured Valentine frontispiece for a February *Illustrated London News*. A year had quickly passed since Evans agreed to publish her book, and during that time Kate had become a constant and welcomed guest at his Witley home. In mid-February she busily prepared dress designs for the Evans children, and wrote to Mrs Evans that the skirt on one must, of course, be pink, with 'pink bows on all things'.[11] She inserted a detailed pen drawing of her design – a girl in mob cap and long bow-trimmed dress like so many of her card designs, but hardly appropriate to the country lives of the Evans children.[12]

Original watercolour design for the omitted witch plate in *Under the Window*.

Her new friends were also interested in the progress of *Under the Window*. In late February Frederick Locker wrote to Caldecott of his delight over Kate's work. Caldecott was pleased to learn they shared a friendship and assured Locker that he too was certain her first book would be a success: 'You speak of Miss Greenaway – there will appear (soon, I suppose) a very pretty book of her children's life and habits and pastimes.'[13]

In March Kate exhibited at the Dudley Gallery two watercolour children's portraits, which the *Athenaeum* singled out for praise. In May she exhibited her portrait of a young girl, *Misses*, at the Royal Academy. While the publicity she received was greater than any given previously, it proved misleading and depressing: the *Athenaeum* attributed the picture to *Mrs* Greenaway: 'a charming study of rich and powerful colour marred by the dirtiness of the flesh'; the comic paper *Fun* commented:

> A Picture by Miss Greenaway (we scarcely like a bit of it)
> Is rightly tilted 'Misses' for she hasn't made a hit of it.

Her most recent black and white commissions brought further disappointments. The first, for William Loftie's 'Art at Home' series, was *Amateur Theatricals*. Kate completed six pencil drawings for it, using her love of Shakespeare's plays to concoct a twisted reinterpretation of the stories: her child-Hamlet delivered his churchyard speech to a turnip rather than to a skull, and others in a similar vein followed. However, the publisher, Macmillan, failed to see the humour and would only accept three of her six drawings, even after repeated attempts to please him.

The subsequent Macmillan commissions were equally difficult. The publisher planned to issue illustrated editions of classic novels for a new sixteen-volume series, of which Kate's were to be the first two: Charlotte Yonge's *The Heir of Redclyffe* and *Heartsease*. Each was over 500 pages long and required careful reading before any illustrations could be planned. As the work progressed Kate found the sheer size of her task placed her under enormous pressure, particularly as she was trying to complete other work as well; then half-way through, she stopped. Despite the fact that she had completed four drawings for the first volume and three for the second, she realized that she was not competent to carry out such work. The books were eventually published, her drawings reinterpreted and engraved by Swain, the *Punch* engraver, but she never again accepted such an ambitious project.

By the autumn of 1879, with review copies of *Under the Window* in the post, Evans began to consider Kate's next book. He first turned to George Eliot, remembering her favourable opinion of Kate's work, and asked her to write a

Pemberton Gardens today, with houses identical to the Greenaways' in 1879.

Alice-inspired Prince Finikin plate to *Under the Window*.

new story for Kate to illustrate. The author surprised him with a polite but firm reply: 'Your proposal does me honour, and I should feel much trust in the charming pencil of Miss Greenaway, but I could never say "I will write this or that" until I had myself the need to do it.'[14] This was a disappointing rebuff, but before Evans had time to reconsider his plans for Kate's future career, he found that her first book had captivated a large and enthusiastic public.

When copies of *Under the Window* reached the shops in time for Christmas sales, the public responded in a phenomenal way. Evans had ordered a staggering 20,000-copy first edition, but even this proved too little. Since the Elementary Education Act of 1870 the children's book market had boomed, and

Henry Stacy Marks, RA.

many publishers had responded with stacks of gaudy, over-produced coloured children's books with elaborate bindings. In contrast, Kate's sparse designs, her stark green cover with delicately outlined children and the pastel-coloured illustrations inside, proved a refreshing surprise, and enthusiastic reviews helped boost sales into regions even Evans had failed to anticipate: the *Athenaeum* praised Evans's colour printing and Kate's first-rate designs, the book was 'sure to be accepted by all, big and little, artistic and "aesthetic", lay and simple'; the *Saturday Review* called it a 'beautiful, fantastic and dainty work', with all the makings of a classic – 'Probably some wise collector will lay up a little stock for future use.' As sales rocketed the first edition sold out before a second could be ordered, and Evans long remembered his amazement at frantic booksellers clamouring for copies priced at six shillings, then selling them at ten shillings. It was a remarkable phenomenon, and with the second edition of 70,000, subsequent reprints and later French and German editions, sales reached over 100,000 copies within Kate's lifetime.

This popularity suggests that Kate had judged her public shrewdly and her book appealed to children as well as to fashion-struck aesthetes of the burgeoning Aesthetic Movement. But her illustrations had their faults, and when a copy was sent to Henry Stacy Marks, the prominent book illustrator, card designer and Royal Academician, he politely, but firmly, pointed these out. In a page by page critique he enumerated examples of what he called her 'naïve defiance of all rules of composition' – how her figures' feet separated from their curious black shadows 'looking in some places like spurs, in others like tadpoles, in others like short stilts'; he advised, 'A cast of any foot placed a little below the level of the eye would teach you how to foreshorten feet better'; and concluded, 'There, I have done! But I know you well enough to feel assured that you would not be content with unqualified praise, and that you are grateful for a little honest criticism.'[15] This was the first real professional criticism Kate had received since she left Ward, and she was genuinely grateful. In following years she sent Stacy Marks a copy of each book as it was published, and awaited his approval and criticism. She was sure that he understood what she was trying to do and would steer her in the right direction.

It was not surprising that Walter Crane greeted the publication of *Under the Window* with severe reservations. Routledge had outraged him by advertising her book as a companion volume to his toybook *The Baby's Opera* (1877), and Crane believed this was a blatant misrepresentation of his intention to illustrate for educational purposes as well as for entertainment value – something which he believed Kate failed to do. Routledge retracted the advertisement, but Crane was wary of his new rival, treating her as a serious threat in the territory he had carefully marked out for himself ten years earlier. Only after *Under the Window* appeared in the shops did they meet, and then it was by chance, at a theatrical evening at the Tennysons'. Kate arrived escorted by Locker, and, as usual, she took her place at the edge of the room, where Crane noticed her and remembered enough of the impression she made on him to record it years later. On this, their only meeting, she appeared 'very quiet and unobtrusive . . . probably quietly observant, self-contained, reserved, with a certain shrewdness'. There was very little to help him understand how she had achieved such a remarkable success with her first book, which he admitted was 'child-like in spirit'. But in his view it was merely surface decoration, 'old-world atmosphere tinted with modern aestheticism', and he concluded, 'May I confess that (for me at least) I think she overdid the big bonnet rather, and at one time her little people were almost lost in their clothes?'[16]

On the other hand, Kate was a long-standing admirer of Crane's work, and had considered it an honour to have had her Valentine designs published with his three years earlier. Each time her paintings hung at the Dudley near one of his or she saw his latest illustrations at Evans's, she declared them 'literally dreams of beauty', and was deeply depressed by her own limited abilities and imagination.

With her first book launched and sales increasing, Kate returned to Witley for a few days before Christmas, where she and Evans discussed plans for her next book. She returned to London prepared for what Evans promised would be a new and exciting experience, now that the long, tedious hours in her studio had at last been rewarded by her remarkable debut as an author-illustrator. With her earnings by the end of the year at £800 (not including *Under the Window* royalties, which one source listed as £1,130), and former publishers cashing in on her success – Cassell's, for example, reissued her *Little Folks* illustrations as outlines for colouring in the *Little Folks Painting Book* – Kate was swept along on an unexpected wave of fame and fortune. No longer a slave to difficult authors, demanding publishers and their engravers, she had found a new independence; and for the remainder of her life she would try to understand this 'new and lovely life' that arrived like a fairy godmother from one of her favourite children's stories.

4   Enter the Master   1880–1883

Oh, little girl, tell us do the Flowers
Tell you secrets when they find you all alone?
Or the Birds and Butterflies whisper
Of things to us unknown?

MARIGOLD GARDEN

Over the next few years Henry Stacy Marks played a prominent role in moulding Kate's career and presenting her work to the public. His letter after the publication of *Under the Window* was of particular importance to her, for it was written by someone familiar with the trials of an illustrator's life – the uncertainties, the promises, the deadlines, the deceptive acclaim. He urged her to enjoy her success; but she must learn to control her enthusiasm or it would control her. He had seen too many colleagues tempted away from an illustrator's career by enthusiastic praise. 'Don't bother about painting too much,' he advised Kate. 'You have a *lay* of your own, and do your best to cultivate it. Think of the large numbers of people you charm and delight by these designs compared with those who can afford to buy paintings. You have a special gift and it is your duty in every sense to make the most of it.' Above all else, she must remain cautious. She was in a vulnerable position – a sensitive woman who had placed her fate in the hands of two professional businessmen and had been overwhelmed by success; she must protect the essential innocence that was the hallmark of the Greenaway style, Stacy Marks concluded: 'One word of advice – although I almost believe you have too much common-sense to need it – don't let *any* success or praise make you puffed up or conceited, but keep humble and try to perfect yourself more in your art each day – and never sell your independence by hasty or badly considered work. I have seen so many spoiled by success that I raise my warning voice to you.'[1]

Kate was flattered by his concern, offered apparently without ulterior motive. She had learned of Stacy Marks's remarkably successful career when she was designing for Marcus Ward (who also used Marks's work). A coachman's son, he had trained as a decorative designer, card designer, illustrator of periodicals and children's books (his illustrations had an acknowledged influence on Walter Crane), then served as art critic of the *Spectator*. By 1878 he had had a great success with his bird paintings, on which he was elected a member of the Royal Academy. At first reluctant to accept Kate's adulation, by 1880 Stacy Marks was flattered by her guileless claims that more than anyone else (including even her father) he had directed her toward her first real success as artist and author. 'You have found a path for yourself, and though you kindly think I have helped to remove some of the obstacles that beset that path, I can claim no credit for having done so.'[2]

Stacy Marks's friendship meant he was willing to promote her work among his artistic and influential literary friends. The most important was the art critic, John Ruskin, once described as 'the mighty-mouthed inventor of reputations',

Kate Greenaway in 1880, from a rare publicity photograph taken by the commercial portrait photographers, Elliot & Fry.

who considered Stacy Marks's paintings equal to those of his revered Turner, his bird pictures comparable to Bewick's. He had become a favourite guest in the artist's home, where the two often discussed their friends' works or the latest discovery to emerge from the galleries. On one such evening, in late 1879, Stacy Marks raised the subject of Kate's drawings for *Under the Window*. Ruskin had apparently seen the book (or the original drawings at the Fine Art Society) and he launched into a lengthy monologue, praising Kate's ability to draw children with such remarkable skill and understanding. Stacy Marks explained his relationship with Kate, and noticed how interested his friend became in his descriptions of her innocent charm. A few days later Kate received a letter from Stacy Marks: 'Mr. Ruskin dined here on Thursday last, and spoke in high terms of your feeling for children, etc. I think it not unlikely that you may have a letter from him soon'[3]

From the beginning, then, Ruskin had very definite ideas about Kate's work and how it could be improved. But he approached the possibility of writing to her with calculated caution, for he knew the hold he could and, indeed, did have over aspiring young artists (particularly young women), and confessed his reservations to Stacy Marks:

> It is a feeling of the same kind which keeps me from writing to Miss Greenaway – the oftener I look at her designs, the more I want a true and deep tone of colour – and a harmony which should distinctly represent either sunshine, or shade, or true local colour. – I do not know how far with black outline this can be done but I would fain see it attempted. And also I want her to make more serious use of her

talent – and show the lovely things that *are*, *and* the terrible which *ought to be known* instead of mere ugly nonsense, like that brown witch [from *Under the Window*] – If she would only do what she naturally feels, and would wish to teach others to feel without any reference to saleableness – she probably would do lovelier things than anyone could tell her – and I could not tell her rightly unless I knew something of her own mind, even what might be immediately suggestive to her, unless perhaps harmfully. Please tell me your own feelings about her things.[4]

Stacy Marks urged Ruskin to lay aside his reticence and help promote Kate's work, and Kate received the promised letter from Ruskin. Dated 'Brantwood Jan. 6 1879' (misdated for 1880), this letter was masterfully constructed, moving from politeness to a series of provocative, critical comments; he revealed his age, his love of children, and suggested that they might become better acquainted. He wrote in a child-like, flippant tone, intended to flatter and to play upon her sympathies: 'I lay awake half (no a quarter) of last night thinking of the hundred things I want to say to you – and never shall get said! – and I'm giddy and weary – and now can't say even half or a quarter of one out of the hundred.' He continued in the tone of an art master addressing a prize pupil:

They're about you – and your gifts – and your graces – and your fancies – and your – yes – perhaps one or two little tiny faults: – and about other people – children, and grey-haired, and what you could do for them – if you once made up your mind for whom you would do it. For children *only* for instance? – or for old people, *me* for instance – and *of* children and old people – whether for those of 1880 – only – or of 18–9–10–11 – 12–20–0–0–0–0, etc. etc. etc. Or simply annual or perennial.

Then followed a series of fifteen questions requiring answers. These were worded to invite further correspondence, and the topics covered reveal Ruskin's wide-ranging interests. He referred to her limitations in drawing children; at the same time he hinted at his obsession with such young children, especially girls of nine or ten, whom he called 'girlies':

Will you please tell me whether you can draw these things out of your head – or could, if you chose, draw them with the necessary modifications from nature? . . . Do you only draw pretty children out of your head? In my parish school there are at least twenty prettier than any in your book – but they are in costumes neither graceful nor comic – they are not like blue china – they are not like mushrooms – they are like – very ill-dressed Angels. Could you draw groups of these as they *are*?

Top Right: Watercolour design for a greeting card.
Bottom Left: 'Flowers and Fancies' series, reissued here as the *Calendar of the Seasons for 1876*, by Marcus Ward.

CALENDAR OF THE SEASONS FOR 1876

MARCUS WARD & CO LONDON & BELFAST

He ended the letter with a series of short, provocative questions designed to discover whether they shared mutual interests: 'Do you ever see the blue sky? and when you do, do you like it?; Do you believe in Fairies?; In ghosts; in Principalities or Powers?; In Heaven?; In anywhere else?; Did you ever see Chartres Cathedral? Did you ever study, there or elsewhere, thirteenth-century glass?; Do you ever go to the MS room of the British Museum?' Finally he suggested, 'Heavy outline will not go with strong colour – but if so, do you never intend to draw with delicate outline?' and closed apologetically: 'Will you please forgive me – and tell me – some of those things I've asked? – Ever gratefully yours, J. Ruskin.'[5]

Kate was deeply impressed, and responded immediately. If she failed adequately to answer all Ruskin's queries in her first letter, she elaborated on her replies in the correspondence that stretched over the next twenty years. She wrote of her admiration for his work, and told him how much she enjoyed reading *Fors Clavigera*, his 'Letters to the Workmen and Labourers of Britain' (1871–8), which explained so much about her own working-class background and filled her with pride. 'Never shall I forget what I felt in first reading *Fors Clavigera* for the first time,' she later wrote a friend, 'and it was the first book of his I had ever read. I longed for each evening to come that I might lose myself in that new wonderful world.'[6]

Ruskin was overjoyed with her reply, and he wrote back nine days later: 'How delightful of you to answer all my questions! – and to read Fors, I never dreamed you were one of my readers – and I had rather you read that than anything else of mine, and rather *you* read it than anybody else.' Knowing that such flattery would assure him her attention, he quickly adopted the role of adviser on her future work. Based on her satisfactory answers to his questions, he explained, 'I think from what you tell me, you will feel with me, in my wanting you to try the experiment of representing any actual piece of nature (however little) as it really is, *yet* in the modified harmony of colour necessary for printing . . .'[7] In stressing studies taken directly from nature, Ruskin was reaffirming the Pre-Raphaelite tenets he had championed for so long. In addition he prepared her to help him in his present state of mental and physical weakness, feeling that her drawings of children were the tonic he needed.

By the 1870s Ruskin was a weary, broken man, famed throughout Britain for his books and lectures, but plagued with fits of madness triggered by overwork and memories of a disastrously painful private past. He felt that his reputation as England's supreme authority on art had been shattered by the Whistler libel action, and in 1879 he resigned his Slade professorship at Oxford. He retired to the peace and solitude of Brantwood, his lakeside retreat near Coniston, Lancashire, where he received a steady stream of well-wishers and maintained a voluminous correspondence with his admirers, particularly young, unmarried women. He treasured these semi-professional, semi-flirtatious relationships with his 'pets', as he called them, and busied himself with their problems and

The Flower Girl, a watercolour painted in Islington using a favourite watercress and violet seller for a model.

John Ruskin. Detail of a watercolour by Sir Hubert Herkomer, 1879.

requests as an attempt to escape memories of his past. But reminders of a
disturbing love affair and the visions of frolicking children he associated with it
continued to haunt his Brantwood days; try as he might, he could not erase
recollections of his ministering angel, the child beauty, Rose La Touche.

The story of Ruskin's love for Rose and its disastrous consequences is
essential to an understanding of his extravagant praise of Kate and her
drawings. Rose La Touche was the nine-year-old daughter of an Irish banker,
when, in 1858, she was presented to Ruskin for drawing lessons. Ruskin, then
thirty-nine and no longer married, was struck by her angelic, childish beauty
and her firm, defiant manner, and he fell deeply in love. Their relationship soon
grew beyond the art master-student role so that when she left for Italy in
1859 she wrote to her 'dearest St. Crumpet', and signed her letters 'ever your
Rose'. Obsessed with her innocence ('She was only a child but even then so wise
and thoughtful'), Ruskin sought reminders of her absent beauty; during
subsequent periods of separation he visited Winnington Hall, a Cheshire girls'
school, where among the fifty girls aged nine upwards he found suitable visual
substitutes for his 'Rosie Posie'. He obtained permission to teach the girls
drawing, read poetry to them and composed the songs to which they danced
and sang, eagerly joining in himself. His brief moments of happiness there
served to sustain him during his separation from Rose; although he wrote to
reassure his mother, 'You need not think I'm in love with any of the girls
here . . . Rose's my only pet.' In 1866, at the age of forty-seven, he could wait
no longer and proposed marriage to Rose, on her seventeenth birthday. Her
parents objected to the difference in their ages, but agreed to a prolonged

engagement until Rose reached twenty-one; and Ruskin remained confident: 'I shall speak of her as my affianced wife to my friends; and I shall wholly regard her as such.'[8] Wherever he went he carried with him her early letters, pressed between sheets of gold. Meanwhile Mrs La Touche consulted a solicitor about Ruskin's previous marriage to Effie Gray (now Millais), in 1848, which had been annulled in 1854. Mrs La Touche explained the details of this to her daughter – particularly Ruskin's wife's claims of her husband's inability to consummate their marriage – and Rose was upset. A deeply religious girl, she was horrified by the idea of physical love, and she accused Ruskin of terrible sins, eventually breaking off their engagement. She sank back into her religious devotions, and alternated between states of madness and physical illness that tortured the few remaining years of her life.

Ruskin was bereft. He had only wanted to be loved 'as a child loves', by someone like the child Rose as she had first appeared to him. Disillusioned by this new rejection, he sought comfort in the company of young children, to whom he now attached spiritual importance, writing in 1873: 'But the purpose of God is that angels should love as angels, and children as children, but maidens as neither of these. And it is because she [Rose] loves only as these, that now she cannot help me, though angels – and children – may.'[9] During Rose's final illness, and after her death in 1875, his devotion to her became an

Punch parody on Ruskin's style of woman with the classic profile.

258   PUNCH, OR THE LONDON CHARIVARI.   [DECEMBER 4, 1880.

WHERE THE SHOE PINCHES.

Eldest Daughter. "I THINK YOU MIGHT LET ME COME OUT, MAMMA! I'M TWENTY, YOU KNOW, AND SURELY I'VE FINISHED MY EDUCATION!"

Festive Mamma (by no means prepared to act the part of Chaperone and Wallflower). "NOT YET, MY LOVE. SOCIETY IS SO HOLLOW! I REALLY MUST PRESERVE THAT SWEET GIRLISH FRESHNESS OF YOURS A LITTLE WHILE LONGER!"

obsession. He began to associate the child Rose with various images – roses, pictures of children, white-frocked young girls with wide eyes and innocent smiles; all triggered his memories of her where ever he went. In Italy he copied evocative paintings – rose details in a Botticelli and a complete copy of Carpaccio's *St Ursula's Dream* (St Ursula being the virgin saint he associated with Rose). But above all, her death left him comforted by a vision of her original child beauty, and this continued to haunt his days.

Ruskin's child-obsession continued at Brantwood, where he surrounded himself with the children of Coniston Parish School. The girls arrived each Saturday for tea and songs with 'the Master'; often at least a dozen appeared, and, according to a frequent visitor, they were not in the least in awe of their host. On later occasions he invited new acquaintances who reminded him of Rose. One was Rosalind Webling, a young girl seen at the theatre who resembled Rose in her appearance and independent manner. She came with her sister for several weeks, after Ruskin's invitation through her father: 'Tell Miss Rosalind that the only toilet needed at Brantwood are a rose in the hair and a frock that won't tear – or won't matter if it does.'[10]

From the very beginning, Ruskin's relationship with Kate was clearly driven by his obsession with Rose. Kate's drawings in *Under the Window* abounded in suggestive images: drawings of pink roses, bowls of rose blossoms, a girl in a pale frock clutching a bouquet of roses ('Will you be my little wife, If I ask you? Do!'), and a wide-eyed infant handing a rose from a window, with Kate's verse below:

> *Little baby, if I threw*
> *This fair blossom down to you,*
> *Would you catch it as you stand,*
> *Holding up each tiny hand,*
> *Looking out of those grey eyes*
> *Where such deep, deep wonder lies?*

Since Kate had the ability to draw those child images so reminiscent of Ruskin's beloved, he was impelled to regulate and direct her talent. But he knew he must tread carefully, for his past dealings with artists had been disastrous: Dante Gabriel Rossetti was an early discovery who later rejected Ruskin's authority; their relationship ended with Ruskin storming: 'I never so long as I live will trust you to do anything again out of my sight.' Edward Burne-Jones was young and impressionable when Ruskin discovered and praised his work; but he and his wife soon learned to brush off Ruskin's autocratic manner, tactfully thanking but ignoring him in their own way. In his bewilderment, Ruskin concluded that the artistic temperament was impossible to control: 'These geniuses are all alike, little and big. I have known five of them – Turner, Watts, Millais, Rossetti, and his girl [Elizabeth Siddal] – and I don't know which was, or which is wrong-headedest. I am with them like the old woman who lived in the shoe, only that I don't want to send them to bed and can't whip them – or else that is what they all want.'[11]

The problem originated in Ruskin's uncompromising manner. He had always been the master of his fate, centre of his universe, the gregarious art critic with an outspoken manner, who lectured and wrote his way to fame. By the 1870s his opinions were quoted, his books read and used by parents and educators to direct young adolescents (particularly women) into adult life. So many women came to his lectures at Oxford that he felt compelled to change his approach and not 'let the bonnets in, on any occasion', by discussing subjects 'of no use to the female mind, . . . they would occupy seats in mere disappointed puzzlement.'[12] While he was at Oxford he established a drawing school which was attended by adoring female art students, and also initiated the elaborate Guild of St George Museum training scheme and schools, with a battalion of artist-assistants willing to make the required copies of his favourite architectural monuments and natural objects. His lessons were exhausting, often without concern for the student's feelings: 'I don't want *any* of these leaves painted,' he instructed one. 'You are to work on them for practise, doing one or two over and over again – fifty times, if needful . . .'[13] According to Arthur Severn (husband of Joan Severn, Ruskin's distant cousin and companion), Ruskin demanded absolute submission to his edicts:

> No one dared contradict him on any subject without his flying into a passion. What he liked was absolute obedience and in return he would pet and flatter. His ideal was a 'kind of feudal system', everyone round him willing to help, to obey, to love him. To all such he would be kind and helpful, but woe betide the man or woman who ventured to differ or put him right. Of course a pretty girl could do it a little and it amused him, but hardly any other kind of human being.[14]

Young women played an even more important role in Ruskin's later life. They were the source of constant comfort during his frequent bouts of depression, and served as reminders of the hold he had over impressionable young minds. An avid letter-writer, Ruskin revelled in the large number of postal relationships formed with such women over the years. His advice to aspiring female artists was often the same as that he offered to Kate: 'Never work for money, it is degradation,' he told one young woman in Oxford. The girl admitted being 'puzzled yet charmed' by his firm, doctrinaire manner when he told her to go to Ireland (Rose's home) and draw only Irish beggar children; but he continued:

> You cannot execute anything of merit if actuated by so mean a motive [as money]. No; you must love art for its own sake. That unhappy system of Kensington has raised up a countless multitude of inferior artists, vainly struggling to live by what will not grow a grain of wheat or stick a rag together. I assure you I would far rather, if I had a daughter, that she were a scullery-maid, or a milkmaid, than a London hack artist.

He concluded in a sterner, more serious tone:

> To succeed you must drudge and love your work. You cannot serve God and Mammon . . . Now, go to Nature, study her lovingly, that is the real teacher. You have a gift for colour; study form; and do

everything as well as you can, even if you give a month's work for half-a-crown; no matter, it is practise and future capital.[15]

Not all of Ruskin's postal relationships were with young women. His letters to ageing single ladies, often wealthy and generous, occupied a considerable portion of his letter-writing day. The most revealing relationship, in terms of his future correspondence with Kate, was formed with his elderly spinster neighbour, Susan Beever, who lived across Coniston Lake at The Thwaite. A cultured woman and an avid nature lover, she had her own childish streak and loved to play Ruskin's games in the over 900 letters that passed between them. A favourite was 'Let's Pretend', during which she quickly became his 'Susie', his 'older sister', and he her 'loving J.R.'.

Ruskin consequently approached Kate in two ways: as an artist in need of advice, and as someone who might qualify as yet another admirer on whom he could rely to restore his strength and confidence. Although letters passed to and from Pemberton Gardens for two years before they actually met, in that time their relationship quickly strengthened, his familiarity and terms of endearment coming as a welcome surprise to Kate, then a spinster in her mid-thirties. His original 'Dear Miss Greenaway' and signature 'Ever gratefully yours' rapidly changed to 'Dearest', 'Darling', or 'Sweetest Katie', signed 'loving J.R.', or 'loving Dinie' (a shortened form of Demonie, meaning he wanted to be her artistic conscience), or the more revealing 'St. C.' ('St. Crumpet'). Kate was thrilled both with these letters, written on the Silurian grey notepaper he favoured, and the telegrams he loved to send. She responded almost daily, keeping a page at her desk on which to record her thoughts, until it filled up and was ready for posting. She often included brief pen sketches, greeting cards on holidays and special occasions, finished watercolours for his birthday, the news of her progress on new books, and, at the end of each year, a presentation copy of her latest publication. She also provided him with a supply of self-addressed envelopes to ensure his prompt reply to her many questions. Her side of the twenty-year correspondence totalled over a thousand letters; he replied only when he had a spare moment or, later, when he was angry enough to object to her ceaseless demands for more letters. Kate kept every scrap he sent her – every brief (often illegible) note, pencil sketch or drawing, while most of hers up to 1887 were destroyed.

Throughout 1880 Kate tried to place her new-found fame into proper perspective and prepare for her next book projects. But interruptions were all too frequent; invitations to private views, afternoon teas and dinner parties given in her honour now flooded her studio. Most of these she ignored. She was not a sociable person, she hated crowds, preferring intimate tea-time chats, and rarely went out alone in public. On the few occasions when she accepted an invitation, she was usually embarrassed by an enthusiastic reception. After attending a children's party given in her honour she wrote a letter to Mrs Evans describing her confused reactions to so much attention. A group of children had sung verses from *Under the Window* ('The songs sounded so well. The 12 Miss Pelicoes very funny, and the processional song pretty . . .'); later she retired to the back of the room, where she overheard rumours about the book's mysterious author: 'The other day I heard I was sixty! – today I hear I am making £2,000 a year!' Most of all Kate regretted her popularity among the followers of the Aesthetic Movement, whom she found affected and embarrassing. At the same party she noted an 'aesthetic artist', who was there to pay his respects to her: she described him as a 'real genuine sort – who drank in the Elgin marbles for recreation. No wonder [George] du Maurier hates them.' On another occasion, at a private view, she by chance met William Loftie, who was immediately taken aback by the sudden change that had come over the shy, quiet woman he had thought her to be. She now bubbled with enthusiasm and smiled and laughed heartily at the lavish attention paid to her. 'The lady who has just left me has been staying in the country and has been to see her cousins,' she explained to Loftie. 'I asked if they were growing up as pretty as they promised. "Yes," she replied, "but they spoil their good looks, you know, by dressing in that absurd Kate Greenaway style" – quite forgetting that she was talking to me!'[16]

One memorable evening Kate accepted a dinner invitation and met some of the literary and artistic giants of her day: Burne-Jones, Frank Dicksee and George du Maurier were among the poets, musicians and politicians proudly assembled by her society hostess. The evening proved an exhilarating experience, and the hostess was so proud of her ability to attract the famous and the recently discovered that she insisted each of her guests should sign the large bamboo fan she waved about during the evening. Pulling it from its silk and sequinned case, she handed it to Kate, who entered her name on one fold, adding two tiny Greenaway children – the emblems of her recent rise to fame.

More frequently, Kate found it necessary to write refusals to unknown authors who requested illustrations. In November 1880 she was firm but polite, clearly honoured by such attention: 'Dear Madam, I should have had much pleasure in making the small drawing you wish, but I have so much on hand, so very much, more than I can possibly get done to time, that it is quite impossible for me to undertake anything fresh at present.'[17] Her tone eventually changed to curtness, then, as deadlines pressed, she turned over to Evans the task of answering all such requests.

The autumn of 1880 saw the publication of *Kate Greenaway's Birthday Book*, with 370 small black and white illustrations and twelve full-page colour illustrations in a tiny format. Evans paid her £151.10s. for the use of her drawings, and assured her that the book would be a success. She wrote to Locker in August, while the book was being printed: 'I think you will be pleased to know that the Birthday Book seems to be going to turn out a selling success. This first edition is 50,000 – so I am looking forward with rejoicing to future pounds and pennies, uncommonly nice possessions.'[18]

The book was an immediate commercial success and eventually produced royalties of £1,100, from a second edition, a French edition of 13,500 copies, a German edition of 8,500 copies; 128,000 English copies alone were sold in Kate's lifetime. The new book secured her position as an influential illustrator and further boosted Evans's reputation. Reviews were enthusiastic, but to Kate the reactions of her friends and advisers were more important. When Stacy Marks received his copy, he wrote that the book only confirmed his early belief in her

Selections from *Kate Greenaway's Birthday Book*, 1880.

abilities; but he still advised caution: '. . . I will say no more than to congratulate you on your success, in which I heartily rejoice – the more so as it does not destroy the simplicity of your nature, or make you relax in your efforts after excellence.'[19]

However, Kate's pleasure and success were flawed when she saw that bookshops and stationers filled their windows and shelves with blatant plagiarisms and books in the Greenaway style. The most objectionable of these appeared in late 1880, with the title *Afternoon Tea*, by J.G. Sowerby. It was a pastiche of the Greenaway style in *Under the Window*, with shocking alterations: a young boy furtively smoked a pipe; a graveyard was depicted in depressing black tones which Kate would never have used. Sowerby had approached Evans with his manuscript, but Evans was so annoyed by such blatant plagiarism that he refused to print it, and the author was forced to farm it out to six separate colour printers before Frederick Warne eventually published it. Kate's reactions were understandable: 'I really feel quite cross as I look at the shop windows and see the imitation books,' she wrote to Locker in November 1880. 'It feels so queer, somehow, to see your ideas taken by someone else and put forth as theirs. I suppose next year they will be all little birthday books, in shape and sort.'[20]

Throughout the autumn Ruskin toured the Continent, with Kate still on his mind, and her last letter 'in the softest recess of my desk throughout the cathedral towns of Picardy'. He returned to find her *Birthday Book* awaiting his criticism and wrote from Brantwood: 'Dear Miss Greenaway – I have just got home and find the lovely little book and the drawing!' But he ignored the book to concentrate on the sketch she had sent with it, done from nature as he had instructed: 'The drawing is so boundlessly more beautiful than the woodcut that I shall have no peace of mind till I've come to see you and seen some more drawings, and told you – face to face – what a great and blessed gift you have – too great, in the case of it, for you to feel yourself . . . I am too ashamed of not writing before.'[21]

Of all her recent press notices, Kate valued her appearance in *Punch* most of all. She had answered the *Punch* cartoonist Linley Sambourne's request for a photograph to help him draw her portrait, and in November sent a photographic negative, all she could spare, 'so what I shall turn out like I dare not think, even if he [Sambourne] could use it at all,' she wrote to Locker. 'I am curious to see what is going to be made of us all – if we are going to have large heads and little bodies, or how we are going to be made funny.'[22] Her tiny portrait appeared in the 4 December issue, floating above a picture of Mr Punch and sharing equal space with the heads of Walter Crane, Stacy Marks, Randolph Caldecott and their respective publishers. Beneath her portrait Mr Punch congratulated Kate on her *Birthday Book*: 'A most dainty little work and a really happy thought for Christmas'. Although it was a good advertisement for the book, some of Kate's friends found her own dark, old-maidish portrait dressed in feather hat and fur muff, offensive; it certainly lacked humour. 'I had the greatest difficulty in finding your portrait,' one wrote to her. 'What a horror! It is actionable really!' But years later Ruskin told Kate how impressed he had been by her first appearance as 'that little girl in *Punch*', and Kate herself was far from upset by the first *Punch* tribute, or the subsequent issues in which she figured.

At the end of the year Kate's correspondence with Ruskin became more frequent and intense. She openly expressed her willingness to submit to his demands to direct her work, and filled her letters with descriptions of her life, her progress on her books, sketches done from nature and paintings of children. At Christmas she sent him a card and drawings and for both she received extravagant praises which were encouraging and misleading in their implications. Writing to her for the last time that year (26 December), he adopted a cautious tone; he still preferred to keep her at a safe distance, yet he clearly aimed at complete control over her future: 'I don't want you to work, even for a

A second parody in *Punch*, 17 December, 1881

moment for me,' he began, but continued: 'but I do want you never to work a moment but in a permanent material and for – "all people who on earth do dwell".' Her Christmas card of a young girl with wide eyes and taunting smile brought an amazing response: 'I have lying on the table as I write, your little Christmas card, "Luck go with you, pretty lass". To my mind it is a greater thing than Raphael's St. Cecilia,' a statement destined to become one of the most quoted and misrepresentative comments he made about her work. His comment was not meant to be taken too seriously, although Kate was not to realize this – Ruskin's ecstatic reaction was coloured by his growing obsession with Greenaway 'girlies'. His letter also stressed the importance of Kate's drawing children in more durable media: 'But you must paint it – paint all things well, and for ever.' It was clear that Ruskin wished to elevate her work, to bring her children out of the nursery and into the realm of his revered Old Masters – with one notable difference: her pictures must remain cheerful and happy: 'Holbein left his bitter legacy to the Eternities – The Dance of Death. Leave you yours – The Dance of Life.'[23]

But Ruskin's encouragement for Kate to create happiness and joy carried forebodings of the depression and gloom that were to overcome him throughout the following winter and spring months, when his spirits plunged to new depths and he was forced to ignore Kate's growing requests for attention. The sad news of his friend Carlyle's declining condition then combined with his own fragile health to bring on a new attack of uncontrollable delirium. This lasted until the following April and meant that he was not responsible for his own actions.

During these months Kate turned her attention to Frederick Locker, in an attempt to mould their relationship into the stronger, more meaningful friendship they both needed. And yet, from the outset, Kate made sure that her affection for Ruskin – a new rival for her attention – was quite clear to Locker: Ruskin was a giant, the most important judge of artistic achievement she had ever known, with a 'certain holiness about his words'. Locker soon realized that he could not compete with such a reputation, or the hold Ruskin had over her; but he could offer well meaning advice, and urged caution in dealing with her new-found public.

> You must be influenced by what the critics say up to a certain point – but not beyond. It is very annoying to be misunderstood and to see critics trying to show off their cleverness, but you are now paying the penalty of *success*, and Tennyson suffers from it, and your friend Ruskin and Carlyle and all who make their mark in works of imagination. I *quite* feel what you say about Ruskin. There *does* seem to be a 'holiness' about his words and ideas. I am very glad he telegraphed to you, and wrote. His opinion is worth all the commonplace critics put together, and worth more than the opinion of nineteen out of twenty Royal Academicians.[24]

Nevertheless, to Kate Ruskin was above reproach and, after reading Carlyle's obituary in April, by associating him with Ruskin, she wrote emphatically to Locker: 'I do like, and I most sincerely hope that whilst I possess life I may

Randolph Caldecott in 1879.

venerate and admire with unstinted admiration, this sort of noble and great men. They seem to me to be so far above and beyond ordinary people, so much worth trying to be a little like – and I feel they talk to such unhearing ears.' She continued rather tactlessly: 'The fact is, most people like to lead the lives that are enjoyment and pleasure to themselves, and pleasing oneself does not make a noble life.' Knowing that Locker was idle, and depressed by his inability to write, she advised reading Carlyle's last chapter in *Sartor Resartus*, 'The Everlasting Yea', which she found so inspiring: 'But indeed Conviction, were it never so excellent is worthless till it convert itself into Conduct . . . Up! Up! Whatsoever thy hand findeth to do, do it with thy whole might . . .'[25]

Locker was enchanted by Kate's naïve approach to life. Like Stacy Marks, he tried to preserve that innocence and whenever possible, to promote her work among his influential friends. He wrote special verses to her greeting cards, criticized her drawings ('Do you think the Bride sitting under the tree is so feeble that she could not stand up?'), corrected her verses ('You ask me to do what Shelley would have had difficulty in doing'), and gave her advice on business matters: '[You] told me you were engaged on two works for his [Evans] house, in one of which you were associated with Crane and Caldecott. Now remember you are to be treated on as handsome terms as those two gentlemen or I shall not be satisfied. We must find out what they are to receive.'[26]

But Locker's motives went further than simple business advice. He longed for an undemanding female companion, a role which his second wife, twenty-five years his junior and a staunch Sabbatarian, apparently did not fill. He described this need in a frank essay, 'Silvio's Complaint', written in 1881, when he was sixty. It began: 'I am prosperous married. I have a rich, young, and affectionate helpmate . . . On the other hand, I am poor and old, and testy, and no longer comely to look upon . . . To speak plainly – I am in search of a self-denying creature – an animal who will talk and be lively when it pleases me, and be satisfied to be silent and subdued if I so desire it.' Earlier, he had directed his frustrations towards a beautiful young girl, but this relationship was brought to an abrupt halt by the girl's irate mother.

When Kate offered her friendship, Locker was willing to make certain modifications in his ideal, as he then admitted: 'She need not be pretty, but I wish her to be interesting looking . . . I may have to be content with a "half-worn" woman.' As an interesting, unpretentious spinster, who loved his poetry, Kate seemed an appropriate choice and Locker eagerly encouraged her. In 1881 he persuaded her to illustrate a new edition of *London Lyrics*, sharing the task with Caldecott. Kate chose the poem 'Little Dinky', inspired by the birth of Dorothy, who became Kate's favourite of the four Locker children. The Locker twins, Maud and Oliver, were a year old when their father persuaded Kate to paint them, asking in his characteristic way:

> *Come fairy Limner, you can thrill,*
> *Our hearts with pink and daffodil*
> *And white rosette and dimpled frill;*
> *Come paint our little Jack and Jill –*
> *And don't be long about it!*

Then followed their only book collaboration, when Kate made a series of forty-five small watercolour sketches to accompany his handwritten verses to *Babies and Blossoms*, intended as a surprise for Mrs Locker.[27]

In London Locker and Kate were often together, looking at the 'darling pictures' in the National Gallery, studying statues in the British Museum, discussing prints at Noseda's in the Strand, Harvey's in St James's, or Colnaghi's in Pall Mall. The letters that passed between them increased in number and intensity; according to Spielmann, these letters ran into hundreds, Locker's written with a 'curious abruptness and irrelevance as though half afraid of his temerity'.

Kate often invited Locker to her studio and in turn she visited his country home, Rowfant, in Sussex. There, in the early part of 1881, she renewed her acquaintance with Randolph Caldecott, another frequent guest. Caldecott by this time was so impressed by Kate's success that he approached the breakfast table one morning with a pen sketch of two children in the Greenaway style, and gleefully told Kate that once he had studied her drawings he could draw nothing but Greenaway children.

By 1881 London was filled with imitation Greenaway books, children's clothes and greeting cards. Those galleries holding annual exhibitions of new card designs inevitably displayed a large number of 'pale imitations of the work of Kate Greenaway', and these were acknowledged as such by art critics. Her books were copied or pirated at home and abroad, and the plagiarism disturbed her. One of her most avid admirers, the poet Austin Dobson, wrote to assure her, 'I have seen some imitations of you lately which convince me – if indeed I need conviction that you have little to fear from rivalry.' But Kate was still upset by her imitators' works. At best they convinced her to work harder to keep one step ahead of her rivals by producing an annual Greenaway volume to preserve her identity.

One of the most memorable tributes to her fame is now found in her diary: 'Sunday July 17 Crown Princess of Germany'. Her invitation to Buckingham Palace was a dream come true, and had been arranged by two new friends, Mrs

Sketch by Caldecott in the Greenaway manner, utilising the twins the two drew together at Witley.

Stanley and Anne Thackeray Ritchie (the novelist's daughter). On arrival, Kate was ushered into a room and sat with her sketchbook ready to entertain the little princes and princesses who hopped about and begged her for drawings. Awed but not quite overwhelmed by this royal attention, Kate managed to remember accurately the details of her visit: she was most impressed by the dashing Crown Prince, who silently entered the room, stood behind his small wife, his hand on her shoulder; then he turned to Kate, modestly stating, 'I am the husband.' After the visit Kate made a habit of sending her latest books and drawings to the Palace, and the Princess would send small tokens of her appreciation in return.[28]

Ideas for new books were essential, and Kate usually kept several small notebooks filled with brief notes and pencil sketches. She also approached Mrs Ritchie (herself the author of stories and essays) for ideas for books, and her friend willingly complied. When Kate suggested a collaboration, Mrs Ritchie accepted, writing in the playful spirit her friend enjoyed: 'When we write our book it shall be called "Treats", I think, and be all about nice things that happen to little girls – don't you think so?' Unfortunately, Kate was forced to abandon the idea when Evans insisted upon a new proposal.

To follow up the remarkable success of the *Birthday Book*, Evans wanted Kate to illustrate a selection of fifty favourite nursery rhymes, to be produced in a small format and called *Mother Goose, or The Old Nursery Rhymes*. This proved to be Kate's most demanding assignment to date. Once the drawings were accepted she specified that they should be reproduced on rough-textured paper. Evans knew that this would make it very difficult to preserve the delicate outlines of her work. Nevertheless, Kate insisted, and he devised an ingenious technique to give her her wish: the rough paper was pressed smooth between copper plates, printed, and then dipped into water to restore the texture. However, determined to produce the book in time for the Christmas market, he refused to show her proofs. In September, when the first copies were sent to her friends, their reactions were as disappointed as Kate's. Locker was surprised by her children's melancholy expressions, similar to those he had

Left: Original watercolour for 'Polly put the kettle on'. *Right*: From the printed book. Both from *Mother Goose*, 1881.

objected to in *Under the Window*, and he urged her to study the children of Romney, Reynolds and Leech. 'I do not think it would suit the style and spirit of your pictures if they were exactly *gay* children,' he wrote. 'But you must make your faces *happy*.' (This problem disturbed her engraver as well: a comparison between the mouth of the original downcast, frowning woman in 'Cross Patch' and the slightly smiling engraved version shows that the engraver did sometimes reinterpret her designs.) *Mother Goose* strengthened Locker's intent to guide her career with greater attention. He was appalled by the uncharacteristic colour and the poor register that resulted in overlapping lines and blurred faces. Kate could only apologize for herself and her printer: 'The deep colour you complain of in some is due to hurry, I'm afraid. There was no time to prove this book, and I never had any proof for correction at all, for Mr. Evans said it was impossible, it must go; and some of the darker ones suffer in consequence. I know you imagine I'm always having them for correction, and sending them back and back again; but that is not so . . .' Her reply reveals how little control she had over the production of her early books. To convince Locker that she was not totally at fault, she presented him with fifty-one original watercolour sketches and thirteen pencil drawings (marked for the printer) for *Mother Goose*.

When Stacy Marks received his copy he wrote to assure her: 'Your work always gives me pleasure – it seems so happy and so fearless of all the conventional rules and ideas that obtain generally about the art.' He added his characteristic page by page comments: 'Where, even in England, do you see such cabbagy trees? . . . How about a centre of gravity, madam? . . . You know I am not conventional, but I am troubled to know why you don't make the hero of your story more conspicuous . . . As instance of fearlessness, I admire the pluck which can place a face directly against a window with each pane made out.' His conclusion emphasized the affection and mutual respect that had grown between them: 'There! now I have finished, but I don't apologize for telling you the truth from my point of view, because I know you are strong enough to bear it and amiable enough to like it. It will always be a source of pride to me to remember (as you told me) that I was, though in the humblest way, partly instrumental in finding you the way your strength lay.'[29]

Commercially, the book was not as successful as the *Birthday Book*, but the press response was as enthusiastic as that to *Under the Window*. The *Magazine of Art* was most extravagant, claiming that the book was 'one of the prettiest, quaintest, most engaging little books imaginable'; in their critic's opinion Kate had become a 'fairy godmother': 'If Miss Greenaway had done no more than *Mother Goose*, she would yet have done enough. Her place among nursery superstitions will be an honourable and good one for many and many a year.'

Before Ruskin could give his critical opinion, another and even less successful Greenaway title was published. *A Day in a Child's Life* was a book of music for the piano, with Kate's children and flowers stretched over the margins. Suggested by Evans, the book was a commercial and critical failure. *The Times* took the opportunity to offer a candid appraisal of Kate's work to date: 'Miss Greenaway seems to be lapsing into a rather lackadaisical prettiness of style. Her little people are somewhat deficient in vitality.'

This review was a presage of what Kate had feared: that her calculated formula might become *passé*, a mere fashion taken up and then dropped by a fickle public. She needed advice from someone who could revive her flagging spirits, and redirect her toward a stronger, more vital purpose.

Fortunately, by Christmas Ruskin had recovered and was ready to advise her. Although he was still depressed by his uncontrollable health, and haunted by images of Rose La Touche, his depression was somewhat relieved by Kate's latest books, which rekindled his interest in her ability to depict children and reminded him of his departed beloved: *Mother Goose* had a title-page drawing of a baby lying in a basket of roses. *A Day in a Child's Life* was even more evocative, with its rose wreath half-title page; a blonde girl lying in bed, so reminiscent of a child Rose on her sick bed; and young girls in white frocks dancing over a hillside to 'A Romp' – so like his Winnington Hall frolics. It is not surprising that he broke his long silence and eagerly wrote to Kate on Christmas Day: 'My dear Miss Greenaway – You are the first friend to whom I write this morning; and among the few to whom I look for real sympathy and help.' He praised her work, and hinted at its therapeutic value: 'You are fast becoming – I believe you are already, except only Edward B[urne] Jones – the helpfullest in showing me that there are yet living souls on earth who can see beauty and peace and Goodwill among men – and rejoice in them.' Of her two books, he was especially grateful for her 'little choir of such angels as are ready to sing, if we will listen, for Christ's being born – every day; and he found the *Day in a Child's Life* songs delightful for their ability to make him especially happy at

'A Romp' from *A Day in a Child's Life*, 1881, with Winnington Hall dance memories
depicted unknowingly by Kate.

this depressing time. Recalling that her books were now sold on the Continent,
he felt encouraged by her fame: 'I trust you may long be spared to do such
lovely things, and be an element of the best happiness in every English
household that still has an English heart, as you are already in the simpler
homes of Germany.' He concluded with a promise to 'write more in a day or two
about many things I want to say respecting the possible range of your
subjects.'[30]

Ruskin's letter marked the end of a long, exhausting year of work for Kate.
Her earnings had rocketed to £1,500 from reproduction fees, royalties from the
German *Under the Window*, two colour frontispieces for children's periodicals, a
full-page engraving in the Christmas *Illustrated London News*. All were sure
signs of her popular appeal, as were the parodies in three separate issues of
Punch that December, and the high praise of Andrew Lang published in *The
Library*.

Ruskin's promised letter did not arrive for nearly a year, during which time
he succumbed to another attack of depression and the mental instability he
would suffer for the rest of his life. Meanwhile Kate spent the early months of
1882 working on her next book. In March she visited Evans and his family at
Witley, where 'It was like June . . . butterflies about in such numbers and the
sun so hot we had to give up a sketch we were doing because we could bear the
heat no longer.'[31] She returned to London, and busily set to work on the first of
her almanacks, refusing all invitations.

Punch parody, with Kate, Stacy Marks, Crane and Caldecott, from 4 December, 1880 issue.

Late in May she visited Evans at his London office to supervise the printing and collect her first almanack proofs. There also she saw and admired Caldecott's designs for the toybook *Hey Diddle Diddle*, which made her feel hopelessly inferior. 'They are so uncommonly clever,' she wrote to Locker, also mentioning Walter Crane's latest book: 'I wish I had such a mind. I'm feeling very low about my own powers just now.'[32]

Locker realized Kate was under considerable strain, and that her work schedule, to a large extent forced on her by Evans, was wearing her down. He tried to bolster her spirits by devising little diversions and outings. Whenever possible he took her to dinner parties, and introduced her to his famous friends – this year the people she met through him included Robert Browning and his sister, companion, Sarianna, and members of the Tennyson family (Locker's daughter Eleanor had married Lionel Tennyson, one of the poet's sons). He also tried to impart to her his interest in collecting antiques and showered her studio with extravagant gifts. In return Kate felt obliged to send him and his family gifts of watercolours, cards and drawings. She also consented to design a book-plate for his famous library at Rowfant, which occupied a considerable amount of her precious work time.

Kate's relationship with Locker was founded on such self-sacrifice, but, as both were strong-willed and opinionated, they had occasional sharp differences, especially when Locker urged her to adopt a more casual, relaxed approach to her work. He had never had to struggle for a living, and Kate certainly realized that there were things about her that Locker would never understand. After learning about her discussions with Evans over the almanack's progress – Evans urged her to hurry and complete the book – Locker gave her opposite advice: 'I hope when you get home you will get to work, but take it quite easily (say two or three hours a day), and try to be beforehand with the publishers, etc., and *not let* anything interfere with or stop your daily moderate work.'[33] Thus Kate was torn between the advice of two friends: on the one hand, Locker feared for her health; on the other hand, Evans feared for her career (and his possible financial losses), if an advertised Greenaway book was not published in time. Frustrated and unable to control her destiny, Kate occasionally lashed out in anger. In mid-December Locker sent her an expensive set of Thomas Stothard prints and some antique brackets – an innocent gesture which Kate interpreted as a threat to her independence. Her sharp response reflects her agitated frame of mind:

> Dear Mr. Locker, It is too dreadful of you and I'm in a raging, soaring temper . . . I thought you promised you wouldn't, never no more and here you are behaving in the most flagrant manner. Have you no sense of honour – *Perhaps* – I shall return them to you – Perhaps – I shall put them on the brackets – and – the illustration opposite strives to portray my true feeling [a pen-sketched self-portrait inscribed 'doubtful face']. Don't do it again or else – I vanish . . .

She signed her name in the most emphatic way possible – a self-portrait figure of a witch about to vanish on her broomstick.[34]

Following this outburst, on Christmas Eve Ruskin conveniently broke his year-long silence to telegram his delight at receiving her Christmas greeting and her new almanack: 'I must thank you today for my best pleasure this year.'[35] At this time he was busy supervising his artist-assistants in making copies of paintings and architectural monuments for the Guild of St George Museum, and he felt in the mood to take on Kate as a new charge. On Christmas Day he decided his intentions were best explained in person, and he invited himself to her studio: 'Dear Miss Greenaway . . . I *must* come to thank you, there's no writing what pleasure your note gives me. When may I come – Wednesday is my first free day – if that will do – and the sunset time (– I know what light must be worth to you, too well to trespass on you earlier –).'[36] She proposed Friday, and he confirmed this on 27 December: 'Friday will do delightfully for me – even better than today – having been tired with Xmas letters and work.' Then he attacked her poorly drawn children, and concluded: 'The drawing on my letter however is perfect! shoes and all – eyes and lips – unspeakable!'[37]

This suggests why Ruskin chose to renew his relationship with Kate now, after two years of sporadic correspondence. During that time they had never met (although he often travelled to London on business), but he had thought a great deal about her work. In the autumn of 1882, while touring Italy, he had met a young, vivacious, American-born artist, Francesca Alexander, who rekindled his interest in children's illustration by aspiring women artists. Francesca immediately impressed him with her unaffected manner – 'such vivid goodness and innocence' – and the tales of local ballads and folk legends which she illustrated with captivating Italian peasant children. He paid her £600 for about a hundred of these (she refused the £1,000 he offered), and he returned to England determined to sell some stocks and publish her work. This he eventually did, under the title of *Roadside Songs of Tuscany*.

With the same enthusiasm Ruskin now turned his attention toward Kate's work. By the end of 1882 he was trying desperately to avoid further depressions, seeking the distraction of his admirers, at least until the new year when he planned to return to the Oxford Slade professorship. This, he reasoned, would bring him closer to London, where he might keep a close eye on Kate's progress.

On the day of Ruskin's visit, Kate's childhood anxieties returned and she grew increasingly nervous, as she clearly recalled in a letter written to him fourteen years later: '. . . before you came I thought so much of your coming it got to be really a pain, and I said I almost wish he was not coming. But then the first moment I saw you, I was glad – so glad.'[38] The Ruskin who arrived was a weary man of sixty-three, suffering from delicate health and, on the day, a sore throat. But he was equally anxious to meet Kate, if only to see what she looked like. Appearances were most important to him; he preferred his women admirers to be tall, slim, willowy and graceful, with fair hair and classical features. Kate was far from his ideal: a short, dark, dowdy, thirty-six-year-old, plainly dressed, who was extremely nervous and rarely smiled. When she spoke she had difficulties in pronouncing her 'm's', and lisped in a tiresome way. But, as Joan Severn later wrote, Ruskin ignored the shortcomings of his new admirer: 'I shall never forget his rapturous delight at first making her acquaintance!' His own reaction appears in a letter almost a year later, when he wrote to Kate (then suffering from a sore throat) that 'You cured mine the first tea ever I had in that dear little room!'[39]

The visit began on a polite note. Kate showed him round the house, then into her studio where they looked at and discussed her pictures; then they took tea and ate muffins at a table set with violets. This was the tea-time ritual that was to continue for several years, each time Ruskin was well enough to come to London. The first visit was an immediate success, and Kate duly entered it in her diary: 'Mr. Ruskin came. First time I ever saw him.' These entries were to increase over the years: the stage was now set for Ruskin to dominate her life, her talent and her career.

5 Kisses, Tears and Sealing Wax
1883–1884

Margery Brown, on the top of the hill,
Why are you standing, waiting still?
Oh, a knight is there, but I can't go down,
For the bells ring strangely in London Town.
UNDER THE WINDOW

From early 1883 onwards, Ruskin became the most important influence in Kate's life. Her diary records his birthday on 8 February, and the subsequent card and watercolour drawings she sent to him were the beginnings of a custom which she continued for the rest of his life. Ten days after receiving her first gift, Ruskin broke a two-month silence to place their relationship on firmer ground:

> My dear Kate, I beg pardon – but I really can't call you anything else, since I've seen you. Now – when can you come and see mountain spring? Another year, you must come for the snow drops; but it must be a year of bright frost, not black rain. But now – there's some hope, (or possibility) – of finer weather – and I want to know what time would be most convenient to you to come: of course – April would be best but I want to be sure of you, and I know you cannot command your time in the chances of book work – so I'll fit my plans to yours.[1]

Although Kate was flattered by this letter, she heard no more for several weeks while Ruskin immersed himself in work at Oxford. Meanwhile she was busy preparing her next book, encouraged by her recent financial success. In late January Evans sent a cheque for £287.17s. 6d., marked 'half profit in 76,403 copies of those books in print' – which included recent German editions of the *Birthday Book* and *Mother Goose*.[2] She accepted Evans's suggestion and planned to illustrate fifty favourite childhood verses by Jane and Ann Taylor, for a book she called *Little Ann and Other Poems*.

Spring at Brantwood made Ruskin irritable, impatient and restless. He instructed Joan Severn to bring Kate to him as quickly as possible despite a whooping cough epidemic at Brantwood. 'Please write and ask if Kate has had it – if so – you and she come on Tuesday anyhow.' They were to take the train for Ulverston, leave it early, and take a carriage fifteen miles on a roundabout route to Brantwood. 'I can't have Kate seeing Windermere before Coniston,' he wrote to Joan.[3] He intended to use Kate's visit for professional reasons as well as pleasure; on 4 April he wrote to the French art critic and Greenaway admirer Ernest Chesneau about his plans to lecture at Oxford the following term on art from 'Hogarth to Kate Greenaway'. 'I think you will be a little envious of me when I tell you that I hope for the *real* "sourire délicieux" [Chesneau's term for Kate] to mingle here with the light of April flowers. She is coming to stay for ten days or a fortnight at Brantwood I hope on the 10th.'[4]

Kate was astonished by Ruskin's urgency. Methodical in her ways, she preferred careful planning to obeying impulses; because of delicate health, she had never travelled far from London. Moreover, she was worried that Ruskin would be disappointed in her if he had a whole fortnight of her company. She carefully discussed the outing with Joan Severn, now a trusted adviser, to whom she had written numerous letters, and had been 'giving no end of trouble but it is your fault you are so kind I am not afraid of you. I am afraid of a good many.' One fear remained insurmountable: '. . . you are not to make so much of me, for I am not in the least a frog Princess. Wouldn't it be nice if I were, to emerge suddenly, brilliantly and splendid?'[5]

Nevertheless, when she arrived on 10 April, dazed, timid and exhausted, she was, like most of Ruskin's visitors, overwhelmed by the beauty of her surroundings. Ruskin had chosen Brantwood for its magnificent mountain scenery and peaceful lakeside setting ('In Cumberland I merely breathe and rest'). 'The mere thought of Coniston Water brings back the peaceful legends and sounds all about Ruskin's house,' Mrs Ritchie remembered of her own visit. 'The wash of the lake, the rustle of the leaves and rushes, the beat of birds on their whirring wings, the flop of water-rats, the many buzzing and splashing and delicious things. A path up a garden of fruit and flowers, of carnation and strawberries leads with gay zigzags to the lawn in front of Brantwood windows.'[6] Inside the house perched high above the lake, Ruskin's favourite Turner watercolours hung over his bed; in his study were shelves of books, paintings, bits of sculpture, a piano, cases of minerals, precious manuscripts, and his own drawings, that lay about in profusion.

Kate arrived thinking she knew Ruskin the myth; she left, not a fortnight, but nearly a month later, feeling she knew Ruskin the man – an enigmatic figure with piercing blue eyes, a caressing voice and the limitless charm that helped her to overcome her timidity and her desire to return to London. He made every possible effort to make her comfortable, and flattered her by listening to her ideas on art, nature and life. During a nervous tea at Ulverston, she remarked on the large tea cups and immediately noticed her mistake, as she later recalled to Ruskin: 'You began to think I was not quite what you thought, that my tastes were a trifle material.' And yet, mesmerized by his voice and impressed by his encyclopaedic knowledge, she forgot her nervousness and willingly fell in with his plans: 'Everything is confused, I never know day or date,' she wrote to Mrs Evans, 'I'm absorbed into a new world altogether.' When Ruskin urged her to extend her stay, she told Mrs Evans: 'Words can hardly say the sort of man he is – perfect – simply . . . Mr. Ruskin wants me to stay, wants me to tell him things about colour, and puts it in such a way I can't well leave, and the few days won't make much difference.'[7]

Ruskin preserved his impressions of her visit in his Brantwood diary. The earliest entries express his characteristic concern for Kate's welfare; yet all the while he watched himself for signs of a new mental breakdown. On 12 April he took Joan and Kate in his boat, *Jumping Jenny*, to visit Susan Beever, while he rowed on to Waterhead and thought of 'old times'. The following day, while walking Kate and Joan 'from tarns, by cascades', he remained silent, preoccupied by the previous night's dream, a 'rather nightmary dream of being

Brantwood, Coniston from the hillside, drawn by Arthur Severn.

besieged by naughty little boys, and running after a redhaired thief with
Baxter. Woke with a bad taste in mouth.' That same day he wrote to Ernest
Chesneau of Kate's safe arrival and described an amusing breakfast-table
incident: Chesneau had sent a long letter praising Kate's work, and Ruskin read
it to her, 'with the double delight of enjoying the beautiful words and thoughts
themselves, and believing what pleasure they must give her; though she looked
very ashamed, and very deprecatory . . .'[8]

The following day was filled with 'exciting talk', although it ended abruptly
with him 'too full of [the] topic'. They walked to Yewdale stream and he led her
to a favourite brookside cottage and pointed out a white rose tree on the roof.
On Sunday it rained, which gave him a chance to begin his Oxford lecture on
Kate's work, and for the next few days he asked to be left alone. Kate wandered
freely about the grounds, drawing flowers or the dancing children of Coniston
Hall; her work only occasionally encouraged by Ruskin. Although he had 'all
kinds of plans in my head for her', he sank back into a growing moodiness that
Kate noticed but tried to ignore.

Because of these strained silences, when her visit ended Ruskin was doubtful
of its results. He wrote in his diary: 'May 8 Tuesday . . . Kate Greenaway went
home yesterday – I fear not much wiser for her visit.'[9] But Kate could only recall
her ecstatic happiness at Brantwood, as she wrote to Lily Evans how she regretted
leaving: 'There was such lots to admire – such wild stretches of country and
then such mountains – such mossy trees and stones – such a lake – such a shore
– such pictures – such books – my mind was entirely content and satisfied, and I
miss it all so much, and grumble and grumble . . .'[10]

The excitement soon died away, leaving Kate depressed and lonely, in need
of reassurance from her 'Master'. She wrote emphasizing her delight at the visit,
and he replied: 'I look forward to our working at Coniston without any sense of

being tortured next time.' Within a few days she planned a visit to Rowfant, where she wanted to finish Dolly Locker's portrait. Ruskin was completing the lecture, and preparing for a display of pencil drawings she had given him. 'My dearest Katie,' he wrote, 'I can't part with the drawings to be india R. [ubbered] – having them by me helps me so.' He also asked whether she had thought any more about their Brantwood discussions: 'I am anxious to know what you have been thinking about colour, and skies, since you got over the first indignation of my tyrannies!'[11]

At Rowfant, Kate gave Locker an enthusiastic account of her Brantwood visit and told him how Ruskin urged her to 'aim at something higher' in her work. Locker listened politely, but he was worried about the hold Ruskin had over her. 'Beware,' he warned; she had a highly individual contribution to make, and must not be distracted by Ruskin's attempts to divert her talent. 'Each has his or her merits, and there is room for all. All I beg, is that you will not rashly change your style. Vary it, but do not change it.'[12] Locker was clearly annoyed by Ruskin's using Kate's vulnerability to achieve his own ends. He had known Ruskin longer than she, and had always found him a difficult, uncompromising individual. Moreover, Ruskin had once confessed to Locker his disillusionment with his own writing: 'It is not my real gift. I ought to be quiet, painting sticks, or straws or stones and moss.' And now, according to Kate, this was exactly what Ruskin planned for her future – to turn her into a proficient but uninspired nature painter – and Locker strongly objected.[13]

While waiting for news of Ruskin's lecture, Kate accepted further commissions. Austin Dobson, who was by this time a great admirer of her work, persuaded her to illustrate two poems he had written that had been inspired by her children. Their collaborations appeared twice, in the January and the May

Ruskin's self-styled moorland garden where Kate spent many difficult hours painting the rocks and tiny plants.

issues of the *Magazine of Art*, the latter being a full page verse description of Kate's inimitable world, with Greenaway children scattered in the margin:

> *Mine be a cot, for the hours of play,*
> *Of the kind that is built by Miss Greenaway,*
> *Where the walls are low, and the roses red,*
> *And the birds are gay in the blue o'er head.*

Kate also worked daily on *Little Ann* and the year's new almanack, all the while looking out for a letter from Ruskin. After almost a week with no word from him, she decided to break the infuriating silence.

His reply was firm and characteristic of the stubborn attitude he adopted towards her while he was absorbed in preparing his own books and lectures. Three days before the lecture, he wrote: 'Dearest Kate . . . it is really very grievous to me that you must think me neglectful and ungrateful when really, I have scarcely an hour now I can call my own, so many people there are who have real claims to my attention – here, and so many old friends in London who want to renew the relations broken off by my illnesses.' His tone then hardened: 'There is no question of preferences to *you* or of one to another among *them*. I must attend to all in turn – or really give deeper pain than I care to think of. There is no chance of my being able to come to see you for many days yet but I hope you will be happy in what I shall be saying of your drawings and you.' However, he was flattered by her continued praises of Brantwood, and signed himself: 'I'm ever your loving and admiring and grateful, J. Ruskin.'[14]

Ruskin's refusal was quite justified. As he prepared 'In Fairyland', his lecture on Kate's work, he was again fearful for his mental stability; to a more intimate friend, Mrs Talbot, he wrote: 'Remember simply this, that *any* day I may go mad, or fall paralysed without having had the least warning of my danger.' His only comfort lay in the fact that his closest friends would not be in his audience. 'It is absolutely necessary – whatever the disappointment that *none* of my friends should at present add to the extreme difficulty and dangerous excitement of my work at Oxford.'[15]

This alarm is apparent in his work. His lecture rambled on for some thirty-five published pages in which he tried to convince his amazed audience that Kate ranked among the most important of old master and contemporary artists. She and Mrs Allingham had given the world the essential element of fancy, which he defined by tracing it from Greek art to the present, 'till at last, bursting out like one of the sweet Surrey fountains, all dazzling and pure, you have the radiance and innocence of re-instated infant divinity showered again among the flowers of English meadows by Mrs. Allingham and Kate Greenaway.' He further confused his audience by a wealth of diverse examples: excerpts from obscure eighteenth-century children's books, Dante's *Inferno*, Shakespeare, the *Odyssey* and a current stage production of Gilbert and Sullivan's *Iolanthe*. Eventually he centred on the work of the 'impressionable Miss Greenaway', and urged his audience: 'to encourage the artist in doing the best she can for you. She will, if you receive it when she does.' He only complained of two major faults: her published work was too ornamental and decorative ('contracted into any corner of a Christmas card, or stretched like an

'The Children's Tea', a watercolour of her family by Helen Allingham.

elastic band round the edges of an almanack'); and it lacked true delicacy ('All great art is delicate; and fine to the uttermost!'). This could be easily corrected by painting 'more descriptive reality, for more convincing simplicity' – the path along which he now led her. He emphasized his enthusiasm (and disturbed his audience) by waving about twelve glass-mounted frames of Kate's tiniest pencil drawings. The bemused undergraduates squinted but failed to see properly; while he taunted them: 'Even I at sixty-four, can see the essential qualities of the work without spectacles.' He concluded that Kate's work had a universal appeal; her flowers and young children restored the element of fantasy and beauty fast disappearing from industrialized England: 'All gold and silver you can dig out of the earth are not worth the kingcups and daisies she gave you of her grace.'

With all its incoherencies and ramblings, the lecture was immensely popular. He delivered it twice in Oxford, then a third time at the London home of the highly cultured Mrs Bishop, where two hundred attended; later he had it privately printed, with illustrations, and it sold extremely well.

When, on 7 June, Kate received a proof copy of the lecture, she began to realize where Ruskin was leading her – how she must submit to his ideas of natural beauty and see the world only in his way. She was to become his Pre-Raphaelite protectress, the Queen of the Fairies, who would feed his fantasies and still obey the strict laws of nature study. Only then could she deliver him, and her public, from the grimness of industrialized England, from the merciless fury which he believed 'today grinds children to dust between millstones, and tears them to pieces on engine wheels'.

Ruskin relished his role as Kate's artistic adviser, and after his lecture he went about his duties with new fervour. Within two days of his London lecture he was scolding her for 'wasting your time and wits' on small, inconsequential sketches ('scattered dew of fancy'), when naturalism was more important. 'You really must gather yourself into a real rivulet between banks in perspective – and reflect everything that you see,' he advised. 'Now be a good girl and draw some flowers that won't look as though their leaves had been in curlpaper all night –

and some more chairs than that one chair – with the shading all right – and then I'll tell you which you must do next, and he's ever your loving, J.R.'[16]

What this did was to revive her art training at Finsbury, those months spent making meticulously accurate pencil and watercolour copies of natural objects. Over the years she had altered these skills, and allowed her imagination to influence her drawing. She was now fond of sketchiness, and left out essential lines which her engraver could add; she might also place a full dress over a half-defined figure, or, worse still, attach the legs and arms to a dress without concern for the form of the figure underneath. Ruskin noticed these careless habits and glaring anatomical errors and, even as his letters increased in affection, he set her a series of exercises designed to correct her faults and redirect her vision. A watercolour copy of a river bank, for example, proved an impossible task – 'but it must be a real river – or rivulet, a bit of canal, or anything that has bank and reflections.' This gave her problems for days and days, until he explained the lesson (writing from Oxford): 'Darling Katie, I'm thinking of you everyday and a great part of the day long, whenever I get out into the fields more and more, anxious everyday that you should resolve on summer's work of utter veracity – drawing – no matter what, – *but* as it *is*. I am certain all your imagination would expand afterwards, like – a rosebud.' As he prepared Francesca Alexander's drawings for publication, he marvelled at her skill in depicting children's facial expressions, and this influenced his judgement of Kate's work. 'But especially I do want more children as they are,' he wrote in the same letter, 'and that you should be able to show a pretty one without mittens and that you should be more interested in phases of character. I want your exquisite feeling given to teach – not merely to amuse.'[17]

Original pencil drawing showing how Kate would draw a figure's dress, then add the feet (here only one).

Ruskin was a firm believer in Kate's ability to teach others, and he stocked his Oxford drawing school not only with prints and drawings by old masters, watercolours by Turner, woodcuts by Bewick, but also with original drawings by Kate and Francesca Alexander. He also believed that her work must be permanently preserved to delight future generations, and made elaborate preparations to transfer a drawing of a Greenaway girl onto glass, 'for some English hall in fairyland', continually reporting the progress of this work to her.

From the start Kate was eager to please Ruskin, and sent as many drawings as she could, pictures of all she imagined or saw around her: a 'doggie carrying a maulstick', a girl looking out to sea, and even a curious self-portrait, much too flattering, with wide, expressive eyes, a clear complexion, and tall, feather-trimmed hat, signed, 'Yours, K.G. 1883'. Ruskin was delighted by this reinterpretation of her plain looks, and wrote: 'The first thing I should have done would have been to [take] the feathers out of your hat! Ah me – if I had had the chance!' Such teasing was quite frequent, as were his demands to hear of 'the progress of the River' – her riverbed study. Moreover, on his frequent travels he kept a sharp eye out for new Greenaway material: 'I saw a boy in a brown jacket with a yellow basket in his hand – looking up wistfully at the sky – in the main street of Worcester,' he wrote to her after a June outing. 'He wanted only a Kate to draw him and [he] would have been immortal.'[18]

When Ernest Chesneau sent Kate a questionnaire, hoping to learn more about her for an article he was writing, Ruskin turned this request into a playful game. He advised Kate to answer the questions, return them to him, and he would send them on to Chesneau, to avoid any unnecessary misunderstandings. But Kate's long, detailed letter, sent with the returned questionnaire, upset Ruskin; and her earnestness annoyed him. 'I didn't mean that you were to write a letter – but yet I thought it possible that you might content yourself with answering it in a frolic – the Frenchman being exceedingly good, and right hearted . . .' Kate had also sent a revised self-portrait, designed to make her appear as she wished to be seen by such a keen admirer: (in Ruskin's words) 'with blue eyes . . . tall . . . lovely white dress and hat and feather'. This second portrait so captivated Ruskin that he refused to send it on to his friend until the very last moment. 'I kept the portrait till I could scarcely bear to part with it. But it's gone today – and I've wreaked my jealousy on M. Chesneau by three pages of abuse of the whole French nation and Academy.'[19]

As he prepared his next Oxford lecture, on the neoclassical in contemporary art – particularly the paintings of Leighton and Alma-Tadema, – Ruskin urged Kate to adopt the neoclassical ideals, to work on figure studies inspired by the Greeks and to raise her children into the realms of High Art. His instructions barely conceal a desire to see young Greenaway 'girlies' in delightfully suggestive poses. Early in July he wrote from Brantwood:

> As we've got so far as taking off hats, I trust we may in time get to take off just a little more – say mittens – and then – perhaps – even shoes! and – (for fairies) even . . . stockings – and then – . . . *Will* you – (it's all for your own good –!) make her [a drawing of a sylph]

A watercolour version of the 1883 self-portrait.

stand up and then draw her for me without a cap – and, without her shoes, – (because of the heels) and without her mittens, and without her – frock and frills? And let me see exactly how tall she is – and – how – round. It will be *so* good of and for you – And to and for me.

To this last remark Joan Severn pencilled in, 'Do nothing of the kind! – J.R.S.', which Ruskin noticed before posting; he added the postscript: 'That naughty Joan got hold of it – never mind her – you see, she doesn't like the word "round" that's all.'[20]

The following day he urged her to keep a small sketchbook in her pocket to record cloud changes and capture the expressions of children 'of more full faces than you – face – usually'. He found the famous, sharply profiled Greenaway child too conventional, and the feet of the figures most disturbing: '. . . you should go to some watering place in August with fine sands, and draw no end of bare feet –.'[21] On 26 July he re-emphasized this need: 'I'm much more anxious about the feet. I want you to go to Boulogne and take a course of fishwives and wading children.' In the same letter he proposed a meeting in London for the following week, and asked to meet the enchanting child model she had described in her letters.[22]

94

In the next few days the post office somehow mixed their letters, and Ruskin was startled to receive from Kate a morose, apologetic letter that made him reconsider his planned visit. Her letter was a frank admission of uncertainty – about her career, her future, and especially her relationship with him. With the letter she had sent a pathetic drawing labelled 'K.G. before the Fates', another watercolour self-portrait, depicting herself kneeling at the feet of the three Fates. It was meant as a plea for reassurance, but Ruskin refused to be serious, and replied: 'I *thought something* had gone wrong about the letters; but couldn't work it out. I can't help being a little glad it did, since I got the lovely begging letter and these delicious Fates by it.'[23]

Then, on the day planned for his departure, Ruskin was too exhausted to leave Brantwood. Three weeks of visitors (including Mrs La Touche and her husband, still family friends) had left him restless, anxious to take up his own work again and unable to face an emotion charged reunion in Kate's studio. He apologized, knowing too well that she would be stunned with disappointment: 'Darling Kate – What will you say to me? What shall I say to you? And you'll be sorry – and feel as if I didn't care for you: and indeed I have been thinking of you ever since you were here, quite to the exclusion of my own work, so anxious am I not to do you harm in any way, and so uncertain how best to use the influence I have over you.' Much of his guilt arose from her recent declaration that she had woken up to his artistic ideals and wanted to follow his instructions to the letter. This total control over her worried him and made him feel responsible for her future when he couldn't control his own. 'All that "waking up" in the sense of complete sympathy is entirely good for you but I don't know what will happen when you begin also to sympathize with me, and to like the colours and forms of things as they *are* . . .' He concluded that it was ridiculous to place so much emphasis on one cancelled visit. 'You know that tea would have been all sipped in a couple of hours and I was forced to be back here next week if I had come . . . Please don't be sorry. Ever your loving, J.R.'[24]

To Kate this was a major setback. She replied in anger and confusion, telling him that not only was she deeply hurt and disappointed, but she felt bitterly let down by his callous behaviour. He had failed to understand how important he now was to her. But if she could not have him in London, at least she could hope for more letters of advice and reassurance. This request, too, upset Ruskin, who defended his position:

> Darlingest Katie, But what *shall* we do if you take on like that. You know, you might get a lot of nice quiet happiness out of it all if you'd take it more quietly – think – if I had fallen really ill again – and couldn't even write you a card? Or if I'd gone to India and been swallowed up? – Or if I didn't like any of your drawings, and were writing critiques on them? Or if you were as old as me and finding your eyes begin to fail?

He urged quiet patience, 'and we can have such lovely teas in October, which will be here before we can think.'[25] Two days later she received his 'many thanks for the sweetness of her letters' and he assured her: 'I know well that you can only do well what you enjoy and that these trials for me must be failures;

but they will be useful failures and lead to better.' And then he urged: 'I do earnestly wish you would take a modest little academy course under any skilled figure draughtsman, and conquer these elementary difficulties finally.'[26]

In September Kate, as usual, conferred with Evans on the progress of her books before printing for the Christmas market. She arrived at Witley early in the month, having left London with Ruskin's admonishment: 'for goodness sake – and badness sake, – (that's *my* sake) and all the girls' sake, and all (little) boys' sake – and all sakes' sake old and new – do rest, and play, and sleep, all the blessed twenty-four hours and if you'll promise to do *nothing* I'll write you a little word of thanks every other day and be oh so grateful and pleased.' Another of the Evans's visitors was Randolph Caldecott, seeking advice for his most recent picture book. To Kate's delight Ruskin's letters arrived at Witley as promised, and she replied to them, enclosing watercolours of the Surrey countryside she now loved. Overjoyed by these, Ruskin forgot that he had urged her to rest, and wrote, 'But all you have been seeing is boundlessly helpful and good for you, and the motives of the sketches you send today are unsurpassable.'[27] Kate told Evans that she wanted to study at the seaside, and he suggested Scarborough. When Ruskin learned this he considered it a further victory and was delighted.

When she returned to London Kate, encouraged by the letters she had received at Witley, pressed Ruskin for yet more attention. He was then entertaining his American friend, Professor Charles Eliot Norton, as well as sorting out old diaries, personal papers and reconsidering aspects of his will that immersed him in thoughts of death. Kate's begging for affectionate, playful letters seemed most inappropriate, and he wrote short, sharp replies to put a stop to her demands – at least until he returned to Oxford in October. In one of these he included a characteristic and revealing assessment of their current relationship:

> My Darling Katie . . . And don't fear that I shall put anything before the seeing [of] you, when I do come, for I feel this affection you bear me puts me in a place of most solemn trust over you – but I do hope you will manage to get it put into a more daughterly and fatherly sort of thing for indeed, Katie – part of the necessary work with this American friend was alloting some bits of my 'will' – and just think what a sad Katie you would be, – as things are with you now – if – you hadn't me to write to you any more. Now be a good girl, and try to get into a quieter – I do not [mean] less deep – feeling to your poor old – Master.[28]

A week later Kate went to Scarborough and took a room in the Grand Hotel on the sea-front. There, each day for a week, she made drawings of the children on the beach and posted them to Ruskin. He was by now in a playful mood: 'I do hope you'll play on the sands and do nothing but what the children do – all day long,' he teased. But Kate knew better, and tried to give him the correctly drawn figures for which he waited. After seven long days struggling in the sun, her working holiday came to a disastrous end when she lost her watercolour box. Tired of the crowds and heat, she took the train to London, where she received an angry, scolding letter from Ruskin, who claimed she had not stayed long enough at Scarborough, and her drawings showed it: 'It would have done you so much good – both to body and mind, to have stayed there all the autumn,' he wrote. 'Suppose I say I'll never write to you in London at all? What would you do?' He was annoyed by her weakness, and he focused his anger on her working on such limited subjects: '[I'm] a little cross with you for always drawing outlines of children and never ships or piers, or cliffs, or cottages, or good-looking Fishermen.'[29] Kate thought this unfair; she had gone to Scarborough only to please Ruskin, not to be diverted by the scenery. A short silence descended between them; only after her drawing appeared in his September issue of *Fors Clavigera* did she feel confident enough to reply to Ruskin's angry letter.

In October Ruskin's letters arrived at daily or two-day intervals, whenever he found a spare moment in his demanding Oxford work schedule. 'I've got two numbers on hand of my History of Christendom – two new *Fors*, one Proserpina, two Oxford lectures – and two books to edit and more letters to answer every day than all the day would answer,' he wrote to her, 'almost giddy' from his work load. Kate responded by sending a new batch of paintings to wherever his peripatetic movements took him. At Kenmure Castle he carefully picked out faults in a recent batch of girlies: 'The two sweeties are indeed beautiful, and only need to be painted larger to become a most glorious picture. I must stand over you while you paint them again with a wide brush . . . And you must give up drawing round hats. It's the hats that always save you from having to do a background – and I'm not going to be put off with them any more.' However, such pictures arrived at well timed intervals in his 'very miserable' work routine and helped to lift his spirits.

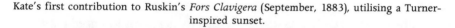

Kate's first contribution to Ruskin's *Fors Clavigera* (September, 1883), utilising a Turner-inspired sunset.

In addition to her drawings of children, Kate now sent recently painted landscape views of Hampstead Heath which she often visited that year. In one letter she let slip a plan to move to a house in Hampstead, near the Heath, and Ruskin was horrified. 'But I am aghast at the house in Hampstead,' he wrote, 'and quite resolved that you *shan't* live in London . . . I'll make your life a burden to you if you live in London! If you had come to Norwood [his childhood home] instead of Hampstead, there would have been some sense in it – I've no patience with you.'[30] It is not clear why Ruskin objected so strongly to Hampstead, although he still remembered her first ecstatic reactions to Brantwood, and had decided her true place was in a country cottage, endlessly drawing studies from nature, undisturbed by London's grimness. Kate agreed and immediately after her return from her first visit to Brantwood she had complained to her brother about the difficulty of living in London. He assured her that Hampstead was the best of two worlds – a country setting near the city. 'I just wanted [to be] taken to a road in the East End of London for a while,' Kate wrote to Lily Evans of her brother's reaction, 'then I should have all the ridiculous nonsense [of moving to the country] knocked out of my head and look upon Hampstead with gratitude – *I daresay*.'[31] With some resignation, she consented to the Hampstead move, and by late 1883 the legal machinery was placed in motion and the house-hunt began.

Kate continued to send drawings of young girls, hoping to buoy Ruskin's low spirits and quell his anger. His delighted reactions disclose the excited state of his mind: a 'heavenly drawing' of a young girl represented 'first love – or perfect love – or the goddess of girl'; others tormented him with their elusive qualities and provocative beauty: 'But for poor – poor me! What have I to do with such dears? or roses – or felicities.'[32] He proposed another visit to her studio and Kate took the opportunity to transform one girlie drawing into a pathetic invitation – a lone girl waving an ivy branch which she inscribed 'Come'. However, Ruskin was still concerned by her relentless need for more of his attention. He planned on this visit to clarify their relationship once and for all, and wrote two frank letters a few days before arriving in London. In the first he confessed:

> I'm terribly anxious about you. Fancy, – if I felt you were drawing feebly – because of me? how dreadful – only it's no use talking till I see you and I don't want to spoil our first tea, neither – only you must for my sake as well as your own, try to be interested in other people – your child pets more than me.

The second letter, written two days later, began:

Three original watercolours from a set of seven to illustrate 'St. Valentine's Day' in the *Illustrated London News*: frontispiece, volume LXXIV, 1879, and in the Supplement, 15 February, 1879.

Darling Katie, What very lovely letters you are writing me just now and I *am* thankful to be able to please you thus and make you 'content' (and I know the feeling well) – but – for both of us, it seems to me that there is a call to a deeply resigned working for other people, and use of our powers with rejoicing, for the myriads we can teach with the beauty we can see. These lovely creatures whom you fancy for me – I have to think of – as only for others – and am much more lonely than you – (but yet – how many would envy the lonelier of each of us?)[33]

Ruskin's second visit to Kate's studio began on this sober note. He had even taken the precaution of bringing along a French book to read in strained silence. As it turned out much of the time was spent discussing topics of mutual interest with her brother. Johnnie was now a distinguished chemist, having abandoned his teaching career for a then unusual post as private adviser to a Guy's Hospital physician. He also maintained a keen interest in amateur photography, and it was this that intrigued Ruskin. He asked Johnnie to prepare photographic enlargements of art works for his Oxford lectures and their collaboration continued for some months, Ruskin sending detailed instructions to Johnnie in his letters to Kate. After tea and muffins it seemed that Ruskin had succeeded in keeping Kate's attentions at bay. He gave a final hug to Mary, Kate's child model, who was also present, and dashed to the station for a train back to Oxford, feeling confident but, as he later wrote to Kate, 'sadly spoiled by the mobcaps and muffins and all the rest of it'. He was even warmed by her attempt to quell her passion. 'I wonder if it's because I tease you so that you care for me – or in spite of it?' he taunted.[34] Kate answered this letter, assuring him that now she had Mary, the model, back in her studio and more book work to do, she was less restless and more confident. For the time being, she felt content.

Ruskin's November letters were filled with urgent pleas such as Kate had never before experienced. He wanted her to play with him a game of 'love letters' at which from the start he knew she would prove the more proficient: 'I am very thankful to be fairly well, still and able for anything I'm to do,' he assured her, writing from Oxford. 'I *can't* write such letters as you would like me to write. I wonder what would become of you, if I did! I *cannot* make out why women ever care for men at all!'[35] This emotionally dangerous game continued as he wrote two days later: 'How I wish I *could* write you a real love-letter! and to think of all the foolish girls everywhere that get them, (– not from me, I mean, but in general –) and poor Kate Greenaway – not one – only lectures and teasers and dreadful silences!' To reassure her he continued, 'But my dear, you should not and must not be afraid of my going away, and being unkind. You shall always have what I *can* give you, that you care for . . .'[36]

Original watercolours, 'For the Dance', 'Supper', both done for a set of twelve drawings appearing in 'Christmas in Little Peopleton Manor', the *Illustrated London News*, Christmas Number, volume LXXV, p.36.

In mid-November Kate prepared her next *Fors* illustration for Ruskin and waited for his promised return to her studio, 'when my beard will be full of Mary all the morning'. Ruskin was now alarmingly irritable – he wrote to Kate, 'my wits are at the far end' – and he was looking forward to the visit as much as she was. In order to comfort him in the interim, Kate sent a watercolour of two young girls trapped in a large teacup. She inscribed it 'Calm in a Teacup', to indicate her own resigned frame of mind, and Ruskin wrote back that it was '. . . far too entrancing, if only I could get imprisoned in the teacup!' He arrived in London and spent the first night with Stacy Marks and his daughters, writing from there to warn Kate that their visit would be much shorter than previously planned. 'I must get away at $\frac{1}{2}$ past three. I'll leave you lots of work to do so that you won't want me back again.' On the day he sent a telegram announcing a further delay: 'Sadly hindered, cannot reach you till about one.'[37] As usual Kate had worked herself into an anxious state waiting for him, but she had taken the precaution of again inviting little Mary to take the edge off their strained conversations, and she secretly hoped the girl would entice Ruskin to stay longer. He arrived with a flurry of apologies, ignored Kate, and turned instead to the mischievous Mary who stepped down from the modelling podium, pulled off her mob cap, tugged at Ruskin's beard and placed the hat on his head. 'There,' Kate laughed, 'you look just like the wolf in Red Riding Hood!'

Kate returned to Witley in early December to discuss her plans for new books and she was met with anxious pleas from Evans for more work. During the year she had produced only two new books, *Little Ann* and the year's almanack. Evans was quite justified in his concern, for Kate's commercial value had reached a new peak, and many other publishers were exploiting it: Marcus Ward had reissued her early card designs in a small volume called *Flowers and Fancies*; Routledge had issued a *Kate Greenaway Calendar* as well as her second almanack, and Swan Sonnenschein had published two early and quite grotesque black and white illustrations in a volume of fairy tales, *Tales from the Edda*, and further infuriated Kate by falsely assigning her initials to a third plate. The press, her large public following, and her professional colleagues held her work in high esteem. The *Magazine of Art* now claimed that she had 'obtained a position of standing among the artists of the present day' and Randolph Caldecott openly admitted that her popularity had cut into his book sales and forced him to sacrifice 'some of the necessary luxuries of life'.

After her return from Witley Kate tried to revive her friendship with Locker and his family. She had dedicated *Little Ann* to the 'Rowfant quartos' – the Locker children – and now sent Mrs Locker a copy of her latest almanack and Locker a watercolour. But Locker had noticeably cooled toward Kate, probably because of her neglect over the past year. It was clear that he was jealous of Ruskin and his influence upon her, and he wrote to say, 'I daresay that Ruskin is sunning his unworthy self in your smiles. I hope he is impressed with his good fortune.' By December he was resigned to living out his old age preparing his autobiography and helping his wife in the building of a large house at Cromer on the Norfolk coast. When he received Kate's elaborate watercolour he was deeply touched, though determined she should do no more for him. 'I was shocked to receive the drawing . . . Why should you waste your

Edmund Evans with his family at Witley, Surrey, about 1876.

time on me? It is heart-breaking to think of, when your spare time is so valuable and you have so little of it. You must send me no more. I say it seriously. No more. I have plenty, plenty to remember you by, and when I am gone, enough to show my children the kind feeling you had for me. Work away, but for yourself – for your new house and for others more worthy.'[38]

Locker's phrase 'others more worthy' was an allusion to Ruskin, who throughout December continued to contemplate death; but he felt encouraged by the hold Kate allowed him over her career. On 2 December he wrote from Brantwood of her 'inestimable gift to me, and if only I thought [of] myself – I could contentedly and proudly keep you drawing nicest girls in blue sashes with soft eyes and blissful lips, to the end of – my poor bit of life.' He enclosed a copy of his favourite Carpaccio painting because 'it shows you *all* I mean, about complete colour'.[39] Three days later, in response to one of her 'exquisite love-letters', he wrote: 'My goodness – do young lovers ever get such I wonder? how mad they'd have driven me, once on a time, if I had ever got anything like them.' He invited her to Brantwood, and added a cautionary suggestion to include 'Mrs. Allingham too, perhaps'. But this was for next summer; now he wanted to be left alone to work in the country and to write to her only when he felt the need. 'You know, when you came to see me, my old ways were all put out of the way for you,' he wrote, 'but really you knew nothing of my life – I had no object then but to be of so much use to you as I could and get as much enjoyment as I could – but when I'm at work I haven't a word to throw at a Cat – or a Kate – or a Katie, or any living thing.'[40]

In the weeks before Christmas Kate tried to elicit more letters by filling her own with elaborate figure compositions ('processionals') of rows of Greenaway maidens joined by flower garlands. These 'girlies' were tailor-made to Ruskin's tastes. Ruskin was then alone at Brantwood, feeling sad and lonely without Joan

103

Frederick Locker and Hannah Jane Locker-Lampson.

Severn or her family to care for him. Kate's contrived drawings easily captured his imagination and sent his spirits soaring. He sat alone in his study, pondering her girlies until he imagined one would 'upset my inkstand and drink my cream and trip me with the hearthrug and pull my hair into my eyes and put everything into the wrong drawer – and do whatever *ever* it likes.' Others he invited for tea, although he feared they 'should all come with toasting forks, and toast me like a muffin – but even then I shouldn't be the better for it – nor you neither,' he wrote to Kate.[41] On Christmas Day, still alone and even more depressed, he telegrammed his praises of her new Christmas drawing; the following day he felt particularly vulnerable and continued his deceptive admiration, adding the pathetic apology: 'I tremble, now, to ask you to draw any other way. I can't tell you not to care for me so much since it makes you draw like that! but I am so ashamed of getting all this grace from you, and being the teasing old brute that I am.'[42]

But it was Stacy Marks who gave her the assurances Ruskin now failed to offer. He wrote to thank her for *Little Ann*, which he thought was 'on the whole, I might say entirely, your best book . . . Your work should be all the more popular after all Ruskin has said of it . . . He is a singular and wayward genius. I tried to get him to admire Caldecott but it was no use –.'[43]

The following year letters passed almost daily between Ruskin and Kate, and when Ruskin felt the need to make an urgent point he sent her a telegram. In so doing, he was using Kate to amuse him and dispel his loneliness; but she had quite different motives. She was by now very much in love; so much so that she was willing to overcome her timidity and describe her longings. The charged atmosphere this created caused turmoil, heartbreak, misunderstandings and a falling off in the quality of Kate's work.

Greenaway book-plate designed for Frederick Locker.

In January Ruskin asked for proper life studies and nothing else. 'When are you going to be *good* and send me a study of anything from nature – the coalscuttle or the dust pan – or a towel or a clothes screen – or the hearth rug or the back of a chair – I'm very cruel, but here's half a year I've been waiting for a bit of Common sense –! There's *none* in *me*! How could there be any left, with you flattering me like that and saying nobody's like me!! . . . I wish you liked my books and wanted more of them and not so much of me.'[44] To emphasize his point, he sent a complete set of his books, specially bound in white leather with white silk and gold arabesque, and included a sketch of 'a coalscuttle in revenge for the bonnets'. This was Ruskin in his most flirtatious, extravagant mood, toying with her earnestness by imposing on her daunting drawing lessons designed to deflect her passion and to help him pass the idle days of January. Kate was understandably confused, but she dutifully sent answers to all his letters and examples of her nature studies. Often she tried to compensate for her failures by sending enticing new girlie drawings, knowing that he would probably not criticize these. 'But how you work me with them – never to see real ones!' he teased in mid-January. 'All the same, they *do* delight me – and are a new life to me –.' Her letters, however, disturbed him with their hints of her growing love, which Ruskin flippantly tried to dismiss: 'You very dear Katie, how terribly you love me – what *have* I done to deserve it all? or to win, for nobody could deserve it – least of all I – hard-hearted Turk that I am.'[45]

Kate now suffered from low spirits and a winter sore throat, which took away her ability to work and gave her time to write passionate letters. Ruskin too was irritable, impatient with her failures and angered by her pleas for affection. 'I'm so cross I must go out and walk it off,' he wrote and then retreated to the Brantwood hills to escape his gloom for 'there's sun!!!' This letter sent Kate into what he called her 'traumatical state', which forced him to apologize two days later. 'I never mean to be cross, but am – but also I'm so sorry when you waste your precious hours in trifling for me.'[46] Ruskin's work was partly to blame for this irritability; he was preparing his next Oxford lecture, 'The Storm Cloud of the Nineteenth Century', and this left him depressed and angry. From his notes of sunrises, sunsets and the movements of clouds made since his youth, he now concluded that an ominous Storm Cloud, 'made of dead men's souls', had descended over England, fed by the smoke from countless factory chimneys. This cloud was a symbol of the moral darkness that held the modern world captive, and he tried to warn his friends and admirers of the danger. When Kate learned of his cloud obsession, she sent a comforting girlie drawing, a 'cloud lady', which he hoped to transfer to glass once she had corrected her poor figure drawing. 'You really *must* draw *her* again for me without any clothes because you've suggested a perfect coalheaver's leg, which I can't think you meant! and you *must* draw your figures now undraped for a while.' To add insult to her injured pride, he enclosed two drawings by Francesca Alexander, the rival for his affections he liked to use on such occasions: 'But you must try to like the Alexanders – for they are Heaven's own doing – as much as Heaven ever allows to be seen of it.'[47]

Emotions became feverish as Kate yearned to declare her love openly, but Ruskin remained wary of the subject. Loving only reminded him of his past. 'I ought to be "good" about everything, for good people love me, – and have

'To the Sun Door', plate from *Marigold Garden*, 1885, contributing to Ruskin's cloud obsession.

loved,' he assured her. In the same letter he told a story about Rose La Touche, who in her religious fervour had prayed a girl friend 'at the point of death' back to health. 'My own dead Rose was – I have told you have not I – a saint in her own way, and was content in the habit of prayer,' he began, and ended with his own conclusion – that since he had loved such a saintly girl, 'mightn't I too be good?'[48] But this was in the past. Kate wanted to express her present longings, and she chose to do so through her drawings. After his return to London in early February, when he briefly visited her studio, she sent him a titillating birthday greeting, a series of young girls painted from her knowledge of what pleased him most. Delighted by the gesture, he wrote the day he received them, 'to tell you how thankful I am to have been spared to get such a drawing on my birthday, and to feel that women can thus care for me'. Three days later the drawing still haunted him, as he studied it in his London hotel room. 'Of course the Queen of them all is the little one in front – but she's just a month or six weeks too young for *me* . . . Then there's the divine one with the darker hair, and the beautific one with the brown, – but I think *they've* got lovers already and have only come to please the rest, and wouldn't be mine if I prayed them ever so.'[49]

Ruskin remained in London for over a month, during which time Kate tried to see as much of him as possible; she devised a scheme to lure him back to her studio for portrait sittings. Flattered, he wrote, 'I wonder how you can bear to think of drawing me – and how you mean to do it!' and eventually he agreed. The sittings were wedged in between their visits to the Grosvenor Gallery and the British Museum, evening discussions on art and his preparations for Oxford. Then, one evening, Kate approached the subject of love. Ruskin reacted angrily and from the safety of his hotel room he wrote the next day: 'How naughty you were last night! For punishment – read every word of [the] enclosed from my Sorella [Francesca Alexander]. Ever your poor, old, cross, J.R.'[50]

As Kate's love grew, Ruskin made elaborate excuses to avoid his portrait sittings and the picture was never completed. He had hoped to leave London as soon as possible, but his doctor discovered renewed symptoms of his disturbing mental illness and urged him to remain. This only further enraged Ruskin and made him feel trapped. He refused to tell Kate about his ill health and, despite her frantic letters, continued to ignore her. Ten days passed before he explained his angry silence, in a letter that betrayed his frightened, confused state: 'No – I never scold! – but I must say what truly ought to be; – and say it more and more firmly; – that I *ought* to be a source of simple and strengthening pleasure to you – and you to me; and that so far as you grieve for my absence, or feel hurt by my being different when I am there, from what you would have me, you "tempt" Heaven to take away from me the power of pleasing you at all.' Ruskin was shaken by his relapse ('not in the least connected with over work – but simply with advancing age'), and said that he could only visit her one more time. 'Would you not have been much happier that I had gone, even without saying good-bye, than that this should be so?' Despite his assurances ('There is nothing of any dangerous moment – but there *is*, what may need some careful treatment, and gives me a good deal of concern'), Kate was alarmed by the news, and told him that she had received it with despair. 'I'm *not going* to hear you writing or talking about "Despair",' he reprimanded three days later. 'It's time enough for that when one's old – blind, deaf, – and forgotten . . . Ever your – Best Adviser! Dino.'[51]

After his departure, in an effort to help to restore his health, she immediately changed the tone of her letters, sending him light-hearted, frivolous descriptions, and drawings of happy children. But when he forgot her birthday in March, she sent a sad, apologetic note, feeling selfish because of her frantic displays of affection, which she hoped had not made him worse. To her the situation was torture – she could not get him out of her mind; her days and nights were now filled only with thoughts for his welfare. He replied calmly from Brantwood, where he had been sorting through his mineral collection and resting. 'But how absurd it is for an old geologist to have to console a dark-eyed Kate and teach her how to bear the love of him!!! – And what strange things these love-instincts are. What is the use of telling you when a letter is coming. How much more to the purpose it would be if it told you when I was thinking of you – and to some extent what I was thinking.' His conclusion re-emphasized her illustrative abilities: 'And how very, very – very wonderful it is that you can draw exactly the creatures that I like so much – and yet haven't the least sympathy with me in liking them?' She told him of a dream she had about him; and, flattered, he added: 'I do so want to know what you dreamed of me. Tell me as soon as you can – Was it a nasty bitter moral moral [sic] lesson then? Poor Katie!'[52]

The man Kate dreamed about and had wanted to paint was not the dashing assured gentleman one might assume from Ruskin's well-documented ability to attract young women. Indeed, the eighteen-year-old Beatrix Potter had found him just the opposite when she met him at the Royal Academy in March 1884. Dismayed by his slovenly appearance and lackadaisical manner, she described him in her diary as 'one of the most ridiculous figures I have ever seen. A very old hat, much necktie and aged coat buttoned up on his neck, humpbacked, not particularly clean looking. He had on high boots, and one of his trousers was tucked up on the top of one. He became aware of this half way round the room, and stood on one leg to put it right, but in so doing hitched up the other trouser worse than the first one had been.'[53] Nevertheless, Kate was deeply in love with this slovenly, toppled giant of the art world and she continued to write letters begging for some sign of reciprocal feeling. When he tired of her endless pleading, he warned her to stop; he threatened to send only letters written by one of his secretaries – curt, business-like letters – because, 'I couldn't promise anything like the correspondence you would be happy in.'[54] Besides, he had other devoted admirers to write to, many of them women.

It is not wholly clear what Kate intended in professing her love to Ruskin. Romance was important to her, a spinster in her late thirties. She once received from an unknown gentleman admirer a Valentine on which appeared a rakish man with a glint in his eye and the suggestive sentiment 'Game for Miss Greenaway'. Even this trifle she carefully preserved all her life, obviously flattered by the attention. And, of course, she treasured all of Ruskin's letters. The question of their romance is puzzling but unresolvable. Rumours of their possible marriage certainly circulated throughout London drawing rooms, and

Kate's friend and confidante Lady Dorothy Nevill wrote in her memoirs: 'I have good reason to believe that at the time the great art critic would not have been at all adverse to marry her, had she felt disposed to think favourably of such an alliance.'[55] However, the editors of Ruskin's *Complete Works* called this 'a piece of gossip which altogether misjudged the situation'. Perhaps more significant is the statement of Kate's great-niece, in her letter to the present author: 'About her friendship with Ruskin, my father [Eddie Dadd junior] *stressed* the fact, that it was entirely platonic – My [great] aunt would have (or even did?) rejected any offer of marriage by a person who was married . . .'[56]

Physically, Kate was not at all the type of woman Ruskin found attractive. Judging by Mrs Loftie's shocked reaction to Kate's plain appearance, she can have made no attempt to alter her appearance to please him: 'her delicate taste in dressing her subjects failed to give any suggestion, or she did not know how or did not take the trouble to make the best of herself.' Now thirty-eight, she had the quality of quaint old-maidishness that Ruskin found particularly objectionable. Besides, his past had given him reason enough to dismiss Kate's advances. As he later wrote in his autobiography, he had learned a valuable lesson: 'The men capable of the highest imaginative passion are always on fiery waves by it.' His relationship with Kate remained to him a frivolous game which was to be indulged in and enjoyed whenever he felt like it – often without concern for her feelings. To him love, romance, and, worst of all, marriage, were not in his thoughts. He seems to have played a cruel game with Kate's emotions; his letters encouraged her with lavish praises; then, when she became too affectionate, he became cool and turned away from her. 'You know I do cry – sometimes at things – you said I did a *little* – once I remember crying because you were cross and you said you *hated* women who cried,' she wrote later when she felt calmer and more resigned to his cruelty.

Unfortunately at this time Kate was determined to make her desires known to Ruskin. Throughout the spring of 1884 she longed for the least sign of hope in his letters, and immersed herself in thoughts of romance. She wrote to him that love was essential to her creative life: it had influenced her early books with illustrations of Pre-Raphaelite suitors and their maiden loves, and now she felt it inspired her to produce passionate lines of mawkish, abrupt verse. In an attempt to express her frustrated feelings for Ruskin, she composed line after line of Pre-Raphaelite-inspired imagery, dwelling on the torture of loving from a distance, the pain of parting unfulfilled.

> *Nothing to do but part dear*
> *Oh love love love, my heart*
> *Is slowly breaking and coldness creeping*
> *Nearer into my every part.*
>
> *Nothing to do but part dear*
> *Look at me before you go*
> *And clasp my hands lightly, Kiss me*
> *Good bye, it's better so.*[57]

Most of these verses remained unfinished, although she often returned to them to rework a phrase or a word, depending on her mood.

Ruskin, on the other hand, was unsure of his feelings, but enjoyed the attention he now received from Kate. He wrote to her, three days after her birthday: 'We *are* not so far apart, for I don't care for any beauty that looks ill-natured, or foolish, nor do I think it a bit more divine in women than in lambs or birds – or crystals –.' In the same letter he told the story of 'a long quarrel with one of my pets once, because I said she was no better to me than a pretty birch tree'. The young girl stormed off in anger, but Ruskin was confident she would return to him, for 'She had to come at last! I can't think how I've such power over women, when it is that I'm never a bit set up by it – but only think them absurd. If I were really a pious monk and didn't care about *them*, I shouldn't wonder – but when they know I'm so naughty and [that I] flirt with every one I can get near!'[58] His remarks were meant to dampen Kate's hopes; instead, they challenged a determined woman to beg for more attention.

At the end of March Kate returned to Witley. There she and Evans planned a book of flower drawings and their symbolic meanings, to be published as *The Language of Flowers*. She also wandered the Surrey countryside, drawing and painting the early spring blossoms; afterwards she wrote to Ruskin, asked him to tell her his favourite flowers, hoping to include them in her new book. Lazy and in a lethargic mood, Ruskin replied at surprising length, listing thirteen favourite flowers and heading the list with the wild rose. When he received her watercolours of some of his favourites he wrote: 'But it will really be worth while to have fallen in love with me, if you fall in love consequently with squills and grape hyacinths.'[59]

When Kate returned to London, she set about writing even more tender letters to lift Ruskin out of what he described as his 'very steady gloom'. For a time she was encouraged – 'I like my Katie for letters'; he was grateful for a grape hyacinth drawing with a new 'lovely long love letter'. 'Write every day for a week,' he urged on 17 April, and invited her to Brantwood, 'when your book's done', and 'we'll do Coniston girls and roses and health – and beautiful purple thistles – and it will be ever so nice.'[60] The letters that followed were the start of an elaborate postal kissing game, in which he sent a number of crosses (kisses) according to his mood. These varied from a single cross and signature, a letter margin edged in crosses, or crosses drawn in perspective, finally to elaborate cross designs. The game continued as long as it amused him, and helped to keep Kate temporarily at bay. 'Yes, that x was for your very own and here are $x_x^x x$ four more for being so *very* good.'[61]

To Kate's surprise, at the end of April Ruskin returned to London, where he warned her to prepare for his visit to her studio. She must not expect too much, only a two-hour stay; but despite his attempt to put her off, Kate had changed very little in her entreaties, and this secretly pleased him. 'You sweet Katie, it's a very wonderful thing to have made any woman love one so – but it's awful too – for what is to become of you!' Ruskin duly arrived at Pemberton Gardens to take tea. 'The cakes delicious! – and such lots of butter – and I rather enjoyed the whole thing!' he acknowledged shortly afterwards.[62] Since he planned a longer stay in London, they hoped to visit the galleries and collaborate on paintings in her studio. But Ruskin fell ill and had to put off their visit to the Grosvenor Gallery, sending Joan Severn to tell Kate the bad news, and

A Surrey Cottage, watercolour by Kate Greenaway, showing the Witley countryside she adopted into many of her paintings.

telegramming his promise to visit her the following day. He arrived as promised and they discussed his latest plan – terracotta Greenaway girlies in the manner of Luca della Robbia. He also reminded her of his Brantwood invitation, and Kate 'behaved quite charmingly', as he wrote to her from Brantwood eight days later.

Afraid that a new depression was about to descend, he felt desperate for light-hearted fun, and asked for fairy tales and Greenaway drawings to lift his spirits. 'Do let us try to get sunshine in ourselves – for the plague wind outside is very cruel,' he begged in a letter signed with twelve kisses.[63] Kate sent an original story with obvious romantic overtones, substituting one of his pets for her part in the story. Her tale ended in marriage, which piqued Ruskin: 'But I'm resolved my pets *shan't* marry – therefore, they mustn't be in love. I've always thought the love in Fairytales quite spoiled them. That's for real life.' Moreover, her affectionate letters made him feel like Bottom in Shakespeare's *A Midsummer Night's Dream* ('especially when my beard tickles').[64] Kate was deeply hurt by this offhand remark, and told him that she was certainly not Titania, mistakenly in love with an ass: he meant more to her than the bumbling Bottom. Ruskin's resigned apology arrived four days later: 'I never dreamed you would take it like that, though of course there was a grain of truth which made it sting worse. I will try not to hurt you, but I can't be on my guard with every word.'[65]

Meanwhile Kate was busy completing *The Language of Flowers* and attending to the construction of her new Hampstead home. 'The little Red House is progressing – not as fast as I could wish, but it has got to actual bricks and mortar now so there's some hope it will be a real home in time.'[66] She continued the kissing game with Ruskin, who asked for news of her Brantwood visit since they planned to collaborate on 'a child's botany based on the language of flowers'. When Kate asked when it would be convenient for her to come, he backed down and tried to put her off. He must first consult Joan Severn, but she was suffering from bleeding spells and exhaustion, so this was impossible. In early June, when Kate wrote in disgust that she could arrive tomorrow week, he hadn't 'the least tested Joan yet'. She was upset by this callous treatment: it

111

seemed Ruskin was not very serious about the visit. In the midst of all this, Brantwood was inundated with a stream of well-wishers and admirers, which proved too embarrassing to stem. 'Things always come in a heap in May and June,' he explained to Kate, who refused to be put off any longer, 'What am I to do?' Then he made the unpardonable mistake of describing and gloating over his visiting female admirers at Brantwood. Kate was especially jealous of Ada Dundas, a forty-four-year-old cripple who, according to Ruskin, 'has got a Kate Greenaway gown just to please me and wants to come and show it [to] me!' She asked why Ruskin could entertain Ada and others and still have to put her off. It was quite intolerable, and Kate sent an angry letter and a 'dreadful threat about vanishing' which left Ruskin confused, frustrated and 'so sorry and puzzled and a little cross'.[67] Trapped by his game of pitting admirers against admirers, without any thought of the consequences, he rejected them all and tried to bury himself in work, greeting only the least offensive or demanding of his guests. Petty differences and vicious jealousies only made him angry, as he wrote to Kate the day after her outburst: 'I am in the very stress of my best spring work – and cannot be interrupted in it – nothing drives me so wild as having my thoughts disturbed when I have important compositions on hand: and I *must* finish what I am doing before I let you come. I can let other people come, whom I don't need to give time to – but *you* must be cared for and seen to, and I am not able, till this spring work is fairly through – nor have I ventured to say a word to Mrs. Severn.'[68] Kate's tantrum brought a second response in a letter a day later: 'Don't *please* dear – don't let yourself fall into that distress so far on the other side of anything I ever meant or thought – is that any reason for resolving never to come here, when I *shall* want you? . . . But I won't – as you tell me not – say more than just – Heaven bless you – and send a little circlet of love, [circle of kisses], Ever your sorrowful, Dinie.'[69]

By this time, Kate had taken on another project, the children's classic, William Mavor's *The English Spelling Book*, originally planned with Randolph Caldecott as co-illustrator. Caldecott had agreed to the commission and produced a preliminary cover design, listing himself and Kate as joint illustrators. Kate had liked the book and willingly accepted the challenge, but a short time later she dramatically changed her mind and told Evans that the book must be hers alone, or she would refuse to continue. Her motives are not known, although Ruskin's influence seems most likely. He had often lamented the inadequacy of educational reading materials for children and was at the time preparing 'Fors Infantiae', his October *Fors Clavigera*, on the very subject of children's books. Perhaps Kate saw the new book as a way to convince Ruskin she could create something more than entertaining picture books for the gift-book market, and Evans had to give in. However, Kate paid heavily for her obstinacy, struggling over the 108 pages, most needing illustrations, until she was frightened that she might not be able to complete it on time. 'I don't get on well with Mavor,' she confessed in a letter to Evans, urging him to leave the engraving 'as long as you could if you fancy I could do better.'[70] But she was determined to overcome her difficulties and she spaced the work over the next few months while still maintaining a voluminous correspondence with, and preparing drawings for Ruskin.

On the other hand, by summer, Ruskin immersed himself in his own work and decided that Kate's letters were impeding his progress. Such letters demanded answers and he hadn't or wasn't willing to spare the time. The safest thing was to burn each new letter, some before opening, 'for fear of their laying about', he wrote to her. This burning of her letters and the cool, reserved tone of the few he wrote led Kate to conclude that he had changed dreadfully towards her, despite his assurances that this was not the case: 'No, the dreadfulness is only in *your* thinking I'm not the same – You're just like a child who thinks the sea's dried up when the tide's down or the sky's all spoiled by a storm.'[71] Instead, it was her over-excited state and her pleas for a precise date to visit Brantwood that had brought on his silence. He was still hard at work and she must keep her distance until he sent for her. 'Alas, nothing can give me pleasure, now in what you do, till you begin to do *right*, and think *rightly*. And until you get out of this overexcited state, I simply *can't* have you near me. I must have my precious summer days let alone – I'm at quiet and strong work, and so shall not be interrupted by nonsense, however disagreeable it may make my letters for a little while –. Do anything you *can*, from nature – and nothing from your head or heart, for neither of them, just now – are good for anything.' If she still loved him – as she said she did – she must see his point of view and stop her selfish demands. This was a valuable lesson, one she had previously overlooked, as he wrote: 'When I am in love, I think of what the people will like that I'm in love with – and don't feel any pleasure myself in being near them if they don't want me to be.'[72]

After this rebuff, Kate tried to finish Mavor, and planned the early stages of her new book, *Marigold Garden*, asking Ruskin's advice on her drawing of four princesses trapped in a tower. This he found a delightful idea, '. . . but the first thing you have to do in this leafy world is to learn to paint a leaf green.' He sent fresh-cut pieces of Brantwood sod, 'not to tease you – but they'll go on growing and being pleasant companions,' and instructed her to 'paint the greens and browns' and draw leaf shapes like the ones sketched in his letter. These nature lessons continued throughout July.

Early in August Kate sent calm and resolute letters to comfort Ruskin, who confessed he was growing despondent at the fading year. On 6 August he invited her to Brantwood, 'from the 16th to the 26th of this month . . . everybody will be glad to see you'; and Kate's spirits rose. On the day she expected to leave, a telegram arrived: 'Your visit must be put off. I am sorry but Mrs. Severn is again seriously unwell.' Despite the disappointment, Kate endeavoured to remain optimistic, and resignedly returned to her work and to plans for her new house in Hampstead. 'The news of the new house is nice – heaven send you health and comfort in it,' Ruskin consoled her in a letter of 28 August, admitting that he was far from well himself.[73]

By September a new wave of despondency appeared in Ruskin's letters to Kate. He was dispirited by his uncertain frame of mind, and by the unavoidable postponement of her visit; he tried to shut himself off from the outsiders he believed intruded on his independence. He wanted only to suffer alone – as he believed he had done throughout his life – and told her that he had never had advice from others, 'or thought of getting it – and knew it couldn't be – [I] only

Eddie Dadd and Mary (?) in rural setting, *c.*1887.

wanted to be let alone to look at things in my own way.' He signed this letter 'Ever your loving Hermit crab'. Kate would have none of this and tried to cheer him with plans for their future visits – the teas and children's parties in her new studio. Ruskin agreed that tea would be extremely pleasant, and even conceded, '. . . I think I shall like the new studio very much – but not so much as the old one. As for the children's parties – alas – no – please – I should see some wretch of a boy dancing with Mary!'[74]

Mary always played an important part in luring Ruskin back to Kate's studio, especially when Kate proved most trying to him. Kate had used Mary from her earliest books and now often paired her with Eddie Dadd, Kate's nephew and perfect Greenaway model, eight years old, with long blonde curls, an angelic face and a mischievous nature. But when, to Ruskin's annoyance, the two were brought together during one of his visits, he instantly became jealous of Eddie's possessive attitude to Mary, and the playful, taunting games they played to exclude him. In time he wanted to know and regulate Mary's every move; even when he was not in London he received constant news of Mary in Kate's letters, and once he wrote, 'Oh, dear, *can't* we keep Mary from going to the other people? I'd pay anything she makes to stop it. Do think about this – it torments me so, and it's so bad for *her*.'[75]

Despite his depression, in October Ruskin returned to lecture at Oxford, also making frequent trips to London, to deliver public readings from *Fors* (to which he invited Kate), and to make one further visit to her studio. Mary was again present, and Ruskin ignored Kate to play with the model, afterwards admitting to Kate that he was 'reprehensible in my attentions to Mary'. But Kate didn't mind; after her anxiety over his health she was happy to see him in such good spirits. She also had the memory of a delightful moonlight omnibus ride back to his Euston Square hotel, when she presented him with a copy of *The Language of Flowers* and her new almanack. The next day he returned to Oxford, promising to send his reactions to the books as soon as possible. Kate waited a few days, then left London for Witley. While she was there his long-awaited letter arrived.

The letter was a scathing criticism not only of the books but of her talent as well, and Kate was shattered by his frankness: 'I shall be most thankful if you will give up everything else and get these books finished and off your mind,' he began, suggesting that her illustration days were over, 'for between them and me, the little mind is going off itself, and you are working at present wholly in vain – There is *no* joy, and very, very little interest in any of the Flower book subjects.' The following day he sent a letter attacking her almanack for its poorly drawn roses, ridiculous figure drawing and disastrous colour printing; above all he concluded he was to blame for 'the funniest illustrations of cheap printing I've yet seen. – The worst of it is, *I'm* at the bottom of all this – all this good of yours goes into the work for me, and you sell the dregs to the public – doing also for *them* everything I forbid you.'[76] Kate apologized, explaining that the printing was not her responsibility.

The attack was a considerable blow to her morale, but Kate realized that Ruskin must again be ill. All his friends were now concerned for his mental condition, especially during his Oxford lectures. A short time later, on another visit to London, he made a brief tea-time stop at Kate's studio, to give her 'rose lessons' and put right her appalling almanack weaknesses. Kate noticed his nervous, jittery state and did not press him for a date for her return to Brantwood. When he left she considered her own needs – how she urgently wanted to be of use to him – and wrote to Joan Severn for advice. She asked about the chance of her coming to Coniston before the year's end and sent a copy of her almanack, apologizing for its weaknesses. 'And you – you do feel quite strong and well again now?' she asked hopefully. 'Remember, when there is a chance I might see you, I'd be *very very very* glad and delighted.'[77]

However, Ruskin insisted that all she could do for him was 'to learn to outline a rose rightly', to draw them less like truffles; his letters avoided any mention of her visit. Instead he telegrammed that his lectures were going well, that he thought his health better; he even sent a watercolour of an Oxford street to Eddie Dadd in an attempt to gain his friendship. In another letter he sent Kate a stack of illegible correspondence from other admirers for her to decipher. After completing his last lecture, he wrote on 1 December that 'I've made a great sensation and done great good in many ways and hope to do much yet.' But he had overworked dangerously, and the electric atmosphere of the lecture hall proved exhilarating and taxing. In mid-December he retired to the peace and solitude of Brantwood, where he guiltily wrote to Kate that 'with a drawer full of the loveliest Kate Greenaways ever anybody saw – . . . how wicked I am to be dull.' As Christmas approached, his letters became more introspective and doleful. Their relationship saddened him, with its clear parallels to what he knew of Carlyle's life: 'My life is a happier one, at its worst than poor Carlyle's! and I don't make people quite so unhappy, except you. If only Mrs. Carlyle had liked him as you like me!'[78]

At this time, Joan Severn – a key figure in their tense, stalemated relationship – was still severely ill at Herne Hill in South London, and Kate proposed to visit her there in early December. Joan had the power to consent to Kate's return to Brantwood and Kate wanted to know how much longer she would have to wait. After the visit she wrote to Joan in the mawkish baby-language usually reserved for Ruskin: 'Dearest Mrs. Severn, – Poor Dear. I'm so sorry. I hope it will be as short in staying as it seems severe. I'm so sorry.' Kate too had not been well ('so absurdly weak'), and confessed 'it is such hard work, isn't it, talking when you don't feel well.' She went on that her mother was ill, too, so she understood family suffering, and ended in a stumbling, yet affectionate, tone: 'Good-bye. How sweet of you to write to me at all, feeling so ill. I hope you're feeling better this morning. With, Dearest, lots of love, Your affectionate, K.G. I'm *very, very, very sorry*. Poor Dear.'[79] During the visit Joan Severn had stressed a concern over Ruskin's deteriorating condition and her fear that he might lapse into madness at any time; this meant that Kate's visit would be impossible this year – a difficult verdict for Kate to accept.

On Christmas Day Ruskin received Kate's carefully composed Yuletide drawing, which warmed his heart during 'the saddest Christmas morning I ever woke in'. The whole day was spent looking at old things, immersed in depression and regret for his past failures with her. In her letter accompanying the sketch, Kate described her Christmas present from the Crown Princess of Germany, and Ruskin replied in jealousy 'how little there's left to be cared for in me', yet 'I wish I was a Prince and could send you pearls and rubies.' He could only wish her a Happy New Year, but added in apology: 'We must get some Brantwood into it this time.'[80]

Kate's publishers continued to exploit her popularity, and at the end of 1884 several gift books had appeared for the Christmas trade. Evans and Routledge chose a selection of line blocks from previous successes to make the Kate Greenaway *Painting Book*, and printed 40,000 copies; Marcus Ward reissued her early card designs in the *Baby's Birthday Book*. There were also a new Greenaway almanack, *The Language of Flowers*, and, just in time for Christmas, Mavor's *The English Spelling Book*. This was not a popular success, although the *Athenaeum* reviewer claimed it further 'increases our debt to Miss Greenaway', her delicate figures and alphabetic drawings done 'in a manner nearer than usual to that of Stothard'. Their comment suggests how much Kate now owed to Ruskin for urging her to draw more delicately, and to Locker for demonstrating the merits of Stothard's work to her.

The press continued to be generous on the whole, and Kate enjoyed her fame, keeping her favourable reviews all her life. Popularity was important, however much she might dismiss it, if only because she now needed the money it brought in to support her parents and help run their new home. Ruskin was still very much a part of her life and was to remain so. But from this time on his influence on her work was secondary; his demands for perfection and unsaleable nature studies were to be met only after she had fulfilled Evans's more financially rewarding requests.

6 Storm Clouds Over Hampstead 1885–1886

Trim your locks, look carefully,
Fate's hid ends no eye can see:
Joy as winged dreams fly fast,
Why should sadness longer last?
ALMANACK FOR 1887

Kate began 1885 in low spirits, brought on by a spate of criticism from Ruskin which left her unable to work. She fretted over her frustrating work on new books; above all she was anxious to complete *Marigold Garden*, and planned that it should have illustrations inspired by Gainsborough. This annoyed Ruskin, who claimed that Gainsborough was 'inimitable and yet a bad master'; she should 'keep steadily to a deep colour and Carpaccio – with white porcelain and Luca [della Robbia] – you may try a Gainsborough now and then for play,' he advised, writing from Brantwood, where he felt neglected, weak and in poor health: 'I get a little less and less bit better every day.'

Despite his attacks and despondent letters, Kate wanted to know more about the autobiography he had begun. 'I write a little bit every morning and am going to label old things it refers to –,' he explained. 'I'm not going to talk of anybody more disagreeable than myself – so there will be nothing for people to snap and growl at. What shall I say about people who I think liked me? that they were very foolish?'[1] These seemingly idle remarks revealed what Ruskin thought was the cause of their present joint failures: his disastrous past with women, and her present failures with books. He advised: 'we must rest and bewail our fates'; then, she should redo *The Language of Flowers* 'in real colours for me'.[2] Curious about the scope of the autobiography, Kate asked how revealing he planned it to be: would he, for instance, forget about his love for Rose La Touche? He replied:

> No – was I likely to have forgotten? But there will be only a few solemn words about her. I have no right to claim to be loved – No hope or knowledge of the future. The main sense with me now [is] of being so unworthy of her. And the auto[biography] won't be a pretty book at all, but merely an account of the business and general meaning of my life. As I work at it every morning, (about half an hour only) I have very bitter feelings about the waste of years and years in merely looking at things – all I've got to say is – I went there – and saw – that. But did nothing. If only I had gone on drawing plants – or clouds – or –.[3]

It seemed to him quite reasonable that he should urge Kate to redeem her past failures by painting plants and clouds, anything from Nature, to make sure that she would be able to review her career with fewer regrets.

However, Ruskin was so immersed in his autobiography that he ignored four of Kate's letters begging for advice, and only broke his silence to answer the particularly significant question she had posed in her last letter, when she pleaded for his candid appraisal of her role in his life:

> No one sees us as we see ourselves – all that first concerns us must be the care that we do see ourselves as far as possible rightly. In general, young people (and children, like you) know very little of themselves; yet *something* that nobody else can know. *My* knowledge of people is extremely limited, continually mistaken – and what is founded on experience, chiefly of young girls, – and this is nearly useless in your case, for you are mixed child and woman, – and therefore extremely puzzling to me. But I think you may safely conclude that – putting aside the artistic power which is unique in its way, the rest of you will probably be seen more truly by an old man of – 165, which is about my age, than by yourself – at almost any age you ever come to.[4]

Kate persisted in her egotistical entreaties, which by mid-January had become exasperating. 'I'm quite *tired* . . . and I've nothing to say – but that I'm your poor old Dinie – and it's been an awful bore to write down this page before I've fell [*sic*] asleep,' he wrote in an almost illegible hand.[5] In other letters he interrupted the frustrating work on his autobiography to attack her publishers, 'You and your publishers are both and all geese –'; or to send useful books and prints with strict instructions to copy in outline carefully selected pages, noting that 'expressional power depends on the rightness, not the delicacy of their outlines.' He tried to be understanding – 'Tell me what the publishers "propose" now, that I may sympathize in your indignation – and "propose" something different'. But she was not in a position to take his ideas about future books too seriously; she remained tied to Evans and Routledge. Moreover, Ruskin's advice was often flippant and impractical. For example, if she didn't like what Routledge or Evans suggested, she should publish her own books, as he did. 'You could produce one easily with the original outlay of – say at the outsidest, £500, which you would sell 50,000 of at a shilling each in a month.'[6] Most of these suggestions she ignored, and sent instead those delicate, time-consuming drawings of Greenaway girlies that she knew he liked. Ruskin, however, refused to be distracted and continued in his demands for proper figure drawing. He sent a book of Holbein's works to copy, with the remark, 'Half the difficulty or $\frac{3}{4}$ of it to you is that you're always straining after a fancy instead of doing the thing as it is – Never mind its being pretty or ugly, but get as much as you can of the facts in a few minutes, and you will find strength and ease and new right coming all together.'[7] He still believed the finest examples of fancy combined with natural beauty were Francesca Alexander's Italian children, and he sent further examples for close examination. When they arrived, Kate puzzled over Ruskin's rapturous praises but could not accept his opinion or learn from her rival's work. This annoyed Ruskin still further. 'I think the reason Miss A.[lexander] puzzles you is that you never make quite a sincere study, you are always making a pretence of striving for an ideal. I want you to learn perfectly – then Miss A. will not puzzle you – though you will do quite different things.'[8]

It was the rebukes in Ruskin's letters that plunged Kate into deep depression; they made her feel inadequate, unable to please Ruskin or to achieve her own ideals, as she believed she had once done. She was exhausted by trying, and tired of his insisting that she accomplish something she failed to understand. To add to her agitation, work on *Marigold Garden* was not going well. Her early attempts to illustrate this book had been attacked by Ruskin for 'unendurable figures' and the 'mere Greenawayism' (by which he meant unnatural quality) of her yellow skies. After that she had resolved not to ask him for advice. Her studied silence on what he felt would be an important book rekindled Ruskin's anger, and he implored her for news before it was too late. 'Why don't you ever send me any proofs, or ask me what to do – or let me have the least tip of my finger in your book pie?'[9] To appease him as she struggled on, she sent new nature studies in time for his birthday. The diversion proved temporarily effective, and he responded with delight on the day: '. . . you are steadily gaining in all that is best – and indeed will do many things heaven sparing you and keeping your heart in peace –.'[10]

On 15 February the Greenaway family moved to the recently completed house in Hampstead. On that morning Ruskin interrupted his work to wish Kate well in her new home, his letter arriving by the afternoon post. Resigned to the situation at last, after a protracted series of postal objections, he remembered his own experiences in renovating Brantwood:

> I hope you are beginning by this time in the afternoon to be very happy in thinking you're really at home on the Hill, now – and that you will find all the drawers slide nicely, corners fit and firesides cosy, and that the chimnies – draw – as well as you . . . the first thing to be seriously thought of in a new house is chimnies, – one can knock windows out – or partitions down – build out oriels – and throw up turrets – but never make a chimney go that don't [sic] choose.

He concluded that the move was of far greater significance to him than Kate could have imagined. He felt it marked a turning-point in their relationship: from the troubled, one-sided romance to a more sympathetic friendship based upon mutual respect and a resigned attitude towards living apart from one another. 'And let us bid, both, farewell to hollow ways, that lead only to disappointment – and know what we're about – and not think truths teasing, but enjoy each other's sympathy and admiration – and think always – how nice we are!' His letter, a cherished house-warming gift, was signed 'Ever your loving Dinie', with three kisses and the postscript, 'I've written to Joan [Severn] about the visit here.'[11]

The move to Hampstead was a momentous step in Kate's life, for reasons other than Ruskin suggested. The new house was the greatest single expense of her career; she paid £2,000 for the acre of land, £150 to the architect and large, unrecorded sums to her builder long after the house was completed. It was a great drain on her savings and in later, more hard-pressed years, she came to regret her extravangance. Not surprisingly, she handled every detail of the transaction herself, from the appeal against unfair property assessment early in 1884, to her letter assuring Mr Rider, the builder, that she would pay

Pen and ink sketch of Norman Shaw's house for Kate, drawn by T. Raffles Davidson,
March, 1885 and Kate's House at 39 Frognal, Hampstead.

him all the money 'at once'. She chose the well-known architect Richard
Norman Shaw, himself a Hampstead resident, who was largely influential in
transforming the neighbourhood into the fashionable 'Queen Anne' style. Kate
was delighted with Shaw's designs and surprised by his conscientiousness in
completing what was, after all, a minor commission. 'It seems to me you have
done a great deal of work for a very little money – I don't know how I'm ever to
thank you enough!' she wrote to him shortly after the move.[12]

Shaw's designs for the house were plain and simple, in the words of one critic
'not guilty of "fussiness" anywhere'. With its plain, red, tile-hung façade
broken only by windows – banks of tiny panes and a long, wide bay that jutted
out and up to the first floor – it was strikingly devoid of the elaborate ironwork,
terracotta sunflowers and beasts that characterized some of the Shaw-designed
houses nearby. The house was set in an open, flower-filled meadow, with
twenty stately elms to the west and the church spire of St John's to the north. It
was considerably larger than Kate's home in Pemberton Gardens, having three
floors of spacious rooms. On the ground floor, to the left of the front door there
was a long, bow-windowed sitting room overlooking the front garden. To the
right a small, square dining room led into a larger drawing room, with space
enough for Kate's piano; behind were a large kitchen and a scullery. The first
floor, reached by a wide staircase in the centre of the house, contained five
bedrooms and a bathroom. The second floor, 'Kate's domain', could be entered
either by the same stairway or by a separate stair from an entrance on the street
(for Kate's models and visiting friends). Her studio dominated the entire front,
its tall, north-facing window opening onto a small balcony. The studio itself
was vast, over forty feet long, a cavernous space warmed by a large open fire at
one end. There was gas lighting for dark winter days, although Kate rarely

The tearoom off the studio where Kate and Ruskin often met but other friends later came rarely, with bric-a-brac given by Locker.

worked by artificial light. Through a doorway lay her favourite room, the tea room, which overlooked the back garden and received very little daylight. Here every effort had been made to create a very private hideaway. Kate decorated it to her own taste, with some of the popular aesthetic paraphernalia, including blue and white china and De Morgan plates, and the fireplace tiles designed by Shaw – her one great extravagance. Here and there on the walls Japanese fans hung boldly alongside old master prints and drawings given by Locker. Elsewhere the most cherished bits of china or books were given special places on the few pieces of furniture. Two wickerwork chairs, heaped with cushions, were set near the fire, a tea table between them, a reminder that all was ready for the Master, if and when he decided to visit.

For weeks Kate supervised the settling-in process, and the frequent interruptions made any work on her books impossible. She was delighted by the neighbourhood, as she wrote to Norman Shaw shortly after the move: 'I believe you're thinking I'm not finding Hampstead to my mind – but that is very far from the case. If you'd ever lived in Pemberton Gardens – you'd know what a comfort this house must be to me and if you had lived in Holloway you would know – what sort of a paradise Hampstead must seem.'[13] She had clearly succumbed to the rural atmosphere that had earlier inspired her beloved Pre-Raphaelites, and her love of Hampstead and its heath never diminished.

Accompanied by the family retriever, Rover, Kate rediscovered her beloved countryside on daily walks to the Heath. At first she felt guilty at ignoring her neighbours ('I shall be a little black sheep in Hampstead . . . I'm very bad'), but it had been 'the most dreary and depressing winter I ever remember' and she needed solitary diversions. She trudged up the muddy cart track outside her house, through the meadow, past the church and on to Redington Road. Every

121

day, after tea, she set out to record the seasonal cycles in climate and vegetation which were sent to Ruskin or used for the landscape backgrounds that appeared in her illustrations and paintings from this time onwards. The Heath was constantly changing and was an endless source of inspiration. The old haystacks just under a row of oaks and the trees in meadows where tired horses were turned loose after their day's work, made this walk a continual fascination for her.[14] She returned via Whitestone Pond, a wide artificial watering hole for the weary horses trekking up the adjacent steep roads on their way to the Heath. There she paused to watch the large crowds of children, in winter skating on the pond or tobogganing down the nearby slopes; in summer splashing water, sailing boats or throwing sticks for their dogs to retrieve. Here, too Rover furiously waged war on the two swans that lived on the pond.

The Greenaway family, too, were happy with their new surroundings, although their lives continued seemingly unaffected by the village atmosphere. Johnnie at this time was sub-editor of the *Journal of the Chemistry Society* and frequently away on business or at his club. John Greenaway struggled on with his engraving work, although his income had dropped rapidly over the past few years, while his wife managed the domestic duties in between frequent illnesses that inevitably spread to the entire household. The family as a whole honoured Kate's strict rules for privacy and quiet, as her brother recalled:

> Of my sister at work, we saw very little. She very wisely made it a fixed rule that, during working hours, no one should come into the studio save on matters of urgency. Her great working time was the morning, so she was always an early riser and finished breakfast by eight o'clock. Her most important work was done between then and luncheon time (1 o'clock). Practically she never went out in the morning. After luncheon she usually worked for an hour or two, unless she was going out anywhere for the afternoon, and then went for a walk on the Heath, and came back for tea. The evenings up to eight o'clock, when we had a meal that was a sort of compromise between dinner and supper, were spent in letter-writing, making dresses for models, occasionally working out schemes and rough sketches for projected books and such-like things; but all finished work was done in the morning or afternoon. After supper she generally lay on a sofa and read until she went to bed at about 10 o'clock. She could not stand late hours and seldom went out in the evening. For the same reason she seldom dined out. Tea-time was always her time for going to see friends, or for them to see her.[15]

This uneventful, at times boring, routine would only be disturbed by a friend paying a call or a long-awaited letter from Ruskin. This goes some way towards explaining why, from the move onwards, Kate renewed her assault on Ruskin's time and attention: quite apart from her romantic aspirations, he represented a necessary break in the monotony of her working life. She used him as a sounding-board when, in March, she was troubled by domestic upsets. He, on the other hand, was dogged by continued poor health and refused to write meaningless, comforting daily letters. 'Darling Katie, . . . did I ever write more letters than I do now? I certainly never in all my life thought of writing daily except to Joan – and she thinks it wonderful I do to her.'[16] Moreover he was too busy to write frivolous notes while he was preparing another series of Oxford lectures, the sombre qualities of which were influenced by the recently completed melancholy sections of his autobiography. A moroseness now darkened his letters to Kate as well. He began her birthday greeting in mid-March, 'I was very very sad, last night – because I felt as if it [his life] had been all in vain.' He felt his sixty-six years and was defeated by his hold over her:

> I don't know how to give you any wish you would care to come true – but I will wish you – every birthday – some new love of – lovely things – and some new forgetfulness of the teasing things and some higher pride in the praising things, and some sweeter place from the worrying things – And longer stay of time – when you are happy – and lighter-flight of days that are unkind. And that your poor Dinie may be able to please you – better next year than this. Ever believe him, your grateful xx changeless – Friend.'[17]

Five days later he resigned his professorship (over the vivisection question) and left Oxford, never to return. His spirits soared as he sought the comfort of Brantwood, to mull over plans for new books, with more time to write his autobiography and to direct Kate's career.

The news of his resignation came as a shock to Kate, who was sure it meant he would remain permanently based at Brantwood, far from London. She thought this was totally unfair and wrote to say so, stressing in her letter the importance of London, 'the centre of all things'. Ruskin's reply was firm: 'As for Oxford being a loss to you – certainly I shall be twice as much in London when I haven't to go *there*. But oh my Katie, how *very* wrong you are in thinking London the centre of things. It is only so as a volcano is the fountain of a fire and earthquake.'[18] He was horrified that she had lost her rural instincts and two days later he wrote: 'Of course you were not wrong in any error of reasoning or fault of feeling – merely living in London you get accustomed to its ugliness and resigned to its misery. To see it with clear eyes out of the sky would be to you exactly like looking into a churchyard field.'[19]

Kate's long-postponed visit to Brantwood had finally been arranged for mid-April, and by the beginning of the month her excitement made it difficult for her to concentrate on her work. 'It's nice you're being so happy about coming,' wrote Ruskin in the first of several encouraging letters. 'What I should have thought – three years ago – if anybody had told me Kate Greenaway would be so wild about coming to Brantwood. I'm not going to be tyrannical a bit but to let you enjoy yourself all you can – only giving you wise advice to lay up for future use!' He was still concerned about *Marigold Garden*, which he believed doomed because he had not seen it. 'Do leave off putting work into that book! The more you put, the worse it'll be.'[20]

There was good reason for the silence surrounding *Marigold Garden*. It was completed when Kate was becoming more and more deeply distressed by the phenomenal number of Greenaway imitations which threatened her livelihood and made her consider giving up book illustration altogether. At the moment this remained only a possibility, for she needed the money books such as

Marigold Garden might earn. This depressing dilemma embittered her, and in a letter forwarding one of the many requests for permission to reproduce her drawings, she described her feelings to Edmund Evans: 'I send you this letter but of course you will say *no*, I never will consent [a] gain – . . . I've seen some of the most shamefully adapted and altered things of mine lately'; and with Ruskin's criticisms of her most recent book failures clearly in mind, she explained, 'I suppose you will do that *one* more book [*Marigold Garden*] if you do no more – I must keep with illustrations for this year anyhow – and I don't want to do any books for other people – I'd rather do other things – still – I must keep on a little longer – things may improve. I have some of the sketches done for Marigold Garden – it has as much chance as any I should think.'[21] Obviously, Kate now looked upon *Marigold Garden*, and indeed all future books, as money-making hackwork, and little else. Those drawings already completed lacked sufficient naturalism to please Ruskin and in places they were quite poor. And so she refused to describe them to the Master, keeping the contents of *Marigold Garden* a secret until publication.

Meanwhile Ruskin grew impatient waiting for her arrival. He planned ideas for new books, in particular a joint botanical volume to make up for the failures he found in her *Language of Flowers*. But at the last moment he discovered that his plan had been anticipated by 'a perfect primrose of a clergyman' whose book 'beat us all to sticks – buds – and roots'. He ordered twelve copies, and vainly tried to initiate a correspondence with its illustrator (who, he hoped, was a young woman). He decided that the time had come to direct Kate towards studio watercolours – paintings of rocks and flowers which would be put on exhibition and restore his faith in London galleries. He felt that true beauty was

John Ruskin in 1882.

being ignored there: at the Royal Academy Burne-Jones was showing what Ruskin called 'a nasty picture of a mermaid clawing somebody'. He ended one of his letters to Kate, 'I am sick of such nonsense. I look to you now only for any comfort in English art . . .'[22] It was a well-timed remark, now that Kate was thinking of doing something other than illustrations. His plans also made her more impatient to be at Brantwood, which Ruskin sensed: 'It is nice to be able to give you such pleasure, for both of us, for indeed I am happy when you do pretty things and I do trust you will see your way this time to never doing such hard work any more.'[23]

Kate travelled with Joan Severn on 17 April and arrived at Brantwood in high spirits. She made her way along the daffodil-lined lakeside and into Ruskin's study. For more than a week she tried valiantly to please him, working harder than he had ever seen before. She did studies of stones and flowers he had brought in from the garden and on inclement days sketched a Luca della Robbia madonna hanging over the fireplace in his study. She was, however, very easily upset and recalled: 'You gave me . . . a beautiful red rose – while the sun was setting behind the mountains and shining across the lake – and, and – when I said I like red roses best – *you said you like pink* ones.' According to Ruskin's diary, Kate collapsed before his 'altar of despair', after failing to master the madonna drawing. She had little to show for her efforts but misery. Three days of pouring rain and strained silences followed, which left him 'wooden and unenjoying . . . full of fault and discomfort', and drove Kate back to London, her expectations shattered. This was not altogether her fault: Ruskin's diary entry for 27 April shows that during her visit he had been in no mood to consider book collaborations or her career, but rather had felt confused and

The Study at Brantwood, showing the Luca della Robbia and cherished bookcases where Ruskin kept Kate's books.

filled with inexplicable guilt. 'I [am] very well – yet not content as I should be, and ashamed of myself for not making the most of this quiet time and restored strength.'[24]

On her return to Hampstead Kate wrote to thank Ruskin for the visit. It was a polite, reserved letter, which increased his sense of guilt. He replied apologetically, three days later: 'Darling Katie, How nice it was though so pitiful, that you saw all those lovely amethysts and opals [his mineral collection] – though only in leaving them. They were all meant, of course, to ask you to come back, and say they were very sorry to have been three days sulking. I'm so glad to hear of the good day's work being done too.'[25] Despite the spring flowers and unusually sunny days, he became impatient and longed to escape from Brantwood. He planned to return to London, where he promised to visit Kate's new house. 'Everybody says *here* I've no business to go at all – and indeed I think it is a shame. Such lovely days,' he wrote to her. It was news that Kate had longed to hear, and she designed an elaborate May Day processional with its twelve Greenaway girlies specially painted to appeal to him. His reaction was as expected: 'You must paint this [one girl in the drawing] some day – in Mays to come, when you're doing all sorts of lovely things at Brantwood.' Four days later he sent a telegram to announce his London plans: 'We will go to see pictures first on Monday and then tea at Hampstead.'[26]

Kate felt slighted by this plan, for surely he could spare more time to visit Frognal and help her with her work. She tried to persuade him into a longer visit and the day before their meeting he replied from Herne Hill, 'What a horrid, sulky, crumpy old Katie it's getting to be! It would serve it quite right if it was a fog and thunderstorm all day long tomorrow – and people couldn't come anywhere at all!'[27] In spite of the mocking tone of this angry reply, he did not change his plans to meet her at the gallery and to accompany her to Hampstead for tea. In his letter of the following day, he was more concerned with her persistent requests for attention than with the suitability of her new house which he had just seen. 'Sweetest Katie, I'm so glad you thought me a little nice – and enjoyed yourself a little –' he wrote after the visit, 'but one's so ashamed of being so much cared about! though it's nice, too – and I am thankful to have the power of encouraging and – partly – even inspiring you – for you certainly do your most beautiful work for me.'[28]

Her constant pleading forced Ruskin to agree, albeit reluctantly, to a second meeting, which he scheduled for Whit Monday. However, on that day a new and severe bout of depression forced him to cancel his visit. Knowing that Kate would be heartbroken, he sent her two long, surprisingly frank letters. In the first he confessed: 'I'm not ill, but in a down heartedness and tiredness which makes it simply dangerous for me to come out.' He could not control his health and this was frightening, '. . . if I caught cold – and went – a little crazy again – think how sorry you'd be.'

His second letter, written later that day and dated 'Whit-Black-Monday', was a further attempt to describe his confusion: '. . . down to very low tide today, and am still, but partly rested, still my head not serving me, – the driving about town continually tires me fearfully, – then I get vexed – then I can't sleep and so it goes on.' He also seemed disturbed by the few *Marigold Garden* illustrations she had shown him in her studio. Their glaring errors and false naturalism represented further evidence of her silent rebellion and clearly indicated that he had lost yet another disciple. *Marigold Garden* was 'no garden, but a mystification . . . And I mourn over your not showing things till it's too late to do anything less or more.' His despondency increased as he referred to what he termed 'the saddest part' of his autobiography, which he was just beginning. This was the part that dealt with his relationships with women. It was a time when he thought 'extremely little of myself – then and now – I was sulky and quarrelled with all life – just because I couldn't get the one thing I chose to fancy. – *Now* – I can get nothing I fancy – all the world ebbing away, and the only question for me now – What next?'[29]

His fears died away and the following day he confessed that his letters had been written in 'a fit of thinking I was going to die', and were not to be taken too seriously. He telegrammed her two days later, 'I want so much to talk it over. Can you be at Academy at two tomorrow?' They met and walked through the gallery, then went on to Hampstead for tea. All the while Ruskin stressed that she was not to worry, and when he left Frognal he had her promise that she would try to understand. But he still felt unsure of his state of mind on this, his 'day of anger', (as he described it in his diary), that ended in a bad nightmare, 'of running frantically round a dark underground cellar. Q. – How much could be hardboiled eggs at K's after fasting and being in puzzle and passion all the way home?'[30]

'Susan Blue', the first page from *Marigold Garden*, 1885, in homage to Gainsborough.

SUSAN BLUE.

OH, Susan Blue,
How do you do?
Please may I go for a walk with you?
Where shall we go?
Oh, I know—
Down in the meadow where the cowslips grow!

Ruskin remained in London until mid-June. By then the first instalment of his autobiography had appeared and he began work on the second of an eventual twenty-eight parts, each published separately. Shortly after publication Kate received the first number, which she eagerly read and praised for the clarity of his descriptions of childhood. She asked about its name, *Praeterita*, which he explained meant 'merely Past Things'; and, despite his avoiding the subject of another visit, she begged him to return to her studio. After some days had passed, he agreed, and, on 11 June, sandwiched her between a poetry reading at two and an Arundel Society meeting at four. With less than two hours to enjoy, Kate resisted the urge to ask him to prolong his visit, served him tea and avoided any subject that might anger or upset him. Ruskin appreciated her concern, and he wrote the following day, 'You were ever so good . . . Really *quite* good, and I liked being there very much and I think tea *did* do me good.'[31]

When Ruskin returned to Brantwood, Kate left for Witley, to discuss future work with Evans. To him she expressed her grave doubts about *Marigold Garden*, no doubt echoing Ruskin's opinion. She also talked about new almanack designs (the annual almanack was by now an unquestioned tradition), and grudgingly considered Evans's plans for new books, refusing a tempting offer from another publisher. Knowing Ruskin would be interested, she kept him informed of these negotiations and her comings and goings. He was angry when he learned how she had made a series of Sunday visits to old friends in the Witley area. 'And what in the name of all that's naughty – do *you* go making "calls" for. I never did hear of anything so absurd – you oughtn't to go to Witley at all.' If Ruskin had his way she would follow his example and become a country recluse with 'a little cottage all to yourself and garden a good deal and have the school children in to tea and draw all the wild flowers growing'.[32]

At the end of June Kate received letters from Brantwood revealing Ruskin's growing euphoria, which, to those who knew the signs, were warning signals. She learned about the surprising light-headedness, the periods of ecstatic delight and optimism, 'at what I can have been and gone and done. I feel so good!'[33] Ruskin's mood revived the idea of their collaboration on a book, and also accounts for the embarrassing praises he lavished on Kate's feeble drawings for it. *Dame Wiggins of Lee and her Seven Wonderful Cats* was an early-nineteenth-century children's story which Ruskin believed had the right mixture of lightness and reassuring elements to merit reprinting. He had the woodcut illustrations of the 1823 edition republished, in line only, so that his readers could colour them, and added four original verses to explain how the cats were educated. Kate provided four crude pencil sketches for the new verses. Her work was slight, and certainly out of keeping with the original heavy-lined woodcuts; nevertheless, Ruskin, in his euphoric mood, decided that the drawings were 'exactly right, and don't want a touch more'. He refused to alter or sharpen her lines, and, moreover, declared that if she could draw cats like these, she could forget his previous attacks on her rat-like dogs and cats, and they would do a second book together, a story about perpetual spring, with his text and Greenaway lamb illustrations. Needless to say, this project never materialized.

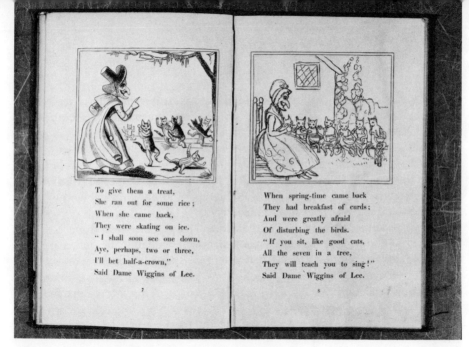

To give them a treat,
She ran out for some rice;
When she came back,
They were skating on ice.
" I shall soon see one down,
Aye, perhaps, two or three,
I'll bet half-a-crown,"
Said Dame Wiggins of Lee.

7

When spring-time came back
They had breakfast of curds;
And were greatly afraid
Of disturbing the birds.
" If you sit, like good cats,
All the seven in a tree,
They will teach you to sing!"
Said Dame Wiggins of Lee.

8

Two pages from *Dame Wiggins of Lee*, 1885. On the right, Kate's design to Ruskin's new verse addition.

By mid-July all seemed well enough for Kate to return to Brantwood. Ruskin's letters urged her to make preparations as quickly as possible: 'the roses are coming out at a great rate, and I mustn't have you miss the main wreaths of them'; if she agreed he promised a happy reunion when 'you'll be in the very gush of the heather and roses.' By then he described himself as 'so dreadfully lazy that I feel as if I should never have the face to set you to do anything'. He explained that Joan Severn had given her blessing to the invitation, and he begged Kate to accept at once, promising that 'you'll be happier than you were last time.'[34] When Kate's letter of acceptance arrived, his response was characteristic: 'You shall do just what you like this time – but your rock is waiting for you – not a bit brambled over. And the wild roses!!! but *they're* too tormenting open and full as you look.'[35]

Kate was too eager to return to Brantwood to worry about the excited tone of his letters or the illegibility of his writing; besides, their whole theme was his urgent need to see *her*. Kate expected to find Brantwood immersed in familiar silence, which she longed again to share with Ruskin alone. Instead, and to her horror, the house was filled with chattering visitors, anxious female admirers like Mrs La Touche and her grand-daughter, Rose's niece (also named Rose). The lakeside echoed with laughter, the house brimming with the anticipation of nervous guests, each hoping to gain a brief moment of Ruskin's time. Ruskin was cordial to his visitors and one day took Kate to a favourite waterfall, made inaccessible by 'two awful tourists'; but whenever possible he slipped into his ground-floor study to add a few more sentences to his autobiography. He refused to neglect this important work, which he believed would alone redeem him from his past. Gradually, however, he became tormented by an increased inability to decide what to put in or leave out. Moreover, his remarks inferred a dangerous irritability, an impatience with himself and those around him, which Joan Severn knew to be sinister. He needed quiet and solitude, and she urged

Mrs La Touche to leave, which she did, although quite unaware of the reason. Joan next asked Kate to follow suit, but Ruskin overheard the request and insisted she must remain. Torn between Joan's anxious pleading and Ruskin's command, Kate chose the latter, thinking she could help lift him out of his gloom. She spent several more days trying to keep out of the way but close enough to give help if it was needed. But there was little response from Ruskin, and towards the end of July his silences and erratic behaviour and her neglected obligations forced her back to London.

At home Kate received frequent letters from Joan describing Ruskin's progress, and dutifully recorded each promising change in her diary. His condition deteriorated into a fourth attack of madness, by far the worst to date: on 31 July Kate recorded, 'He is much worse today'; on 11 August, almost two weeks later, when he was 'still as ill', she sent a copy of her latest almanack, and inserted in it a painting of a little Greenaway girlie in a white dress, with white roses in her hand. On the first page of the almanack, printed opposite a single rose, Ruskin found her reassurance:

> Be you Foe or be you Friend,
> I once more on you attend.

He was still too ill to respond. On 13 August there was 'no change, still so quiet'; but the following day his condition improved slightly. Fourteen days later Kate jubilantly recorded that he was strong enough to go out in the garden alone – the end to three weeks of worry. Despite that time Ruskin had remained oblivious to his condition and to the enormous amount of public attention it had caused. Joan Severn kept him isolated, protected from all disturbances, such as the daily presence of newspaper reporters who besieged the house, and the many telegrams and letters that came from anxious admirers. She kept Kate informed of any changes in Ruskin's condition, and after one encouraging

Untitled watercolour done after Kate's return from Brantwood, using the local hills and Ruskin's moorland garden setting.

report, Kate replied: 'It is consoling in a way but I do miss him so – I've no doubt he does feel in ways we can't imagine – such [a] strange illness may well have strange after effects . . . . I wish I could be content – but I do miss him all ways and every way so that nothing else seems of any use – or worth caring about – I go out to see people thinking it will be better – and – I come home almost disliking them – I am happiest at home quite quiet – I never knew or thought – how very much difference it would make –'[36]

By September, when Ruskin was well enough to consider work (although Joan Severn prohibited it), he managed a few letters to close friends, but none to Kate for many months. During that time *Dame Wiggins* appeared, published in October, with Ruskin's apologetic introduction: 'My rhymes do not ring like the real ones; and I would not allow Miss Greenaway to subdue the grace of her first sketches to the formality of the earlier work.' Still, he was pleased with this slim volume. He recommended it to children and adults, 'because it relates nothing that is sad, and portrays nothing that is ugly'. Later he called it his 'calf-milk of books on the lighter side' and distributed copies to his dearest female pets; others were sold through his new publisher, George Allen.

Marigold Garden appeared in November, the end of Kate's two-year struggle. A surviving notebook, filled with pencil sketches, brief themes and possible ideas for pages, suggests that it was an especially difficult work to complete. The published book was a jumble of inconsistent styles, page designs and confused verses. Her figures are either set in fully developed gardens or left adrift in space, balanced only by the odd flower border. Even more curious was the introductory page, implying the social awareness Kate most certainly learned from Ruskin's *Fors*, feebly expressed by two Greenaway children, a tiny girl in a white gown bearing a bouquet of lilies, symbolic of wealth; opposite, a poverty-stricken boy in rags, straddling a stream. Below the girl appeared the dedication:

> YOU *little girl,*
> You *little boy,*
> What *wondering eyes, that kindly look*
> In *honour of two noble names*
> I *send the offering of this book.*

The lively verses and escapist pictures, 'beautiful in colour, fresh and naïve in design', were praised by the *Athenaeum* critic. He finished by stating that Kate had not lost her ability to charm and transport her readers into a more carefree world. Sales, however, were another matter. *Marigold Garden* was Kate's most expensive book to date and had to compete with Caldecott's latest publications, *The Panjandrum Picture Book* (a reissue of his four popular picture books done for Evans and Routledge) and his illustrated edition of Mrs Ewing's last story, *Lob Lie-by-the-Fire*, as well as with a startling number of new Greenaway imitation titles. Only 6,500 copies of *Marigold Garden* were sold in England, 7,500 in America and 3,500 in France. It seemed that Kate's original reservations, the resigned attitude she took in completing the book – not to mention Ruskin's fears – had proved well founded; the poor reception of *Marigold Garden* was a depressing omen.

'Ring-a-ring'. Detail of final page to *Marigold Garden* 1885, adapted from an eighteenth century arcadian theme.

The new almanack was equally disappointing. Kate's year-long struggles to complete *Marigold Garden* and *Dame Wiggins*, as well as her worry over Ruskin's health, had seriously hampered her work on new illustrations. No doubt recognizing the almanack for what it was – a purely commercial venture – she chose to use drawings previously printed in *Under the Window* and *A Day in a Child's Life*. This attitude further influenced two Greenaway titles produced this year: *Kate Greenaway's Alphabet*, a tiny gift book composed of reissued alphabet letters from the poor-selling *English Spelling Book*; and *Kate Greenaway's Album*, compiled from the tiniest of her used and unused drawings in a small format, which Evans bound in leather and gilt. He printed eight copies, but Kate was upset by the slight, often faintly printed drawings. She still strove for quality, and she urged him to abandon the project; the book was never published.

After a very disappointing year, some consolation came when Ruskin renewed his correspondence with Kate. Despondent and lonely, she had written to Joan Severn in early December: '. . . if only only only – he didn't think I was a little stone instead of a human live thing.' His letters, filled with perfunctory good wishes and a false optimism, were of momentary comfort, but little practical use. Ruskin had again changed; his weak health left him resigned. 'I am contented – henceforth to live – if I may – as the old trees do, content with the sunshine and the rain so that I may be no more cut down to the roots for pride,' he wrote to one woman friend.[37] Similarly, on New Year's Day, he broke his six-month silence to wish Kate well. 'I wish you a busy and prosperous New Year – and as much happiness as heaven pleases – but I shan't be happy about you till you draw properly and colour deeply and richly.' It was the familiar voice of the Master who, despite his illness, longed to continue to dominate Kate's work. 'And you may write now and tell me when you have plans in hand, for book or picture – if you'd like to.' Again, he wanted attention, but on his own terms; while he urged her to write often, he stressed the importance of his own silence: 'I have entirely forbidden all useless talk by letter or lip to all my feminine friends – hereafter – but I like to hear how they are working.' Such one-sidedness infuriated Kate, and after receiving this letter

132

she wrote to Joan Severn that she 'could not and would not answer it, but then I had better thoughts come – for indeed of what value is affection – unless – it is to put away care for yourself.' Finally she sent 'a plain, matter of fact answer.'[38]

Then began her repeated pleas for guidance in a further effort to find a new direction for her career. She was modelling Greenaway figures in bas-relief, using his favourite Luca della Robbia for inspiration; one of his January letters contained the cryptic comment, 'I believe that it is the right way out of it and into it – for you and that we shall have the loveliest Catherine della Robbias.' But on the whole Ruskin's coolness continued to distress Kate. 'I only wish it did make me happier,' she confessed to Joan Severn, 'but it is deeply painful to me – it isn't the friend I used to know – it is some other quite – oh quite.'[39] She also received and commented at length upon the latest – the eighth – instalment of his autobiography. Her enthusiasm pleased Ruskin, especially her interest in accounts of his past loves, 'for I was afraid it would begin to shock people,' he explained. She eagerly awaited the ninth instalment, which he promised 'without the naughty things in it', and reread the earlier passages that she found so natural. Pleased with this response, he replied, it was 'the "natural" me – only of course peeled carefully – It is different from what else I write because – you – know – I seldom have had to describe any but heroic – or evil – characters –.'[40]

'The Four Princesses', a plate from *Marigold Garden* with four 'Rosies' to tantalize Ruskin.

THE FOUR PRINCESSES.

FOUR Princesses lived in a Green Tower—
A Bright Green Tower in the middle of the sea;
And no one could think—oh, no one could think—
Who the Four Princesses could be.

One looked to the North, and one to the South,
And one to the East, and one to the West;
They were all so pretty, so very pretty,
You could not tell which was the prettiest.

'The Ungrateful Lamb'. Dog-like lamb drawn for *Marigold Garden*, 1885.

Removed from Ruskin's complete attention, Kate was irritable and frustrated. She longed to occupy more of his thoughts, but when a long-awaited letter arrived from Brantwood it either proved disappointingly vague, or lacked the depth she felt she deserved. On the other hand, Ruskin continued his campaign for clearer, truer colour and greater naturalism; this, to her horror, he concluded could best be achieved apart from his erratic influence. After a two-week silence, he wrote to Kate: 'I am finally convinced that you must go your own way and not care what either I or anybody else thinks – but tell me always what you are about.'[41] He made it clear that he wanted her to relinquish all attachment to him, for her good and his own; he believed his weak health and uncertain future could not stand up to her repeated demands. Kate's frantic reply begged him not to abandon her, and had its desired effect; after two days Ruskin replied, first blaming her failure as a naturalist for his decision: 'I tell you I like purple and blue-greens, and you send me yellow and sap-greens – What can you expect?' However, her pleading letter had made him reconsider: 'Do you really still keep missing me like that? I'm always here myself just the same, and as ready as ever to give you sympathy in everything you are doing.' Above all, she must remember that independence was essential. She must work hard, 'set the heart free again'; only then would 'your great genius . . . have joy in its own power'.[42]

Dazed by his threats and the fear of his abandonment, Kate sensed her world gradually slipping beyond her reach. The news of the sudden death of her old friend Randolph Caldecott was an additional blow, which Kate took as yet another augury of the demise of her profession. After a brief excursion into London in mid-February, she explained her reactions to Joan Severn. 'It looks quite horrid to see the black-bordered card with his books in the shop windows

– it feels horrid to want to sell his books somehow, just yet. I'm very sorry.'[43] By then her spirits had reached a dangerous low, and this left her easy prey to winter colds, sore throats and influenza, which forced her to bed. Where, unable to work, she wondered about Ruskin, and reread passages from *Praeterita*. She was especially taken by his account of an early love, Adèle Domecq, a young French beauty who kept Ruskin dangling, hopelessly in love for four years, before she thwarted his passionate advances and ungentlemanly attempts to write her verses, and married a baron. Then followed the tragic story of Miss Wardell, who died following Ruskin's selfish rejection of her love. Ruskin concluded in *Praeterita* that he had acted selflessly in this disastrous affair, 'literally to *please* her, for that is, indeed, my hope with all girls, in spite of what I have above related of my mistaken ways of recommending myself.'[44] His clear descriptions of two important young women in his life – two beautiful Greenaway maidens – gave Kate the idea that she might try to illustrate a future edition of *Praeterita*; her idea was no doubt encouraged when Ruskin remarked that Adèle Domecq and her sisters 'were exactly like one of your own groups'. Ruskin greeted her proposal with severe reservations and urged her to wait for future instalments. 'I fear it will not be cheerful enough. I'll try and keep it as Katish as – the *very* truth can be,' he promised her.[45] The collaboration was soon forgotten and, despite Kate's efforts, she had nothing more to do with *Praeterita*, despite Ruskin's unfulfilled promise to include her in the closing chapters.

March brought an easing of tempers. Kate's spirits always soared with the coming of spring and she now prepared preliminary drawings for *A Apple Pie*. Ruskin found time to send frequent, light-hearted letters in reply to those he enjoyed from her. He urged her to send 'crumbs of the merest notion – Literally I mean the room sweeping' with each of her replies. After puzzling over what he might want with scraps pulled from her waste basket she carefully wrapped the bits of paper, unfinished sketches and scraps of verse and posted them to Brantwood. Her regular packets proved a new delight for what they might contain – the unexpected line or well drawn arm to prove that she could succeed on her own. Furthermore, they provided relief for Ruskin as he worked on painful new passages of *Praeterita*. A passage from the end of the section on his struggles to understand love, gives an indication of his attitude both towards Kate and towards his past: '. . . having never at any time been in the slightest degree blinded by love, as I perceive other men are, out of my critic nature. And day followed day, and month on month, of complex absurdity, pain, error, wasted affection and rewardless semi-virtue, which I am content to sweep out of the way of what better things I can recollect at this time, into the smallest possible size of dust heap, and wish the Dustman Oblivion good clearance to them.'[46] By mid-March Ruskin found that he was relying heavily upon Kate's bundles, her remnants from a different, less tragic dust heap. They provided an excuse to write misleadingly affectionate replies: 'Your letters are ever so nice and good just now – I wonder how long this good fit will last! The little white scraps are precious.'[47]

At the end of the month, Kate returned to Witley and devoted much of her visit to the nature studies that Ruskin now hoped would become more important than illustration; and she sent him the recent studies of Witley flowers for his approval. Unfortunately, he rarely even acknowledged these, since her letters were among the twenty he confessed receiving each day, of which he found time to reply to only twelve. Her detailed letters, filled with lengthy leading questions, were for the most part ignored, although he revelled in the attention. 'I'm printing a circular however to say I won't write any more letters – Would you like to see one?' he teased.[48] This was Ruskin in a playful, spring mood; but by early April it had dramatically changed to one of gloom. He spent long, sleepless nights mulling over his past and tortured days writing about it in *Praeterita*. When Kate sent a new batch of nature studies – of his favourite violets – he dismissed her gift as callous. 'My good depends simply on my not tiring myself. We both of us can please ourselves in our own way. I know how to please *you* also – in *your* way, but you are too apt to think that my old age can be revived with violets.'[49] Kate continued to stress her need to see him. She desperately beseeched him to come to her in Hampstead where she was lonely, had a sore throat, and could not work. It was this letter that proved the last straw, turning Ruskin's mildly caustic letters into bitter attacks on her selfishness. He felt victimized, his work threatened by her needs and senseless demands. 'Do you think when I have to bury my dead of the last forty years of Wildness – that I am inclined for streets of London?' he began, in an unusually long reply; then continued, 'My dear Kate, there is not the remotest chance or possibility of you or anybody else in London seeing me this year and if you begin snewsing [*sic*] and probing again – I close correspondence on the instant. – I don't want to see anybody and I won't be bothered. I am grimly busy – angry – and entirely resolved to say no word but what I please to the outside world. You ought to have known my *heart* world is dead – long ago.' He was also angry at the news that she planned to adapt her processionals into card designs for publication as *Queen Victoria's Jubilee Garland*. The book, he believed, would 'disgrace yourself, and me – and the cause of goodness and beauty'.[50] Nevertheless, Kate completed her designs and the book appeared in time for the celebrations the following year.

It took three days for Ruskin's anger to cool enough for him to write an apology. 'I'm rather relieved that you haven't been throwing yourself into Hampstead ponds, or the like – for really that Thursday flash was a bad double one. I'm in a horrid electric state just now – a mere brass knob that if people put their knuckles too near – they get a start.' All he could do was ask for sympathetic understanding. 'But I'm ever your loving Dinie for all that – and think a little how nasty it has been for *me*, all my life to have Turner – Millais – Rossetti – [Holman] Hunt – [Burne] Jones – and Kate Greenaway, never one of them doing a single thing I say they should!'[51]

This letter put Kate in a difficult position: she yearned to please Ruskin and was willing to sacrifice valuable working time to do so; yet she needed the money only illustrations would provide, even though her interest in such work was gone. When she tried to explain her dilemma to Ruskin, he replied with surprising candour, 'I knew the cause of your having to work so hard, – don't think I forgot it for a moment – but that is no reason for your wasting time drawing feasts of pretty girls to please me, who are of no use to publish –.'[52]

136

Kate's confusion made her weak and eventually ill. Bedridden and in need of encouragement, on Good Friday she wrote to suggest an idea for collaboration with Ruskin. To her astonishment, he willingly agreed. 'It is lovely your thinking of doing books with me. There is nothing you could do, I believe more happily or useful than illustrating children's books of my choice.' As always, such a collaboration had to be on his terms; his decision was made to relieve her immediate fears rather than from any faith in such future books. He selected *Beauty and the Beast* as her first project, and regarded himself as the Beast; she was the Beauty who refused to abandon him.

This plan seemed to be the answer to Kate's immediate problems. She could complete a book which, with Ruskin's sanction, was sure to sell and might please him as well. She abandoned all other work to make her preliminary watercolour sketches for *Beauty*, based upon Ruskin's instructions to concentrate 'at any moment of the courtship you liked'. Their business relationship was unlike any Kate had previously experienced and it seemed, at least to her, a welcome game, with Ruskin her publisher and she his employee. 'Only you're not to tease and say you don't like me to be only your publisher – because that's the way it's to be, and there an end,' he warned her, half in earnest, half in playfulness.[53] But, as so often in the past, the book proved a false hope, a futile promise of something that could never be. *Beauty and the Beast* never progressed beyond Kate's watercolour drawings of Beauty rushing about Kate's Hampstead garden.

Kate's garden, now a year old, had become an essential retreat for her. There she posed and painted models, grew flowers for backgrounds, and completed nature studies for Ruskin. A keen gardener, she once described her garden plans to an equally keen Ruskin and he replied, 'I will wait at the garden gate – *any* time!' Flowers were especially important to Kate: 'It is curious, but certain flowers are to me almost like books I like that every now and then I feel I must read over again. . . . I must possess some – to look at for a day or two – it's the feeling of seeing someone you care for again.' Her garden was a very private world, surrounded by a high brick wall and entered along a footpath at the right side of the house, between a hawthorn and a flowering almond tree. Five or six steps up from the entrance stretched a broad green lawn, which was, according to one enthusiastic visitor, 'the very place in which you would expect to see dainty maidens tripping merrily about, or picking up the apples from beneath the standards, which stood here and there on the grass, a joy of blossom in spring and of ruddy colour later on'. A second path, along either side of the creeper-lined brick walls, led to a raised flower garden, its borders edged in box, the beds filled with childhood favourites: nasturtiums, love-in-a-mist, hollyhocks, poppies, stocks, irises, the tall madonna lilies loved by the aesthetes, and a pink mound of carnations often covered in a cloud of yellow butterflies. The plants were allowed to grow in wild profusion, without pruning or trimming, to give her garden a carefree, haphazard look, rather like the cottage gardens Kate had loved since her childhood. Despite the horrified looks of those visitors who favoured more formal gardens, Kate refused to conform: hers was to be a natural setting. 'A nice idea! my cherished garden made the exact replica of every one in Frognal,' she exclaimed to a friend.

'Nothing should induce me to consent to such desecration.' Even when matters appeared to grow out of control – 'we have larger and more varied weeds in our garden than you have in yours – in fact our garden has forgotten that it is a garden and is trying to be a field again' – she refused to have it cut down by an over-zealous gardener.[54] Instead, when plants became too tangled and the lawn too insect-ridden, she adopted natural means of dealing with the problem. To control the insects, for example, she and Eddie Dadd made visits to the Hampstead ponds with a wicker basket, to collect frogs and toads which they placed among the plants at Frognal. The idea seemed to work, and it amused Ruskin, who gleefully wrote, 'I expect Frognal will have more frogs for tea. I'm sure that you'd find even the tadpoles cheerful,' suggesting that frog collecting was a way of keeping her mind off him and her loneliness.[55]

The garden in May proved an ideal retreat, where Kate, seated under her blossoming apple tree, mulled over her future, wrote letters to Ruskin, and pondered his new series of puzzling requests. 'I wonder if you could put in writing about any particular face – what it is that makes it pretty?' he asked.[56] She tried to comply, but her work on a commissioned book left little time for theoretical discussions. The book was, to some extent, a surprising one, for it demanded of her what she had vowed never to do again. *The Queen of the Pirate Isle* was not her story, but the work of the American expatriate writer, Bret Harte, suggested by a new publisher, Chatto and Windus. This was the first time Kate had strayed from Evans and Routledge; she did so reluctantly and, one must assume, only out of financial need. Evans remained a lifelong friend and he had managed to instil in Kate, as well as his other illustrators, a staunch loyalty, despite the fact that he often exploited them.

Kate found the story a difficult one to illustrate. It required a considerable amount of research, being set in a decidedly unfamiliar California gold-mining area, with an Oriental character (the only Greenaway Oriental ever drawn), and gold miners she eventually depicted as innocent adolescents 'aged' with rather feeble chin whiskers. She did not meet the story's author until 1894, so she turned for advice to Ruskin, who offered little comfort, other than the fact that he liked the book's title. Work progressed very slowly, until the commission had become an exasperating, depressing burden, which left little chance for other, more pleasurable diversions. By the beginning of June, Ruskin had heard enough and he advised, 'Please don't think of anything else till Bret Harte is off your mind –.'[57] Working under pressure to complete the book and to impress a new publisher, Kate found the strain too much; she suffered bouts of trembling nervousness and eventually fainting spells, which undermined her confidence. This time Ruskin came to her aid to reassure her that he knew the consequences of overwork from his own experience. 'The excitability is not weakness in that form. It is weakness not to be able to bear it – but all my books are written and much of my life passed in fierce excitement, the fiercer when I am stronger. The weakness shows chiefly in not feeling interest in things . . . Now *you* are to get well and have no can't standing fits [her frequent fainting attacks] and to begin *singing again*.'[58]

Kate's recovery was slow, and not much helped by Ruskin's light-hearted, entertaining letters, filled with hopelessly difficult instructions. 'Do coloured creatures transparently – I don't know how it's to be done, but it *can* be done.' He advised her to sharpen her naturalism by studying some of his own early watercolours, ten of which he enclosed with the letter, instructing her to select one to keep, 'returning me mine till further orders!' It was the first of several such packets that arrived during the summer, and the selection of the one to be kept eventually involved the entire Greenaway household. This was more than Ruskin had hoped for; he revelled in the attention his exercise had caused and wrote uncharacteristically modest letters to her, claiming that the sketchy, unfinished watercolours were 'such mere hints of what I want to do, or syllables of what I saw, that I never think – or at least never thought, they could give the least pleasure to any one but myself –.' Gradually, Kate improved enough for her to suggest a return to Brantwood, using the excuse of her poor health; and, to her astonishment, Ruskin agreed. He must have felt partially responsible for her illness, and wrote, 'It all depends on my health – but if I go on as I am now, I could let you come in the heathery days of this year.'[59] To this Kate replied that there were even more important reasons why a reunion should take place – it would give her new hope and confidence in her future, which at the moment looked bleak and uncertain. Ruskin, touched by her sincerity, promised a letter every day to record his health's progress, and that he would 'do all I can for you poor little Katie'.

Work on the Bret Harte book continued, but it was fraught with difficulties; even the cover design (on which she misspelt 'Brete' Harte) gave her unexpected problems. Again Kate complained to Ruskin and he teased, 'Yes, covers are an awful trouble – . . . But your covers are always successes. *In a whisper*, sometimes the pictures inside look a little like covers too!' He was now 'ever your teasing Dinie', and, in contrast to her gloomy depression, pronounced his life at Brantwood pleasant and calm.[60] He sent her the next instalment of *Praeterita*, which she again praised for its vivid descriptions, and in return she sent proofs of the Bret Harte book. Ruskin was enchanted by the story of Polly, Queen of the Pirate Isle, and her exploits with Hickory Hunt and Wan Lee, the Chinese page. Their discovery of the famous old lode of Red Mountain, a legendary gold vein in the California hills, delighted his geological leanings and he wrote to Kate, 'Bret Harte *is* worth drawing for – how that story stays with me!'[61]

Kate found the wait for her visit to Brantwood frustrating. Once she had finished Bret Harte she was idle, and she spent most of the time selecting further watercolour sketches from Brantwood, reading Ruskin's autobiography and answering the increasing number of letters she received from him. Each of these proved a surprise and taken together they chart the early stages of a dangerous change in mood. His excitement and expectation turned to giddiness and eventually incomprehensibility – signs that something was again dreadfully wrong. His first letters described his frustration at not finding rosebuds in the garden; next he urged her to paint new pictures in seventeen distinct reds and planned to invent a red paint to help her. Then followed a series of ominously illegible letters; and on 2 July he warned, 'I'm in a sea of troubles and I want to be on a white bird with a crest like a lawyer's wig.' The next day he tried hard to keep his mind on her visit, not wanting to disappoint her, but could only

John Ruskin in 1885 at Brantwood.

conclude, 'I hope to *be* quite myself again.'[62] No further letters arrived from Brantwood and Ruskin slipped silently out of reach.

Kate was left to guess the reason, and when no news came from Brantwood, she grew impatient: 'I have said all I can and dare,' she wrote in disgust to Joan Severn, 'I often feel it is impertinent of me to say so much – but it is so dreadful to pay such a fearful penalty.' When she learned it was yet another attack of Ruskin's madness, she was contrite, promised to get her work done quickly and paint 'sods and flowers that will interest him – I shall try.'[63] Although it proved less violent than previous bouts, it was nevertheless worrying to Joan Severn and the Brantwood household. Ruskin sprained his wrist struggling with his male nurses and he tormented Joan Severn, telling her he knew her every thought simply by listening to the baa-ing of lambs outside. He sent her away with a message for the Queen, assuring her that it would be properly delivered when she played a song on the downstairs piano. Also, in his delirium, he mumbled his concen over Kate's cancelled visit: 'The only person I am sorry to disappoint is Miss Greenaway.'

The attack lasted a month. Then, in late August, Kate received a remarkable letter containing a pathetic apology:

> Darling Katie, Yes; please write again now and tell me all you care to tell of yourself and your work. I am extremely sorrowful at having

been ill again – and more because no one will tell me exactly what happens, but all seem frightened at me – and for me – more than they should, certainly: and far more than I am for myself – yet though this last illness was to me more terrible than any yet – and the gloom succeeding, not in weakness, but in deliberate measure of the time I lose and the pain I cause to all who care for me, – is heavier on me than ever before. Your little flower at the corner of this note is one of the loveliest you have ever done and I have lost none of my faculty of admiration nor I hope of sympathy. Ever your loving, Dinie.[64]

Kate received several more such letters, imploring attention and seeking to regain the influence he had once had on her work. He needed this incentive, at least until he was sufficiently recovered. Kate respected his requests, but worded her replies cautiously so as not to upset him. In an attempt to lift him out of his depression she also sent special watercolours, and to some extent this worked. He received each new letter gratefully and when he had the chance and the strength, he replied in glowing terms.[65] He clearly needed her letters to restore his confidence and to fill the long hours of enforced idleness. A brief visit to the seaside at Heysham provided an excuse to write even longer, more confessional letters, and as the boredom at the end of the month grew excruciating, he complained that he didn't know what to do with himself. Work was forbidden and letter-writing was becoming a great bore. 'Not knowing what to do with myself means, I don't care to walk – nor to draw, nor to read, nor to write, nor to eat – nor to think,' he wrote to Kate, wanting only sympathy. Instead, she proposed a visit to help cheer him up, for, as she explained, she too needed a change. Horrified that she might arrive unannounced and see him in his helpless state, he wrote a firm refusal.[66]

It seemed now Kate had served Ruskin's purpose, he wanted her only for an occasional letter. No further word arrived from Brantwood and Kate spent all of September and October sulking in Hampstead. In early November she sent him a copy of the recently published *A Apple Pie*, a book he knew nothing about. It can have been no surprise that Ruskin objected to the book, done without his advice or approval. He considered the project a personal affront, an insult to their friendship. He wrote a series of outraged letters: 'I am considerably vexed about Apple Pie,' he began. 'I really think you ought to consult me before determining the lettering of things so important.' The book was the largest-format Greenaway book, with enormous red letters and figures, often poorly drawn, stretched across each page; the oblong shape itself upset Ruskin, who hated books that protruded from his bookshelf. Also, with time to study each page in detail, he made a list of her glaring mistakes, pointed out the flaws in her figures' feet – 'literal paddles or flappers' – and found the lettering 'simple bill-sticking of the vulgarest sort, over the drawings – nor is there one of those that has the least melodious charm as a colour design – All your faults are gaining on you, every hour that you don't fight them –.'[67] He continued his attack four days later, after receiving her apologetic letter and plea for less scolding. 'But I never *do* scold you! never think of such a thing! I only say I'm – sorry.' Still obviously disgusted with *A Apple Pie*, he concluded, 'Why do you do it to the public?'[68]

Kate was shaken by such strong criticism of a book which, after all, had only been done for the money she now needed. To quell his anger she promised to send the recently published Bret Harte book he had liked so much in proof stage. The day it arrived he wrote yet another stinging letter about *A Apple Pie*. 'My dear, you must always send me all you do: If I don't like it – the public will, – if I do there's always one more pleasure in my disconsolate life. And you ought to feel that when I do like it – nobody likes it so much! – nor half nor a quarter so much.' At this point he laid down his pen to open the packet containing *The Queen of the Pirate Isle*, leafed quickly through it, then returned to his letter. The book was 'lovely. The best thing you have ever done – it is so real and natural.' In an attempt to preserve the little left of his hold over her work, he concluded, 'You may do more colour, however, next time.'[69]

Public reactions to both books were lukewarm. Kate received from Frederick Locker a copy of the 11 December *Athenaeum* ('full of your praises'), in which she read that her Bret Harte illustrations were done 'with admirable spirit and humour', but were not as good as previous work; she had fallen victim to 'the grotesque inspiration and rather rough fun of the author'. However, in the same issue *A Apple Pie* was praised for the 'Englishness' of its figures which 'more than justify her reputation'. Other similarly mixed reviews, and low sales figures, convinced Kate that her illustrations had lost their appeal.

After Ruskin's series of attacks on *A Apple Pie*, Kate believed he too had changed toward her, and she openly expressed this most serious fear to him: 'You always crush me by speaking as if I changed, or were changed. There is no change whatever in me,' he insisted, signing this letter, 'Ever your loving – much lectured – can't help it – Dinie'.[70] Both felt like victims of unfulfilled promises, the year's disappointments and misunderstandings. But Ruskin made a daring attempt to revive Kate's flagging spirits, by once again proposing a collaboration. He wanted a Greenaway-designed cover for Francesca Alexander's new book, *Christ's Folk in the Apennines*, which he was preparing for publication. It was a galling request to help promote the work of the woman Kate regarded as her rival for Ruskin's esteem. Nevertheless, Kate swallowed her pride and accepted the challenge. Ruskin was overjoyed, and wrote, 'It's so dear of you to do this cover for me,' also sending a flower book to help her with the fleur-de-lis he wanted on the cover. Kate struggled for over two weeks on this elementary exercise and she failed. It was as if she had developed a mental block against helping Francesca in any way and the whole disastrous project gave her 'colded headaches and achy colds'. Ruskin accepted the news philosophically and wrote to Kate in mid-December: '*You* have been certainly out of tune in drawing these irises – I never knew you do anything so clumsy before. I've given up the idea at once and am going to print a plain title in printer's letters. It is not your fault but my grotesque ill-fortune; I never yet had luck in these little things.'[71]

By the end of December Kate was immersed in such gloom that even Ruskin could not dissipate it. The year had been a great disappointment with so many dashed hopes, that she was left more than ever uncertain about the future. Of the books published this year, only her almanack proved a financial success, and that simply because America ordered 45,000 copies. At home her fame

Francesca Alexander's impression of Ruskin's Rose – 'Santa Rosa', which he published in *Christ's Folk in the Apennines* (1886).

continued to fade, what remained resting on the first fresh picture books, such as *Under the Window* and *Mother Goose*. When she sought encouragement, the alternatives for earning the living she still had to make seemed equally limited: she could follow Ruskin's erratic and all too often misleading advice; or she could return to illustrating the work of other writers. Then Ruskin decided to stop writing to her; his silence added an infuriating new worry. When a letter finally arrived from Brantwood, in reply to the several she sent pleading for answers, it was only to scold her, to call her his 'very sulky little Katie', and, worst of all, to urge her to work on alone. She reminded him that they had not seen each other for over a year; she had been put off numerous times, and now there was little hope for a future reunion. All she wanted was a promise, a glimmer of hope to give her something to think about. Ruskin was obviously touched by her affection but he only taunted, 'But certainly a year is long to wait. In my trial time [his engagement to Rose] I waited three and did not get what I had waited for.' Eventually he promised that, if all went well, she could visit him at Brantwood for his birthday in early February, 'to watch all the spring flowers come out . . . and we'd have shortbread and muffins for tea – and I don't think I should be being cross or horrid – so please try!'[72]

This new invitation left Kate slightly sceptical, since such arrangements in the past had had a way of never materializing. But it gave her some slight hope with which to start the new year.

7 Fate Takes Command
1887–1889

Gather ye rose-buds while ye may!
Old time is still a-flying:
And this same flower that smiled today,
Tomorrow will be dying.
Robert Herrick, quoted in Kate
Greenaway's ALMANACK FOR 1889

Throughout January 1887 Kate was delighted with Ruskin's daily letters designed to tighten his hold on her work. 'It's nice to be able to make foolish people happy with scratches like this! But I must and will have some colour studies of things that *are*, done while – I'm still among people that are. I have just been writing to [Stacy] Marks – "If only you and I could keep her in order!" '[1] It was during these weeks that Kate realized he was in low spirits, with only the prospect of her February visit to brighten the gloomy winter. Kate admitted that she too was anxious and would drop everything to escape to Brantwood. Worried about upsetting her in his present condition, he tried to prepare her. 'It *is* nice to make you so happy – and truly I hope to be well enough to give neither Joan nor you any anxiety for me while you are here – But you must be prepared for a weary and listless Dinie quite different from the one you last saw. I can't walk up hills carrying musical stones in my pockets any more!'[2] Despite this warning, Kate believed that her return to Brantwood would help revive her own flagging spirits. Her recent book was not going well, and she found comfort only in long, self-indulgent evenings spent reading *Praeterita*.

From past experience, Kate knew that it was the few days immediately preceding a visit to Brantwood that proved most crucial: her spirits would soar in expectation, but she could easily be plunged into a despair of disappointment at the last moment, with the arrival of a dreaded telegram announcing that he was again ill, and unable to see her. This time, when the expected telegram arrived, it proved a surprise: 'No change of plans. You carry on your work without fear of interruption and arrange for what time you like.'[3]

Although Kate arrived at Brantwood in high spirits, she immediately found that Ruskin's warnings about the change he had undergone had been well founded: he was now a wizened old man with an iron-grey beard and gnarled face. However, he too was in an expectant mood, having just completed a new chapter of *Praeterita*, and, although he had several more planned, he was anxious for a break. This set the visit off on a good start, and both Kate and Ruskin enjoyed themselves. Over the past few months Ruskin had made a habit of inviting the local Coniston schoolgirls to Saturday afternoon tea and lessons, when he read to them from Shakespeare and the Scriptures, and taught them bell-ringing, botany, and even to sing his verses from *Dame Wiggins*. He revelled in what seemed an innocent diversion and while Kate was there he insisted on her joining in. When they were alone, Kate would discuss her views on art and help Ruskin to reorganize his mineral cabinet, all the while apologizing to Ruskin for her devotion and saying he was 'a saint for bearing it.' She returned to London revived and confident that she would be able to carry on with new work.

After such a heavy dose of Kate's affection Ruskin felt that he had earned a slight rest from her appeals, and he ignored her letters, recoiling from responsibilities that she still looked upon as essential to her well being. He wanted only to be left alone to continue *Praeterita*; and he urged her to work for herself and for others who, unlike him, were not susceptible to unpredictable illnesses and depressions. 'Spring is coming – and your only hope is in making the most of every hour as it passes, – and not wishing for others, or times, or places. Fix your heart on your work – and on the poor, who need affection – and don't when you grow old – feel – as I do that you have thrown it away.'[4] However, the visit had not only given Kate renewed hope of advice, but had also increased her craving for more frequent letters. She had not learned the lesson that while he worked he did not want to be disturbed or made to feel guilty for not answering her letters. Actually, as he confessed to her, all he now wanted was 'to sleep and forget all I can'. To get round the impasse, Kate proposed a new and extremely appropriate book to be done entirely under his guidance. This was Robert Browning's *The Pied Piper of Hamelin*, which she had considered two years earlier. She had gone so far as to write to Browning and had received permission to illustrate a new edition; but only now did she consider it seriously.[5] It was a shrewd choice: Ruskin's revived interest suggests that this book meant a great deal to him. Indeed, Kate's *Piper* became for him a project of sufficient importance to be placed on a par with his own work on *Praeterita*.

Kate decided that the illustrations should be in the Pre-Raphaelite style Ruskin would approve. She sent him long, detailed letters to describe her progress, and she soon learned that one scene in particular was important to Ruskin. This was what he called the 'paradise scene', the final episode in the story, where the Piper plays in a perfect 'celestial garden', with Greenaway children dancing round. He supervised her work on this one scene with unswerving dedication, to make sure that Kate got every figure and pose right. 'Yes, that is just what it must be, the piper sitting in the garden playing. It perfects the whole story, while it changes it into a new one,' he wrote in early March, by then having in mind that the paradise scene should represent his idea of heaven – at least as heaven might appear through Kate's eyes.[6] Of secondary, yet crucial importance were the book's architectural settings. Ruskin decided that these must be drawn in true perspective so as not to detract from the overall impact of detailed Pre-Raphaelite accuracy. Perspective, however, was not one of Kate's strong points: when her *Under the Window* drawings had been exhibited at the Fine Art Society years earlier, one astonished critic had noted, 'She has one point of sight here, and another here! and here! and here! Why she has five distinct points of sight!' At that time Kate's father had tried to help correct her errors, but with little success. Now her brother decided to try, with Ruskin's blessing.[7] It quickly became clear to Johnnie that Kate's failure to learn perspective was physiological – the result of the short-sightedness that forced

Three Girls in White. Unfinished watercolour adopting Ruskin's springtime demands for a suitable garden setting for the Piper.

her to study objects at close range. But Ruskin refused to accept such a simple explanation. He was confident that Kate could and would conquer the rules of perspective, and he took up where Johnnie left off, revelling in this opportunity to experience again the art lessons once given to his beloved Rose La Touche and his other young pupils. They became a challenge with deep, hidden significance; and he attacked each new lesson – always sent by post – with renewed interest. He knew exactly where to find simple yet pertinent examples, and he sent Kate copies of his favourite paintings to study. He claimed that the key to perspective drawing was intuitive, not mechanical. 'One never *uses* the rules, one only feels them – and defies if one likes – like John Bellini. But we should first know and enjoy them.' To which Kate argued that if painters like Bellini could defy the rules of perspective, why shouldn't she? Annoyed, Ruskin replied, 'Perspective won't put up with you – if you tread on her toes – but will concede half her power to you if you can look her in the eyes. I won't tell you more till you're across that river.'[8]

It would be wrong to assume that Kate did not want to succeed with her perspective lessons. On the contrary, she spent most of her time trying to master Ruskin's tasks, copying intricate, lettered diagrams of steps and archways, and finally mice (or, as Ruskin called them, rats). These proved especially difficult, but Ruskin refused to let her rest. 'Finished the rats have you! but you ought to do dozens of rats – in perspective with radiating tails'; he included a crude ink sketch of a pile of rats. It is strange that Kate, who had been trained to make accurate copies of architectural ornament and stuffed animals at art school, should have had such difficulties, but throughout her life she had problems with perspective, and she never quite understood its complexities. And, while for a long time she had managed to avoid making too many errors, now, with such a keen instructor, she felt trapped into having to learn what she had previously neglected.

Ruskin's demands on Kate's time went beyond lessons in perspective. As a personal favour he asked her to design a dress for the May Queen ceremony he had initiated at Whitelands Girls College, Chelsea in 1881. This rite, by now a recognized annual event in the school calendar, had its roots in Ruskin's

146

attempts to realize his fantasies with young girls. In mid-March Kate sent her eagerly awaited designs for Ruskin's opinion and he selected two of the simplest, with embroidered bottom hem, sleeves and neckline, but otherwise pure white toga-like gowns. If these would not fit, he explained to Joan Severn, 'anything will do – her bedgown would and barefeet!' Clearly Kate's designs were not as important as he had led her to believe.

At the same time Kate was weary of her lessons in perspective, which to her horror, seemed to have affected her eyesight. In April she sought the advice of her doctor, Elizabeth Garrett Anderson, now a Hampstead neighbour, who willingly became another mentor; but the advice she gave was more disturbing than any Kate could have imagined: to relieve her eyestrain she was to work only indoors, avoid the cold, paint much larger pictures and, worst of all, to take a prescribed medicine no less than nine times each day. This medicine proved the greatest obstacle to her work; needing to have it always to hand limited her movements and made her feel an invalid. In despair she wrote to Ruskin, who, understanding such things, viewed the diagnosis as a new obstacle which he could share with her. Infuriated with being so restricted, she wanted sympathy, but Ruskin offered only bracing advice: 'I am so *very* glad you have been to that appalling Doctress and have been bullied – and have things to take 9 times a day.' But he concluded his letter, 'If I'm at all well I'll come and do something beside you – or at least – just [sit in?] the corner!'[9] Despite such calming reactions, Kate could not escape the debilitating presence of her medicine; it was a symptom that something was terribly wrong. In fact it was the first sign of treatment for an undiagnosed disease which left her susceptible to continual colds, bouts of influenza and rheumatic pains for the rest of her life.

The Piper's paradise garden, final plate to the *Pied Piper of Hamelin*, 1888.

The *Piper* had progressed to the all-important paradise scene and Ruskin again stepped in to make sure all was done correctly. The young girls were to be dressed in white gowns – not unlike the May Queen dresses – and the Piper seated in a garden of 'celestial spring'. 'The only difficulty to me is the sort of frocks people will wear in the next world,' he explained. 'But you must keep up heart for the piper. The last scene with *him* will be exactly the right preface for the Book of Heaven.' Kate dutifully sent preliminary sketches for the dresses and Ruskin replied, knowing exactly what he wanted from her. 'I *think* we might go the length of expecting the frocks to come off sometimes – when it was very warm? you know.'[10] However, limited by her eyestrain and daunted by his vague instructions, Kate made only halting progress on the book.

In addition, the daily letters Kate now received began to suggest a recurrence of giddiness and confusion brewing in Ruskin's mind. By Easter Tuesday he was 'extremely sad and helpless – and want to be seven years old again'.[11] The news of the tragic death of one of his secretaries, Laurence Hilliard,[12] plunged him deeper into a melancholy from which he found only brief relief in Kate's letters. It is significant that, from this point onwards, Ruskin began to preserve Kate's letters, locking them away in his 'Greenaway drawer' and resorting to them for further consolation. Most of these letters were later destroyed by Joan Severn, but the following survives, to show the uncertain, child-like language Kate used in writing to Ruskin. She knew what he liked, yet hoped to steer his attention closer to her own, more personal interests.

> My Dear, My Dear Dinie – I am very sorry to hear your sad news and sorry too, for the shock to you, just now – when you are not well – it is very sad – how often it seems to happen – to people who are – not strong. – I'm very sorry for All of you – but Dear Dinie I hope you won't trouble about it more than you can help – though I know – you are very grieved – Poor – dear – . . . Yes Dinie – I'll be very good – I don't think I've been – naughty – have I? . . . I'm doing the steps [of] one of the Pipers today – it's getting on, but they have a great deal of work in them, so many figures and so much background – . . . You say you are much the same – I wish dear – you – could – begin to feel better – but I hope it won't be long now before you do – Oh, Dinie Dear. I'm afraid you are very grieved and trouble over this – I am so sorry for your sorrow, and theirs – poor Dear Dinie . . . I do so wish I could say things to comfort you – but you tell me to be so quiet – but Dear I may hope you are better today and if you have it so mild – you will go out and that will do you good – Good bye my Dear Dear Dino – may all things bless and Comfort you Dear. With all my love, Katie.[13]

However feeble her language and pitiful her intentions, this letter provided Ruskin with some comfort. The following day Kate received a telegram: 'All well at Coniston. John Ruskin.' Joan Severn helped nurse him back to health, as did the local schoolgirls on their Saturday visits. Slowly his spirits rose and Kate waited patiently. Then she received a letter explaining that the past few weeks had not been a bad attack, although he was 'obliged to be on my guard against the exact conditions of danger of last year – and I must not let myself be put

Left: Kate Greenaway's *The Old Farm-house*, using cottage themes like those in (*right:*) Helen Allingham's *The Elder Bush, Brook Lane*, Witley, 1887

under hospital attendants again . . . Therefore I must write to *nobody*.'[14] This was an unexpected blow to Kate's morale; she had depended on even the smallest piece of news from Brantwood. What was even more difficult to accept was the fact that her brother was now constantly receiving letters from Ruskin, containing instructions on photographic work and asking for scientific advice; but no letters arrived for Kate. 'Love to Katie though she'll be savage with me for not reading her letters just now,' was written at the end of one letter to Johnnie. Ruskin was doing what he had long threatened to do: cut her off completely. Kate was frantic, her letters filled with angry pleas for even the briefest reply; and still the silence continued. 'Tell your sister please that I'm – just as I was and shall probably be, and that as for finding things to write about to please me – the only thing she can do to please me at present is to write about Nothing,' he instructed Johnnie.[15]

Ruskin's silence continued for two months. During that time Kate escaped from her studio and visited Witley. There she tried to restore her weak eyesight and overcome her depression. Evans later recalled how the Surrey countryside had the power to restore her sagging spirits. 'I remember her seeing a field of daffodils, looking at and admiring it, then she said, "it was worth living to see this sight".'[16]

Late in June, while still at Witley, Kate received a long-awaited letter from Ruskin. In it he tried to explain his past silence, but failed to mention his recent fits of anger and irrationality, the traumatic battle with Joan Severn that had left him miserable, or the extravagant purchases he had made with money he didn't have. Finally, feeling threatened by Brantwood – scene of so much past anguish – he had moved to the local Waterhead Hotel, taking with him only his precious Turner watercolours. There he remained for several days, then moved on to lodgings, where he wrote to Joan (who was too ill to move from Brantwood) that she and her family must leave his home immediately. When they finally complied, in early June, Ruskin deeply regretted his behaviour, particularly his callous treatment of his 'darling Joanie'. He moved back to Brantwood, where alone, irritable and longing for affection, he chose to write to Kate. 'My poor Katie, Fain would I write and comfort you but there is no comfort in me. The whole time since my birthday has been of increasing difficulty and danger – my heart is broken for poor Joanie – be what you can to *her* – there is no help for me at present but in my own resignation.'[17] This was the first of a series of affectionate letters written with a view toward providing him with comfort. Kate was now the one person he was sure still loved him; her letters he received in response proved he was not far wrong. Overjoyed by her affection, he replied to one, 'My poor Katie, *What* a love you have given me! Here is clear writing once more to tell you how well I know it – and have known. Heaven keep you in its hand and lead you – and strengthen you to be – yourself, and the joy of myriads in the fair Earth.'[18]

These tender letters were a short-lived phenomenon and, following this last one, a six-month silence descended. Throughout that time Kate still wrote long, detailed letters, describing her life in Hampstead, her garden flowers, the books she read, the galleries she occasionally visited; but Ruskin never responded. 'I feel dull,' Kate confessed to Joan Severn, yet thoughts of Ruskin, despite his unpredictability, seemed to help: 'I never feel angry with him now whatever he does – I'm too sorry – besides he can't help it. Poor dear.' She was compelled to make money and, while she continued to worry about Ruskin, she poured more energy into two new and very commercial books: the year's almanack, with designs based upon an open window theme, and *Queen Victoria's Jubilee Garland*, published as a series of processional drawings to accompany verses descriptive of important events during the Queen's fifty-year reign. When she was not working, Kate derived some comfort from her family, especially her young niece, Catherine Dadd. Catherine's striking appearance made her a favourite model, as Kate once exlaimed to Ruskin: 'My sister's little girl is good to contemplate. Her profile a cheerful Burne-Jones!' Kate found time to take Catherine and her brother Eddie on frequent excursions into London to see the Jubilee celebrations. The streets were filled with foreign visitors and the shop windows, lit for the first time by electric lights, were bursting with memorabilia, Greenaway cards and books. Then there was a call on John Greenaway's new office in the Strand, and a visit to a children's play. Kate was not then in the mood for light-hearted fun; after the play she wrote to Ruskin that such frivolous productions lacked the depth she needed: 'I think I like going deeper into things, I think I like deeper motives for things than what Society *thinks*.'[19]

Ruskin ignored these letters, often refusing even to open them; he preferred to spend the long, despondent summer and autumn in isolation at Brantwood. At last, however, its atmosphere became too oppressive and he set out with his valet for France. At a Folkestone hotel his behaviour became so erratic that it was decided they could go no further. Still refusing to return to Brantwood, Ruskin remained trapped in Folkestone, until a few days later he was moved to Sandgate, taking lodgings near the sea. There he sat and watched the waves outside his window, wrote wildly abusive letters to admirers and friends, and felt sorry for himself.

Kate's annual Christmas greeting card and almanack were sent to Sandgate, and fortunately they arrived at an appropriate time, with Ruskin nursing feelings of rejection. These stemmed from his relationship with a new young art student pet, Kathleen Olander, whom he had coached in painting, but who had refused his invitation to visit him while on the Kent coast. He broke his long silence to write to Kate on Boxing Day: 'I have had a dreadful time to pass through of which I could not write to – anyone that would have suffered with me, or been afraid – as I was for myself. Least of all to poor Katie.' He continued to send her affectionate letters throughout January 1888. By then he was extremely bored with his seaside exile and initiated involved correspondence with several admirers, including Kathleen Olander, now 'my dearest Kathleen'. A comparison between the letters written to Kate and those to Kathleen indicates that, while Kathleen stirred in him long-dormant romantic feelings, he regarded Kate as an ageing, devoted friend, to whom he turned whenever he needed reassurance, or to boost his sense of importance by criticizing her latest trifle.

Kate, however, wanted reassurance, and again she begged Ruskin for more frequent letters. He believed these would be a waste of time, time better spent working while he still had the strength; and he wrote to scold her. It was clear to Ruskin that Kate did not understand his fears for his health, and the possible return, at any time, of his madness. Indeed, she chose to ignore all mention of it in her letters. This lack of comprehension was infuriating to him, since he was still very much afraid, and quite aware that the slightest upset might precipitate a relapse: 'Remember that this life is never in Sunlight – only in frosty Starlight! *You* are absolutely independent of me as an artist.' Six days later, when his anger had abated, he wrote: 'But had you no idea then how sad I always was – how the pain and failure of age torment me – what an agony of longing there is in me for the days of youth – of childhood – here every one of your drawings is as of heaven into which I can never enter –?' His anger towards her was the result of a crushing melancholy: 'My illnesses are all the intensity of this sadness,' he confessed and wanted 'only to be me by *quiet* work on things I can do – not by complaining as I do now – still less by trying to be – what I would be – I am always the same in care for you.'[20] This was all painful to him: he knew her love for him and found great comfort in it; and yet he felt that for her own good he must try to break with her. This would most certainly deprive him of one of his last real pleasures – namely her letters – but at the risk of hurting her again, as well as of bringing on a new attack of his madness, he begged to break his hold over her. To clarify the situation he wrote, 'Whatever state I fall into – the pride of being loved as you love me remains. Sometimes it is almost the only pride I have left.'[21] She must accept the break, 'looking everything clearly in the front – and resolving not to defy, but to make the best of it – good *humouredly* though sorrowfully . . .'[22] Kate wanted to believe him, to accept his sincerity; but she must have questioned his motives. She now knew (from Ruskin's own letters) that he had made several brief visits to London over the past weeks, mainly to see Kathleen Olander, and had made no effort to contact her.

When she wrote to express her pain at this new humiliation, Ruskin chose to ignore her pleas, and filled his days at Sandgate writing more of *Praeterita*. This also left him guilt-ridden, but for a different reason, as it recalled his past as one long failure. Kate's friendship was yet another instance of his personal failure: her childish innocence had turned to old-maidishness; her relentless demands for affection and her refusal to abandon him despite his callous behaviour, increased his distress. He looked upon her as a paragon of virtue, a model of family devotion which outshone all his attempts at doing good: 'My poor Katie – you don't know what a blessing it is to you – that you have nothing to repent of – but have done for Father and Mother and brother, and for me, every dutiful and loving deed – I am in a fearful fit of remorse just now for all the selfishness and anger and extravagance of my life.'[23] Moved by this genuineness, Kate sent a parcel of light-hearted letters to assure him that she understood his predicament; but these only proved to be reminders of her virtuous life, and tormented him further. He wished he had her childish fantasies: 'You cannot conceive how in my present state, I envy – that is to say only in the strongest way, long for – the least vestige of imagination, such as yours. When nothing shows itself to me – all day long – but the dull room or the wild sea and I think what it must be to you to have far sight into dreamlands of truth – and to be able to see such scenes of the most exquisite grace and life and quaint vivacity – whether you draw them or not, what a blessing to have them there – at your call . . . Heaven keep you Katie, and restore you from the sorrow about your poor Dinie.'[24]

Kate's pitiful touchiness and longing to help Ruskin were heightened by such poignancy in his letters. She pondered each line, tried to read beyond each word, to understand his true feelings for her. But, as always, she was a victim of her own fantasies, and in refusing to believe that Ruskin's suffering could not be cured with 'sweetness and violets', she was waiting for her chance to nurse him back to health. However, he was still out of reach at Sandgate and her efforts had to be confined to therapeutic Greenaway drawings and long, affectionate letters. She drew new Greenaway girlies, spent hours perfecting the faces she knew he enjoyed, and sent them with motherly advice: he must, for example, take lots of chicken broth and afterwards reread those of her letters that reminded him of their relaxed, happy times together. Her vivid memory enabled her to recall in great detail past events and her reactions to them, such as the first time he arrived in her studio, and her first visit to Brantwood. To some extent this part of her advice worked, and Ruskin carefully preserved her most poignant recollections. In one letter she entertained him with an original, and vaguely suggestive story: 'A little child was ill in bed, and so they asked it what it would have for its dinner. "An angel's egg" said the child. There was a picture of an Angel with great wings above the bed.' Cryptic and mawkish in style, the letter continues as if she were speaking to him directly, again in a motherly tone:

> Well, and so you go to sleep do you – and the cat goes to sleep – and nobody talks – poor Dinie, only I expect you don't want anyone to talk – not like we used to at those happy violet teas – and the beautiful teas at Brantwood, when you used to read Byron and I was so happy living in a new world. How I did love it – how satisfied I was. The need, so long wished for, granted at last, surrounded by Art – consoled by friendship and books – inside – and out – such loveliness – I still walked among the Gods (or rather with one) in a new spring – with mountains seen for the first time – and now – what wonder I am held – and it all *might be, might be,* beautiful yet – oh the deep pity of it. Goodbye – my poor Dear, Dear Dinie with all my love, Katie.[25]

152

Scene from the *Pied Piper of Hamelin*, 1888, adopting Kate's perspective lessons in its architectural backgrounds.

Such caring letters further aggravated Ruskin's guilt, and he broke his resolve not to ask for news of her work, so that he might again advise her. When she sent him outline proofs of the *Piper* illustrations, which were just what he needed to take his mind off himself, his reaction was that of the Master criticizing one of her early books:

> It is all as good and nice as it can be, and you really have got through your rats with credit – and the Piper is sublime – and the children lovely. But I am more disappointed in the 'Paradise' than I expected to be – a *real* view of Hampstead ponds in spring would have been more celestial to me than this customary flat of yours with the trees stuck into it at regular distances – And not a Peacock! [his favourite bird] – or a flying horse!![26]

Over-all he was delighted with the book, and the same day surprised her with a second letter – an invitation to come to Sandgate 'as soon as possible'.

Ruskin preserved her ecstatic answer to this invitation, a letter that rambles on for four full pages. She began:

> I am glad to get so well out of it [the *Piper*] I was very fearful of what you would say. I *know* the Paradise is bad. I was very ill indeed – and tired out when I did it – then it is so difficult to do Pictures with backgrounds full of colour that they can print well – still I know it is not good and very sorry I was at the time and am now – I could not leave the one unfinished – because for one thing I wanted the money – and could not feel at rest till it was off my mind – but it was foolish – I might have done a far better one after a long rest – I am only thankful you can like the other part – for I was *very very* tired – My Dinie.

She apologized for forgetting the peacock and the flying horse, then continued,

And if you think I've said all I've got to say to you – why you're a mistaken Dinie – I don't know how long letters you'll get – only I have to work – and also – I fear you might stop short in the *reading* you know . . . And now – is it – I am really to come – is it true – *real true* – I can't let myself believe it till I know Dino Dear – is it really going to be seaweed my Dear – [his invitation was conditional on her painting him green seaweed] why? Are not there mermaids above the lovely green water – and I – ah, Dino – you Dear – I could toast muffins after all – and – write the story out and it would – (or let it be *will*) be so joyful. My Dear, oh I shall be so glad, so glad – to see you – one whole year full of those months and weeks and days – have I waited. Surely . . . if the wind would cease to howl – one could have hopes how soon I shall come – with all my love Dear – Katie.[27]

Ruskin was pleased that she felt so strongly about the reunion, and he told Joan Severn not to return to Sandgate without her. Joan reluctantly agreed. Meanwhile Ruskin assured Kate that all was ready and nothing should prevent her arrival. 'Yes, it's quite real this time . . . and we'll have a time of it.' He warned her not to expect the same person; he had changed yet again, and was even more susceptible to violent fits and angry tempers. This, although it worried Kate, was not enough to put her off. Indeed, she somewhat selfishly urged him to be especially careful now, to avoid minor upsets and most of all to avoid the cold she believed brought on his illness. Rather annoyed he replied, 'It wasn't the cold that made me ill. It makes me sulky as it does you; but the bad time that was on me was simply a phase of the real illness, which had always held on me more or less, now – the result of old sorrow – and new – fear alike of Death – and Life – lest in living I become only a burden of those who love me.'[28]

When she arrived with Joan Severn, despite the warnings about the change that had come over Ruskin, Kate was shocked. She had never before seen him quite like this: his actions were at times familiar, at other times erratic; those of a stranger thrown into fits of anger over the least offensive phrase. Throughout her visit, she was forced to choose her words carefully, even more than she had done while writing to him. Joan Severn was worried, recognizing the symptoms of a fresh attack of madness; she urged Kate to leave before things became more difficult. At this point memories of the months spent anticipating this visit to Ruskin got the better of Kate and she refused; she reminded Joan of how Ruskin had begged her to come and she stood her ground. It proved the most painful and shattering decision in Kate's relationship with the Master.

She guilelessly approached Ruskin, not knowing what to expect, confident all the while that with her love she could get through to him. Joan pointed out the signs of madness that now slowly returned: the nightmare rage alternating with reasonable behaviour; the reckless promises, extravagant gifts and misleading letters of affection. From the beginning Joan had tried to censor most of these before they were sent, thinking them cruel; but Kate's invitation had unfortunately slipped through, leading to this further complication. After a tortured week spent in constant fear that Ruskin would break down at any moment, Joan desperately wanted to leave; and she again urged Kate to go with her. The idea of leaving Ruskin alone to endure an unimaginable fate horrified

Kate, and still she refused. Infuriated by the stalemate, Joan Severn described her frustrations to Lady Simon, writing on 7 March, 'He would ask me to bring Kate Greenaway on a visit, and her influence and presence have I fear not soothed and comforted, or helped the position of things. And of course she's been miserable – and Heaven knows so have I – but as she won't leave as long as I am here, I'm determined to take her back today – and when we're gone, I hope he'll get better.'[29]

Eventually they both left, but it was Kate's possessiveness, her stubborn refusal to accept her helplessness, that most annoyed Joan Severn. She wrote to Lady Simon, 'Of course the poor Coz [Ruskin] was both cruel and foolish in having K.G. on a visit, but I believe she pestered him into it, and is herself so foolish in the matter – and quite asserts she has a right to expect all sorts of favours from him after the way he has gone on with her – and perhaps she is right, but oh the sorrow and perplexity of it all . . . It is all inexpressibly sad.'[30] Just three days after her return to London Kate received a letter from Ruskin, written in obvious confusion, the envelope addressed to his secretary, so that it had to be rerouted to Hampstead, with Ruskin's pencilled instructions to Kate to pay the twopence postage due. The enclosed message was short and almost illegible: 'It's not "all over" at all!! Where are my Sarah Walker [a favourite Greenaway girlie] and mermaids? Ever your loving Dinie.'[31] This plea to Kate not to forget him ended his correspondence with her that year. He slowly recovered at Sandgate, made one brief trip to London to see Kathleen Olander, then went abroad, and did not return until December.

It was this single, pathetic letter followed by silence, that left Kate miserable and confused. Her efforts to restore Ruskin's health had been a failure and, moreover, her professional reputation was fast waning. Work on illustrations for books now seemed dispiriting, and she did it solely for the money. For consolation and patronage she turned to old and by now long-neglected friends, accepting private commissions from Lady Dorothy Nevill, Lady Northcote and Gerald Ponsonby. She agreed to supply a title page of fourteen Greenaway children for one of William Loftie's projects, the third edition of the *Orient Line Guide*, a curiously inappropriate introduction to a steamship company's guidebook. The fact that the firm's chairman was James Anderson, who was married to her doctor, Elizabeth Garrett Anderson, perhaps had something to do with it, and with his satisfaction with the finished design. It is ironic that while Kate needed the money from this commission, and did it at the behest of her old friend Loftie, she refused payment. The care she devoted to even this minor commission ('It seems a pity it is not done in colour . . .') shows that she was still concerned about how her illustrations appeared to whatever public she could find.[32]

The void of the spring and summer of 1888 was to some extent filled by an old art school acquaintance, Helen Paterson, who, before her marriage to the poet William Allingham, had been a successful black and white illustrator. She still maintained her reputation as a landscape watercolourist and regularly exhibited in the London galleries. Kate had met Helen during evening classes at the Slade about fifteen years earlier; later they were formally introduced by Frederick Locker at the home of the Tennysons. In 1886 Kate sold William

155

Title page to the *Orient Line Guide*, done for the Reverend Loftie and the Pears Soap advertisement illustration.

Allingham the use of her picture *Bubbles* for his book *Rhymes for the Young Folk*; and now, in the spring of 1888, when Kate visited Helen's home at Witley (in Helen's words) they 'became *really* friends'. Kate looked to her old acquaintance for the stability and direction she now lacked; and together they made frequent excursions into the nearby copses and lanes to paint the trees and flowers they both loved. When the Allinghams moved to Hampstead in the autumn, Helen and her husband became frequent guests in Kate's studio, where, as Helen wrote later, they had intimate tea-time chats 'in the cosy little tea room or in the great studio full of interesting things . . . When the time came for saying good-night she would always come down to the hall-door and generally pull on a hat hanging in the hall and come as far as the gate for more friendly last words.'[33] There Kate lingered over these last precious moments spent with her friend, before facing the darkness of her studio and her uncertain future. She gained inspiration from and respected Helen's skill as a painter, which Ruskin had long believed far superior to her own. He had praised Helen in his Oxford lecture on Kate's work and afterwards urged Kate to be humble and learn from her. Then, as now, Kate had swallowed her pride and recognized her better, replying to Ruskin, 'I always feel I like her so much whenever I see her.'[34]

Conversations during Helen's visits frequently turned to Ruskin. Helen had been acquainted with Ruskin for some time, but she did not like him. She remembered his scathing criticism of her watercolour portrait of his beloved Carlyle, 'painted like a lamb when he ought to appear like a lion', and his outrageous suggestion that she should repaint it according to his ideas. This she flatly refused to do, for her painting was true to her impression of her husband's friend as a kind and gentle man, 'certainly not in leonine garb!' she told Ruskin. Similarly, when Ruskin visited her studio a short time later, he had astonished her by pulling out a pocket microscope to search her latest landscape for the dangerous grey skies he hated, 'The Devil sends them!' Such eccentric behaviour left Helen doubtful about Ruskin's critical faculties, and she must have explained this to Kate. Other topics of conversation included all the artistic and literary acquaintance they shared – the Tennysons, Evans, George Eliot. Kate occasionally accompanied William and Helen to the galleries where, as William recorded in his diary, he had first met Kate. There, at the Royal Academy, he was astonished to learn that 'K.G. was a real person', and afterwards, like his wife, he fell under the spell of her innocent charms. Helen often discussed her friendship with Kate; and she frequently praised her works, claiming in particular that, 'No one could draw roses like Kate Greenaway.'[35]

In October, presentation and review copies of *The Pied Piper* were sent to friends and critics. Kate sent one to Robert Browning, specially inscribed with a meticulously painted Greenaway girl with mob cap and basket of flowers on its half-title page. When Stacy Marks received his now customary copy, he wrote to congratulate her as one of the few who knew about Kate's difficulties with Ruskin over the book. 'You have far exceeded my expectations in carrying through what must have been a strange and difficult task.'[36] Even Walter Crane forgot his usual reservations about Kate's formalized children, and praised the book as a good interpretation of his favourite story. Writing to Evans (from whom he received his copy) he called it 'very charming, and beautifully printed. It is a subject after her heart I should say. I remember contemplating it

Inscribed half-title on a copy of the Piper given to Browning by Kate.

myself years ago.'[37] The book arrived in the shops in time for the Christmas trade and received its reviews accordingly. The *Athenaeum* (24 November 1888), the magazine that had earlier championed the Greenaway style in the face of rampant imitations, now decided that 'the artist cannot be said to have exceeded herself, although the subject undoubtedly suited her vein of taste and lent itself to sympathetic treatment of children and quaint figures'; but it attacked the *Piper* children as 'needlessly stupid and dull'. The equally important *Art Journal* was also dismissive. Their reviewer considered that Kate· had chosen a subject which was unsuitable to her powers; she had been seriously hampered 'in her attempt to render the pseudo-German medievalism on a large scale'. However, by now Kate had learned that the importance of the American sales was paramount and, fortunately, reviews there were far more encouraging. One admirer claimed, 'You have more followers in the States than ever the Pied Piper of Hamelin had;' and the New York *Critic* (8 December 1888) declared her book 'one of the "star" books of the season . . . The artist's name upon the cover is doubtless the book's best recommendation. If there is anything to be said in criticism, it is that the thing is almost too dainty for the mischievous digits of the little vandals for whom it is intended.'

Further, the December sales of her new almanack proved cheering. A *Pall Mall Gazette* article (4 December 1888, found among her papers after her death), claimed that the almanack was among Routledge's most important and best-selling titles. By early December Routledge had already sold 30,000 copies – equal to the combined sales of the Routledge editions of *Swiss Family Robinson*, *Hans Andersen's Fairy Tales* and *Robinson Crusoe*. From this 30,000, 20,000 copies had been sent to America, still leaving an unusually large 10,000 for the English market. This was certainly the encouraging news Kate needed. It didn't seem to matter that the almanack was among her most startling, with each figure given an uncharacteristic black background. Here too, the Piper reappeared, opposite the January page and alongside several rose-inspired illustrations–just to show Ruskin she had taken his interests to heart.

The early months of 1889 were a disappointment after the successes of December, since Kate received no news from Ruskin. Although he had returned from his Continental tour before the end of the previous year, he was now recovering from another, unexpected mental relapse. Consequently she had only new projects to fill in the winter's solitude. She consulted one of her old notebooks in which the idea of a book of children's games appeared several times, and began work on this in earnest. She also accepted more illustration work, this time on *The Royal Progress of King Pepito*, a book by the travel writer Beatrice Cresswell, to be published by the Society for the Promotion of Christian Knowledge. Here, yet again Kate had to please a new editor, a daunting challenge when one remembers her struggles over the Bret Harte book. However, the SPCK were well known publishers of massive numbers of 'improving' books such as those of the redoubtable Mrs Ewing, and Kate's friends Mrs Locker and William Loftie; the chances of large sales for the new Greenaway title were therefore very good indeed.

Despite the silence from Brantwood, Kate continued to send letters to Ruskin. She sent her customary birthday greeting with a pathetic reminder of 'what might have been' – by now a favourite phrase. 'I wish I was going to be there to see all the lovely flowers you are going to have. If I were there you should ask me to tea – I think – Yes, I think you ought to ask me to tea – and we'd have raspberry jam for tea – a muffin, some violets and a Turner to look at – oh yes, I think you should ask me to tea.'[38] It was clear that she still felt Ruskin owed her some show of affection, some small hint that he thought of her. But he preferred silence; until at last, on May Day, surrounded by daffodils and the blue gentians running in a border from his study to the lake, and with a vase of the early rosebuds Joan had placed on his desk, he decided the time was right to write to Kate. Indeed, he spent most of the day writing and renewing postal relationships (notably with Francesca Alexander) and recalling past pleasures. He rummaged through his Greenaway drawer, crammed full of letters and drawings, 'so long unopened – most thankfully today unlocked again – and sending balm and rose and lily sweetness all through the old study', he wrote to Kate. Then he pulled the *Piper* down from his bookshelf, leafed through it to refresh his memory, and continued, 'of course the Piper is the best book you ever did – the Piper himself unsurpassable – and I feel as if he had piped me back out of the hill again, and would give some spring times yet to rejoice in your lovely work and its witness to them.' Reminded of their times together at Brantwood, he hoped there was still time for her to return.

> I wonder if you would care to come down in the wild rose time – and draw a branch or two, with the blue hills seen through them, and perhaps study a little falling water – or running – in the green shadows. I wouldn't set you to horrid work in the study, you should even draw any quantity of those things that you liked – in the forenoon – and have tea in the study . . . – and poor Joanie will be so thankful to have somebody to look after me a little, as well as her: – and so – perhaps you'll come, won't you?[39]

Kate was taken aback by receiving not only a letter but a further invitation. She agreed in principle to the visit, but the urgency in his reply to her letter of acceptance worried her: 'At present we're all right and I want you to come as soon as may be.' She wanted, above all, to avoid another embarrassing Sandgate dilemma, without hinting as much to Ruskin.

Kate was at this time considering the pressing problem of augmenting her income. She attended a spring showing of Helen Allingham's watercolour landscapes at the Fine Art Society and returned home with the idea that she too might renew her gallery career. It had been years since she exhibited in London, but it now seemed the answer to her problems: by exhibiting landscapes and flower paintings she could please Ruskin, as well as earn money she badly needed. However, this work would take time; much more time than illustrations, which did not require the painstaking work needed to produce a finished surface. She decided to put Ruskin's invitation off, at least until she had started on her new career. He was obviously disappointed, but agreed with her reasons. 'I *am* so sorry you can't come sooner, to see gentians – but I suppose they contrive ways of growing them now even in London.' And he was comforted by the fact that with Greenaway pictures exhibited in the London

Helen Allingham.

galleries he despised for their ignorance of true Beauty, all might again come
right. 'Well, if you can't come yet you can't – but you must read a little bit of *me*
every day – to keep you steady against the horrible mob of animals calling
themselves painters nowadays (– I could paint better than they by merely
throwing my ink bottle at them – if I thought them *worth* the ink).'[40]

Temporarily freed from Ruskin's demands, Kate pursued her gallery career
with dedication and a refreshing new sense of purpose. In June she sent thirteen
frames of original book illustrations to the International Exhibition in Paris,
where there was still keen interest in her work. Despite the fact that her tiny
drawings hung near the more impressive paintings of her contemporaries,
Whistler, Alma-Tadema and Millais, the critics singled her work out for praise.
Special emphasis was given to her influence on French fashions in *la mode
Greenaway*, which the critics linked with the aesthetic paraphernalia exhibited
by Liberty's.

Later in the year she was elected a member of the Royal Institute of Painters
in Watercolour. This was a less august institution than the Royal Academy or
the Royal Watercolour Society; but still the initials 'RI' were an indication of an
artist's status (although Kate never used them, claiming her signature 'was
already so well known'). Helen Allingham had achieved more distinction as
ARWS in 1875; but many noted colleagues, such as Randolph Caldecott, Walter
Crane, Arthur Severn (Joan's husband), Kate's distant relative Frank Dadd and
Elizabeth Thompson, her old art school companion, had exhibited there. True,
most of these exhibitors had resigned by 1889, to take up membership at more
exalted institutions; but Kate's appearance at the Royal Institute marked an
important step upwards in her gallery career.

Throughout the summer and autumn of 1889, whenever the weather
permitted, Kate escaped to the countryside, where, often accompanied by
Helen Allingham, she prepared work for exhibition. The two painters made
frequent day trips to Pinner, Chesham and Amersham, taking the early
morning local train to benefit from a full day's light. They discovered the
picturesque villages, cottages, river banks edged in willows and cottage
gardens that feature prominently in their pictures. They emerged from the train
like two laughing, truant schoolgirls in love with the countryside, to disappear

along the hedgerows and down lonely country lanes. Helen later remembered that on one day of intense work they were suddenly astonished that they had not noticed storm clouds looming overhead, threatening to drench their work. Undeterred by being miles from shelter, she and Kate waited and then seized the first opportunity to escape. 'We hailed a baker's cart that was going towards our station and we agreed that it gave us a capital view of the country over the high hedges.'[41]

Kate was so immersed in her painting outdoors that in August the letter cancelling her visit to Brantwood came as a great relief, rather than the disappointment Ruskin had feared. In the intervening weeks he had suffered a sixth attack of madness that left him not knowing where he was, and unable to recognize those around him. Significantly, Kate had no further letters from him: his nine-year correspondence with her had come to an end. Instead she now turned to Joan Severn, for advice and letters which were often filled with hopeful news of the Master. Their friendship, once threatened by Kate's stubbornness, now grew stronger through their mutual love for Ruskin. Joan's letters to Kate always contained enquiries about her work, and she would pass on news of it to the now silent Ruskin. Flowers from Brantwood were occasionally packed and sent off to Hampstead to remind Kate of her visits; later in the year Christmas turkeys and plants would arrive. The greatest comfort came from the slightest bit of news that Ruskin's health was improving. 'It must have been nice to have seen him so himself, I wish I'd been there to see also . . . It does seem to have been such a long hopeless time.'[42] Then, after Joan had spent three months diligently nursing Ruskin, she wanted a break to be with her husband in London. Kate wrote sympathetically: 'I think you are so wise to go away sometimes to live your own life as much as you can, and besides the little changes help you to bear the terrible times when they come.'[43] This

'Le Bon Esprit' from *Little Ann*. Original watercolour exhibited at the Paris Exhibition in 1889, inspiring a French Greenaway boom.

Detail of King Pepito from *The Royal Progress of King Pepito*, 1889, and detail of 'Hop Scotch' from *Kate Greenaway's Book of Games*, showing her favourite Hampstead street, Church Row.

letter, and subsequent advice meant for Joan rather than for Ruskin, indicate Kate's realization that there was little either could do to strengthen Ruskin's failing health.

Kate's depression returned in November, with Hampstead daily shrouded in thick fogs that, according to Kate, made 'all painting . . . quite impossible'; she was 'quite in despair at wasting so much time'.[44]

The year's end found Kate immersed in sorrow and loneliness, with little news from Brantwood, where Ruskin had recovered briefly, but not enough to raise her hopes. Of her three books for the Christmas market, the almanack, again with black backgrounds, and *King Pepito* both proved critical failures, the latter being attacked for its 'mannered and conventional' little boy dressed in lace-trimmed frock. Only the *Book of Games* was a moderate success with the book reviewers: the *Athenaeum* claimed it was 'equal to the lady's best while nearly all of them are as true, graceful, and fresh as Sothards'. Sales were another matter. Only about 10,000 copies of each were printed, and at that they had to compete with recent reissues of classic books by Crane and Caldecott. One final work of note this year was Kate's full-page drawing for the periodical *Holly Leaves*, destined to be the last of her works engraved by her father. Still in need of money, Kate accepted Locker's suggestion and sold her drawing *Bubbles* to his dear friend Mr Pears, the soap manufacturer. It was engraved and printed in colour on an advertising handbill, opposite Millais's *Bubbles*. However degrading such advertising seemed, Kate accepted the fact that this bought her valuable time to sort out her priorities. She had set her sights out of the nursery and into the galleries, determined to succeed at what some regarded as a late start to her true artistic career.

8   The Loneliness of Gleaning
1890–1895

A lonely soul, I am ever alone.
If love ever comes it is quickly gone –
Nothing abides and nothing stays.
I think I have found it, but only to know
How very soon it is all to go.
The sunshine is followed by falling snow.

KATE GREENAWAY

News of Ruskin's health arrived in the letters Joan Severn sent to Kate throughout the winter of 1889–90. Kate followed his progress – the temporary relapses, the surprising improvements – with intense interest. It gave her something to think about during a very depressing winter, with her own bouts of illness, enlivened only by the brief visits of her fourteen-year-old nephew, Eddie Dadd, and the enchanting Lily Severn, Joan's nineteen-year-old daughter, now at school in London. They both provided Kate with brief glimpses of the youthful spirit she had once sought in her models. She especially loved Lily's visits for Saturday afternoon tea, and afterwards described her guest's lady-like manners in the letters she sent to Joan at Brantwood. Lily captivated Kate by her naïve charm and her constant attempts to be more grown-up. It was her defiance of convention that most appealed to Kate, as her young guest pranced round the studio, mimicking the dowagers seen in society and expounding her outrageous plans for the future. The two often laughed over Lily's tales of her own impracticality, such as the time she comforted her near-fainting mother by emptying a whole bottle of smelling salts into her mouth. However, as the visits went on, Kate would become afraid her young guest might be bored – a fear she often had while entertaining – and always hoped to take her out for a walk to amuse her in some other way.

In early January news arrived that Ruskin was delirious; all Kate's hopes for his recovery were destroyed. In despair, she wrote to Joan, 'how distressing it is if he seems to get on a little [and] he is back again so soon. There seems no hope now. I wish someone would know of something to make him get better again. The delusions – are so sad, they make all recovery seem so far off.' His ups and downs and the uncertainty of his sanity were traumatic, even though Kate was not told all the details. 'Things are one long anxiety, aren't they?' she concluded in one letter to Joan Severn, begging for a few lines on a postcard, just to know how he was. She was more concerned over Ruskin's health than by her own inability to work, feeling 'faithless when I don't write – and worrying when I do – so [I] don't feel at Peace anyway.'[1]

But work had to be done, if only to further her career exhibiting in the London galleries. She prepared four new children's portraits for exhibition at the Royal Institute in March, but admitted to Joan they 'shan't do much credit to the institute this year!' Her intention was that they should reintroduce her name into the London gallery circles, and 'in a year or two I hope I shall improve a little. I'm very disgusted with myself – not to do better now.' After all four were left unsold, she tried to hide her disappointment, claiming that she felt 'none were worth buying. I certainly would not buy them myself'.[2] But she was shaken, nonetheless.

Slowly her confidence returned, and her spirits were buoyed by the unseasonably warm January weather, with polyanthus and primroses in bloom in her garden: promises of spring, her best working season. In addition, news arrived that Ruskin was well enough for Joan Severn to take a holiday, which Kate advised. But Kate's cheerfulness was short-lived. Young, charming Eddie Dadd had to return to his family in Germany and a deep feeling of loneliness overcame her: 'I feel I am a changed person and shall never be my old self any more. I often wonder at the way I do miss *Him* [Ruskin] it is such an unutterable loss as if the best of everything has gone and nothing so nice or so happy or so interesting again. You would think in all this time I should have got used to it – used to doing without him – but I have not one bit – ,' she moaned to Joan Severn.[3] The consolation she badly needed fortunately came from her work and her ability to lose herself in her fantasies – especially those romantic daydreams based on her love for Ruskin. The memories of their time spent together, of crying over his angry letters and his apologetic responses, now helped her to fill a notebook with page after page of intense, love-lorn verses. Many were based on the painful theme of her undying love of the Master:

> *It is so glorious just to say*
> *I loved him all at once – one day –*
> *A winter's day. Then came the spring*
> *And only deepened the thing.*
> *I think it deepen'd – I'm not sure*
> *If there was room to love you more.*
> *Then summer followed – and my love*
> *Took colour from the skies above.*
> *Then weeks – and months – and years there came,*
> *And I, well, loved on – just the same.*
> *Then, Dear stretch out your hands – and let me lie*
> *Within them as I slowly die,*
> *Then stoop your head to mine and give –*
> *Ah, not a kiss – or I should live.*[4]

To Kate, steeped in thoughts of everlasting love, Ruskin's silence took on a greater, more spiritual importance. It became a sacrifice; a necessary trial which, like her loneliness, she was forced to endure. But although her letters clearly show how she tried to disguise her depression – for example, by describing happy visits with friends and relatives – she failed to hide from him the bitterness and pain that still plagued her life. In mid-January she suffered an especially painful relapse in her illness, so severe that she lacked the strength

Original watercolour to 'Cross Patch', for *Mother Goose*, 1881, showing a dejected maiden in an aesthetic interior. She smiled in the original version.

even to write to Joan Severn. When she was better she wrote, 'I've got such a cold in my head I can hardly hold up – (it isn't influenza). So very tiresome for it is a perfect picture of a morning, sun out, lovely.' Still suffering enough that she could barely lift her pen, she ended the short letter: 'Goodbye. Head too bad to go on.'[5] Typically, she was not completely frank about the cause of her illness, not even to Joan. Instead she went on to explain how Stacy Marks and his wife had visited her studio and, albeit reluctantly, had given valuable advice on how she should redirect her talent towards successful exhibiting. Then, too, in January a royal messenger had delivered a portrait medallion from the Empress Frederick, in return for her Christmas almanack. Such displays of concern and affection from old friends and acquaintances naturally meant a great deal to her. They were important enough to describe in detail to Joan Severn, who in turn related them to Ruskin.

The news that Ruskin spent most of his days muttering about young girls, but failed to mention Kate, came as no real surprise. At last she had accepted his amazingly neglectful and callous behaviour. She was convinced that he could not help himself: it was to be attributed entirely to his illness – 'all madness as all things are that ever he does unkindly' – and not to any lack of affection. Kate explained to Joan how her primary concern remained the fact that she could not see him: 'If only he could be himself again and I could see him . . .'[6] A short time later, startled by a rumour that Ruskin was unconscious, Kate wrote a frantic plea for news. Believing the reports to be true, she felt that Joan Severn had betrayed her by not writing sooner of this important development. Several days later, a reassuring letter arrived from Joan, explaining that all was well at Brantwood, and that she had in fact spent the last few hours rearranging Ruskin's bedroom ('quite a wonderful day's work'), though she was uncertain whether it would go unnoticed or be appreciated. During the interim Kate had worked herself into a frenzied state; she described herself as nervous and exhausted, 'till my head – feels quite excited . . . Then it won't keep still inside or feels as if it won't – and it has got into dark days again. So very trying.'[7] This trauma was caused by worry and the fear that Ruskin might slip silently away, leaving her helpless and even more alone than she already was. She yearned to make one final effort to show her deep affection, especially now she felt she had dreadfully neglected him over the past few weeks. She sent a specially constructed birthday card, consisting of two of his favourite Greenaway girlies holding a rose wreath over the head of a tiny young blonde child, labelled 'Rosie' – to make sure that he understood she represented Rose La Touche. In return, Joan Severn sent a detailed description of Ruskin's reactions, saying that he was 'just that much himself again'; and Kate burst into tears of joy.

Kate's anxiety over Ruskin's health made it difficult for her to cope with her own illness. Each time a fresh attack threatened her, she bore it silently, describing it to friends as 'mere rheumatism'. The pain was often intense, her

'Girl and Two Babies', original watercolour frontispiece to *A Day in a Child's Life*, 1881.

167

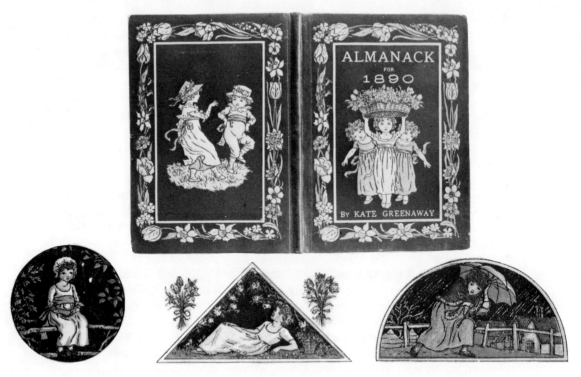

Almanack for 1890 with black background: cover and three geometric designs.

nights sleepless, making her irritable and depressed. She felt slightly better with the spring-like weather and she was cheered by reading extracts from Ruskin's writings that were published in the papers.[8]

Spring brought renewed energy and further plans, as well as the chance to paint outdoors. At Easter Kate joined Helen Allingham and her children at Freshwater, on the Isle of Wight. Helen stayed with the Tennysons, and Kate took rooms nearby, calling daily upon Helen. As Helen later recalled, she would then lead her friend to a favourite spot, 'either to some pretty old thatched cottages around Farringford or to the old dairy in the grounds, when we often had a friendly visit from the great poet himself, or from Mr. Hallam Tennyson, with an invitation to come up to tea.'[9] Kate loved to visit the poet who was 'very quick and says *astonishing* things'; and she thoroughly enjoyed working outdoors, despite the extreme cold. Most important of all, she derived comfort and confidence from painting alongside her much-admired colleague, whose work the *Times* had once claimed was 'the very model of what an English watercolour should be'.

On her return to London she exhibited two new works at the Royal Academy, the first time she had shown there for ten years. These were a portrait head of a little boy, and the picture an *Athenaeum* critic called 'a charmingly ingenious and bright "Girl's Head"'. Her painting trips to the countryside with Helen Allingham continued, but during their long summer afternoon sessions, working side by side sketching the same subjects ('generally silent – for she was a very earnest, hard worker', Helen remembered), it became clear that Kate's pictures lacked the individuality she sought. In fact they often appeared as poor, though at first unconscious, imitations of Helen's work, her landscapes drawn and painted in the same meticulous manner, her figures dressed and placed in similar poses and identical settings. Kate's struggles with her short-sightedness presented an additional problem, as Helen recalled: 'I remember her exclaiming one day at Pinner, "What am I to do? When I look at the roof it is all a red blur – when I put on my spectacles I see every crack in the tiles."' In consequence, Kate decided it would be best, at least for her, if the two stopped painting together, and pursued their careers separately. According to Helen later, their separation was friendly, and 'whether days or months passed between our meetings, I was always sure of the same hearty greeting from her.'[10] Kate had made this new decision – a painful one, for she loved Helen's companionship – out of concern for her future as a gallery artist, and her reasoning was simple. She had achieved her success in the past by working completely alone, without distractions (apart from Ruskin); and now, with the same belief in her abilities, she preferred to struggle privately to develop her own watercolour style.

In August Kate's worst fears for a lonely future began to be realized, when her dearly beloved father contracted pneumonia. Kate stopped all painting and cancelled a visit to Witley, in order to devote her days to nursing him. But his condition gradually worsened, and on 26 August John Greenaway died, aged seventy-three. His was a particularly depressing death, coming at the end of a long and hard-fought career. With the rise of photo-engraving, his business had gradually deteriorated, so that he and his wife were almost totally dependent upon Kate. However, right up until his death John Greenaway had held a position of respect among his engraving and publishing colleagues, as a friend and associate at the *Illustrated London News* made clear: 'He has left behind him

Helen Allingham and Kate in Kate's Hampstead garden. Even here Kate betrays an aversion to photography while looking admiringly at Helen.

Out for a walk, a watercolour in the style Kate used in painting under the influence of Helen Allingham.

an unblemished character and a respected name.' This was little consolation to Kate, now beside herself with grief. She never really recovered from his loss, and her mother was plunged into a depression that drained her of the will to live. Fortunately, Kate's brother Johnnie was still living with her, and when he was at home he provided much-needed comfort. But, as he was editor of an important chemistry journal and a prolific author of chemistry textbooks, his work often took him away from the house of mourning. Moreover, John Greenaway's death also brought financial worries. In his will he left his wife a mere £295.3*s.*, a pitiful amount that could not go far in paying his wife's or Kate's medical bills, or in running the large Hampstead house.

It was a time of personal and professional crisis. Bereft of her trusted confidant, Kate felt alone; but the practicality she inherited from her mother helped her to prepare for her responsibilities in supporting the family. She spent a day sorting through her studio cupboards and decided that there were works enough for an exhibition of old drawings, illustrations and paintings which could be sold to alleviate the financial distress. Her frank, business-like letter to the Fine Art Society, proposing the exhibition idea, was hastily written and suggests she did not want to think too long, or she might change her mind about the sale.[11] It was clearly painful for her to have to sell off the works that had propelled her to fame, for they had both sentimental and morale-boosting value.

The Fine Art Society made hurried arrangements, and Kate's first solo exhibition opened to the public a month later, on 7 February 1891. With 150 exhibits, all for sale, this was the largest showing of her works during her lifetime. The motivation behind the exhibition was not only financial, for, according to the eloquent catalogue essay, it was also intended to re-establish her importance in the art world. The essay attacked the Greenaway imitators, 'a number of so-called artists, thinking to reap where she had sown', noting that they were particularly prevalent in Germany. 'Has she founded a school, or only started a fashion?' the essayist asked, then urged visitors to decide for themselves by studying and buying works 'touched with genius'.[12] She shared the gallery with Hugh Thomson, a recently acclaimed illustrator working in the style of Caldecott. Thomson had made his reputation with illustrations for Macmillan's edition of *The Vicar of Wakefield*, and his original drawings hung in a gallery adjacent to Kate's. Crowds of friends and admirers ignored an unusually heavy winter fog that day to attend the tea-time viewing, and when Hugh Thomson arrived at four, he and his wife discovered that 'the rooms were crowded and we could scarcely force our way through'; although he conceded that the crowds were 'most, of course to see Miss Greenaway's drawings'.[13]

Altogether, sales brought in £1,350, of which Kate received £964. While this was encouraging, the sale had cleared Kate's studio of many cherished works that had taken months, even years, to complete; and all for an amount not even near to that she had earned from her first successful book. It was even more depressing to find that a large number of the new watercolour landscapes – those done under Helen Allingham's keen direction – remained unsold. Moreover, reviews of her exhibition dwelt at length on her earlier career, and her new watercolours were for the most part ignored. The *Athenaeum* critic dismissed the exhibition in one sentence: 'The collection of drawings by Miss Greenaway is exactly such as all her admirers could wish to see.' No mention was made of superlative technical skill, accurate natural detail or keen sense of observation – qualities she had struggled to put into her work. Kate could not accept her critics' verdict and, undeterred, she spent her time during the next two years preparing new and more ambitious works for exhibition. Determined, she refused to be distracted from her goal, even when her doctor's husband suggested that she take a restful cruise on one of his steamships. It shows that while her doctor believed such a rest was important to restore her patient's health, Kate felt her career was more important than a needless and expensive (in time if not in money) excursion abroad. As a result, almost all her time was spent painting and completing the new almanack illustrations.

In early autumn, exhausted and in need of a rest, Kate did accept the invitation of a friend and patron, the Hon. Gerald Ponsonby and his wife, who asked her to spend some time with them at their Bournemouth summer home. This was the first of a series of annual autumn visits to Bournemouth; it was too crowded for her liking, but its pretty seaside gardens and the nearby picturesque villages of Christchurch and Poole were a great pleasure. This year she painted portraits of the Ponsonby girls; and this and every year after, she and Gerald Ponsonby enjoyed long discussions about art, antiques and books. Ponsonby was a respected connoisseur, who advised several people on antiques, and was an active member of the Burlington Fine Art Club. Seventeen years Kate's senior, he held a position in her life not unlike that earlier occupied

Brother and Sister, a watercolour placing meticulously drawn figures in a rough, unfinished springtime setting, thereby showing how Kate first completed her figures, then painted in the backgrounds.

by Frederick Locker. Ponsonby and his delightful wife, Lady Maria, had all the grace and charm Kate admired. When conversation turned gloomy and Kate began to complain – something she found very difficult to avoid, although she feared it would alienate her friends – Lady Maria was adept at steering the subject back to more pleasant things. Content in their company, Kate always found leaving Bournemouth difficult, and she usually took with her reminders of the pleasant times in the form of flowers or cuttings from exotic plants in the Ponsonby garden, which she transplanted to Frognal.

Her return to London, refreshed and restored, gave her the energy to plunge whole-heartedly into her painting. In late November, she received a request from an editor of the children's magazine *The Youth's Companion*, asking for an article on children's dress, which she flatly refused. 'I have never written anything of the sort – and at the present time – I have not time to spare for anything of the sort.'[14] Work continued throughout the spring and summer of 1892, interrupted only in August, again to visit the Ponsonbys. The previous six months had been hard, working long hours in her studio, undisturbed for weeks on end, with no news from Brantwood and only her own 'increasing neuralgia' to worry her. And so, shortly after her visit to Bournemouth, Kate decided to renew her correspondence with Joan Severn, then still nursing Ruskin at Brantwood. Kate's letter was thoughtful and considerate: 'I had a very nice time at Bournemouth – I don't love the place – but I do the people . . . I had a very happy time with the kindest of people.' But it soon became clear that her real reason for writing was to re-establish contact with a trusted friend. She needed someone who would understand her fears as she now endured alarming bouts of pain. The hot weather, which usually brought comfort, had this year caused a recurrence of her mysterious illness: 'It was very warm so I do not I am sorry to say feel much better,' she confessed. 'I shall I expect have to wait for a little cooler weather for that.'[15]

In the middle of an uninspired September she also began to feel the strain of again nursing her ill mother while her brother was away on holiday, leaving her to cope alone. She felt trapped by her domestic duties, but even more so by her professional obligations. She resented having to make her living now that her fame would not pay for a badly needed rest. Only the heartening news that Ruskin was much better helped to revive her spirits. She wrote to Joan: 'It is almost strange *now* after so long to think of him as so well, though I suppose he can do no work – make no effort – Can he read – does he still care to – do you think he feels content?' As soon as her mother showed signs of recovery, Kate planned to have a holiday, this time at Newhaven Court, Cromer, the seaside home of the Locker-Lampson family (Locker had changed his name in 1885, in order to benefit under the terms of his father-in-law's will). Kate found the waiting strenuous for, as she complained to Joan Severn, 'I feel tired and done up – I am generally away at this time and I miss it – and have constant neuralgia in consequence.'[16]

She arrived at Cromer with autographed copies of *The Language of Flowers* and her latest almanack to give to Dolly, her favourite of the four Locker-Lampson children. She was by then in acute pain, which she tried to hide by filling her visit with activity – giving Dolly drawing lessons, playing games with Maud and the two boys, wandering the seaside cliffs with them to watch the sun sink into the sea, or walking on the beach, stopping to make sketches with the end of her umbrella dipped in the sand. All the while Kate kept a shrewd eye out for a young child to sketch; she loved to watch the tiny infants in prams on the beach, or their older brothers and sisters paddling along the shore. She often pointed out the absurd antics of some plump gentleman bather floundering in the waves, and sometimes she would boldly march up to a child to ask his name and listen to his impressions of the sea. 'I can see her now, apparelled for a walk in a rather short skirt, with a plain little cape gathered about her shoulders and wide-brimmed felt hat on her head; she looked something like a gnome,' Oliver Locker-Lampson recalled years later of his walks with Kate at Cromer. It was her unassuming appearance, combined with her childish spirits that found release in rippling laughter and giggles of delight, that endeared Kate to the Locker-Lampson children. She became a trusted comrade, willing to dash about the hedgerow below the house playing hide and seek, or to bake potatoes in the revolving summerhouse perched on a hillside in the garden. She willingly drew them pictures, pulling faces while she worked to keep their attention; and, when one of the children was ill, she would write entertaining illustrated letters to send to the sick room until the invalid recovered.

These delights apart, Kate chose to visit Cromer for her health. As a seaside retreat, with bracing North Sea breezes appreciated by a select few since the early 1800s, Cromer offered a chance for Kate to recover from her painful attacks of muscular rheumatism. Her hostess ordered hot seawater baths (climbing the steep cliff walkway, a local workman brought up the water in buckets suspended from a yoke around his neck). In the evenings roaring log fires warmed the huge Queen Anne style house famous among its guests for its surprises – the huge stuffed owl hung on wires over the entry, the spring-hung doors that shot open at a touch, leading to large, draughty rooms and cold hallways. Kate always felt the cold and at Newhaven Court constantly fell victim to the damp. But she loved the house, its relaxed atmosphere and the Norfolk seaside, where 'the propriety I have been used to seems thrown to the winds – but one easily gets hardened, I find.'

Kate stayed at Cromer for three enchanted weeks, until it became evident that, instead of improving, her pain was growing worse. Nothing could ease her suffering, and in her vulnerable and easily irritated state she had an argument with Locker about her future. He insisted that she must not stop illustrating and she insisted that it was impossible for her to go on. She returned to Hampstead dazed, considerably weaker, and apologetic, and wrote to Locker: 'I was irritable and you were – irrational. That is not the right word – but you enunciated opinions that I thought were not quite sound, and I was stupid enough not to agree with you. Time is too short for these arguments, at least so I think, so let us have no more of them.'[17] Above all she missed the 'nice noise' of the waves and the children's laughter, and she continued her letters to Dolly ('I can't tell you how much I miss you and Maud'), sent with books and drawing lessons which were to be returned to her for correction.

Gradually the pain subsided, and early in November she felt well enough to make plans for a second Fine Art Society exhibition. She had also agreed to a brief exhibition of twenty watercolours at Messrs Van Baerle, Glasgow – the first and only showing of her works in Scotland. In addition, she completed drawings for a new almanack; but, again, these were repetitive and uninspired. She was plagued by the very real threat of her health breaking down, taking away her ability to paint and crippling her future. It was a horrifying prospect.

News that Ruskin was much better – which meant that her return to Brantwood was a possibility – helped to revive her spirits, and old memories flooded back. She spent a day dreaming about it and clearly remembered the last time: '. . . it was in the summer in June when the wild roses were out and the irises in the garden. It feels very long ago,' she wrote to Joan Severn.[18] First, however, her work had to be finished. She declined to send new pictures to the Royal Institute in March, directing all her energy into paintings for the more important Fine Art Society exhibition.

By late December Kate was worn out with having to comfort her mother, as well as being harassed by her own struggles to paint against time as the hours of daylight decreased. As a result, she had neither the time nor the energy to prepare Ruskin's Christmas drawing, which left her feeling guilty. 'I am considerably done up – it is too stupid and tiresome,' she apologized to Joan Severn, her default made even more embarrassing by the fact that Joan had sent a Christmas turkey from Brantwood. To make amends, she set aside the time to paint a tiny New Year's drawing, which she sent with her apologies that it was not better, 'but *I am* overdone just now . . . and it takes so much of my time.'[19]

The depressing winter days of 1893 left a trail of illness in the Greenaway family. It was only at the end of January, after nearly a month's suffering, that Kate found enough time to describe her woes to Joan Severn. 'We've been very dull of late years, almost feeling – that existence at all is a mistake,' she wrote, before listing her problems: her mother was still very ill; Johnnie had a bad cold and sore throat which she feared she would also get; both her sister Fanny and her sister Lizzie's husband were very ill. Besides nursing her mother and brother, Kate was struggling to maintain her output, managing to work on new almanack illustrations as well as finalizing plans for the exhibition. She broke a long silence with Helen Allingham and invited her for tea to discuss gallery percentages and framing costs; but when Helen arrived, armed with all the facts, her efficient replies made Kate feel hopelessly inadequate. Kate hated business details, the scraping about for money, and found Helen (now supporting her family by her painting) 'so very (*near frightfully*) businesslike –'. Moreover, the current unsettled state of the art market and the previous year's poor sales figures, made her especially concerned about her exhibition; and she complained to Joan Severn about how it had been 'a frightful year for *everything* – art, business, everything – I do hope times will get better – .'[20]

The exhibition catalogue provided unexpected problems as well. Kate wanted each work described in the catalogue, and on labels in the gallery, with comments on intent and origins. One early watercolour of a rock, done under Ruskin's sharp supervision at Brantwood – 'Ah, many have begun it,' he had challenged – now gave her special difficulties. She could not remember the specific incident surrounding the picture, and wrote to ask Ruskin for help. 'I am quite at a loss what to say – I wonder if Mr. Ruskin remembers all about it – ' she asked Joan Severn.[21] But Ruskin remained silent, and in the catalogue the picture was described only briefly, Then, with the preparations near completion, Kate somehow managed to send a small watercolour for Ruskin's birthday, although again she found it necessary to apologize for its size, 'but I have no time to help it'.[22] In addition to her work, in early spring she had forced herself to visit the London galleries to survey her competition; there she found encouraging signs of a change in attitude: works by her favourite Pre-Raphaelites, once out of favour, were now being reassessed, as were the old master painters Ruskin had taught her to admire. She knew how pleased he would be with this turn-about in taste, and it gave her hope for her own exhibition.

Spring brought a re-evaluation of her progress and a reminder of what still needed to be done before the showing. She was horrified to discover that her painting retreat at the Evans's house at Witley was now threatened. Business had not been good for her old friend after the process engravers, with their faster, more efficient techniques of photo-engraving, had begun to take away important commissions. Then, earlier in the year, Evans had suffered a cerebral haemorrhage which had left him weak and unable to work. The once familiar spirit and ambition quickly drained from him. All he wanted was to retire to peaceful surroundings, and he intended to sell the Witley house to finance the move; a decision which placed a further, unexpected strain on Kate. She had come to rely on her spring visits to the Evans household; not only did the Witley countryside provide unlimited painting subjects, but the Evans family helped to revive her spirit. The immediate requirement, however, was to get her Witley-inspired landscapes ready for her exhibition, and Kate decided to make quick painting trips to the country, hoping to finish her paintings before Evans sold his house. Each week she made preliminary sketches in the fields and returned to Hampstead to complete the picture, her hectic pace continuing for several months. 'This year is certainly not my own,' she wrote to Joan

The Fable of the Girl and her Milk Pail. A watercolour exhibited at the Fine Art Society, 1894, where it sold for 45 guineas.

Severn, during one spell at home for her birthday on St Patrick's Day. Joan had sent a birthday packet specially prepared to mark both occasions, enclosing a shamrock and a fresh lock of Ruskin's hair. The latter was, of course, received with raptures, as Kate wrote:

> What beautiful fine hair it is. I had a little piece that you gave me once before – but I much liked having this – it made me feel all the old times back – the sight of it – and think of the pity of it all and what he might yet be if only Fate had been kind instead of cruel. I so often come across beautiful pieces of his writing and when I feel he might still be saying those things – it is oh so great a misfortune![23]

In another letter she thanked Joan for the Brantwood daffodils. 'I wish I could have seen them growing – and all of it – the primroses – the lake – the mountains – the moor – the stone walls with the pretty little things growing on them – the flower field when the white narcissus are out on the slope – it is all so beautiful and I know so well how it would all look.' For the first time she acknowledged that time might now have placed an impassable barrier between Ruskin and herself, and this made her less anxious to visit him. She worried that he might not recognize her now she was greying, and she admitted to Joan, 'It is a curious feeling to think of seeing him again. I fear I shall feel him much changed. I do not see how I can help it.'[24]

176

At the end of a year devoted almost entirely to her exhibition (her only book work had been the drawings for the now inevitable almanack), Kate was confident all was ready. It had been a difficult time, with new 'fainting spells' and worries about finance so much uninterrupting her painting. She had paid for it from a variety of sources, including forty-five guineas for five pictures sold at the Columbian Exhibition, Chicago, as well as money from the sale of her original drawings for the previous year's almanack to the Manchester stationers, Palmer, Howe and Company, who afterwards used them for 'sanitary nursery wallpapers'. They were advertised as authorized by the artist, and to Kate's delight, these were impressively printed. After such an effort to make her exhibition a success, Kate was depressed that in early December the dates were still not fixed. Then, on 29 December, after what she described to Gerald Ponsonby as about nine plan changes, the date had 'at LAST' been set for 20 January 1894:

> First they couldn't, then they could. First the small room and then the big one. HE [Marcus Huish, gallery director] suggested palms to fill up the corners. Think of my poor little works floating about in that big room. I wrote a beautiful letter, suggesting that a considerable amount of palms seemed inevitable – but the letter was not allowed to be sent, my brother considered it FLIPPANT and unbusiness-like. I thought this rather hard, as I had abstained from remarking that a few apple trees or roses might be more in accordance with the sentiment of my drawings than plants of an oriental character. However I am going to have the small room.[25]

The small room was just as well, for the exhibition was thirty frames smaller than the previous one. The gallery was again shared, this time with two artists: Alfred Parsons showed book illustrations and the Earl of Dunmore travel pictures. Kate's 120 watercolours and drawings included what remained of her illustrations from *Under the Window* to her latest almanack, as well as the Witley landscapes. The large number of these paintings shows that Kate was trying to establish herself as a studio artist: a plan which, unfortunately, did not altogether succeed. The critics were still unwilling to forget her past reputation. The *Athenaeum* (27 January 1894) claimed that the pictures were 'such as half Europe and America have delighted in . . . they do not differ from what Miss Greenaway has done before'. Worse still, the shrewd reviewer pointed out that Kate's new style was not wholly her own, but relied on that of another, technically more proficient artist: 'The manifest disproportions of some of her landscapes containing houses and figures indicate the present limits of her powers. Some of her cottages are rather too much in Mrs. Allingham's vein.' The *Magazine of Art* review was equally unenthusiastic. More importantly, sales were disappointing, and a distinct falling off from last time. £1,067.16s. was taken, of which Kate received £799; and this came mostly from well meaning friends such as Joan Severn, who paid £36 for the beautifully finished watercolour *At a Garden Door*, or Frederick Locker-Lampson, who paid £10 for *A Girl's Head*. The *Illustrated London News* believed it a fitting tribute to their deceased employee, John Greenaway, to help his struggling daughter at this time, and purchased two pictures for a total of £35.

On 2 February a new jolt brought more pressing worries. After a long and distressing series of illnesses, Mrs Greenaway died, aged eighty-one. Kate had been expecting this, and had forced herself to sit by her mother and watch her slip away. 'She has no pain but it feels dreadful to me to feel she is going to die and that nothing can help it,' she had written in despair to Joan Severn late in January. The sudden reality of the situation plunged her deeper into what now seemed an inescapable loneliness; it was almost too much to bear. Even her brother, still so often away on business, failed to brighten the gloom. Apart from occasional letters and calls from a few friends, Kate was now left completely alone in a rapidly emptying studio.

In the week immediately following her mother's funeral, Kate understandably turned from a household deep in mourning to seek the company of friends like the Ponsonbys, who had offered sympathy and compassion in the past. She wrote to Gerald Ponsonby: 'You and Lady Maria have been *so kind* – I can't tell you *how* much it has been to me to feel I have such friends as you always are to me . . . We certainly do feel desolate and strange but I know in time the very dreadful feeling will pass off though I also know life must be forever a different feeling for I have never felt the same since my father died.' Longing to escape her gloom, she begged an invitation to tea, reassuring them 'you will find me grateful for the good tea I hope,' and promising not to talk of death – which now greatly preoccupied her. Afterwards she returned to Hampstead in good spirits and prepared to carry on working; her recovery was characteristic of the determination she often displayed despite upsets.[26]

But, from this time on, Kate only half-heartedly continued her painting, as the loss of her mother weighed heavily on her mind: 'I seem to miss my mother more and more instead of less – but I know this is often the case with me.' For most of this year she preferred visiting old friends and making new and hopefully valuable acquaintances, whose names she duly entered in her address book. Some felt that she had changed, abandoning her natural shyness to grasp these brief opportunities to enjoy herself and try to forget her problems. For example, in April she was a guest for a country weekend in Berkshire, at Lady Jeune's home, Arlington Manor. There, among the large number of society lions and lionesses gathered by this famous hostess, Kate, to the surprise of her friend, opened up and enjoyed herself, taking down the names of prospective patrons in the process. She had in fact allowed her painting to fall by the wayside, a girl's portrait head exhibited at the Royal Institute being the year's only attempt to further her career. When requests for illustrations arrived she politely, but curtly, replied, 'I am sorry to be unable to help you. I am illustrating *no books* at present. It is difficult to say what ideas are likely to take now.' Similarly, when Joan Severn sent her an unfavourable review of the new almanack, she attacked her critics: 'They make me so angry because they say you do it like this one or that – it is all very well to wish to draw for books but if people won't buy the books what is to be done? –'[27] She seemed to want to forget about earning her living, until the shock of her mother's death had worn off.

While she was in this despondent mood a more persuasive request was made; one which, despite her objections, she found she could not refuse. It came from the indefatigable young editor of the Philadelphia *Ladies' Home Journal,*

Edward Bok, who, in April, was in England to collect material for his magazine. He had succeeded in making the *Ladies' Home Journal* a very popular periodical among American women readers, both single and married, by promoting a wholesome, motherly image in its pages. He now wanted a series of articles written and illustrated by prominent figures in English children's literature. His first target was the indomitable Charles Lutwidge Dodgson (Lewis Carroll), and he hoped to commission a sequel to the *Alice* books for his magazine. Despite Bok's enthusiasm, and his claim that Dodgson was disappointing 'the thousands of American children who love you and who would gladly welcome "Lewis Carroll" back', Dodgson categorically refused him, at one time even disavowing authorship of *Alice*. To the stubborn Bok, this was a surprising blow. He returned to London and to more disappointment when Florence Nightingale refused his request for an autobiographical article, sending her refusal through a servant, who returned his business card with a curt, 'Miss Nightingale never receives strangers.' His ego wounded, yet determined not to go home until he had succeeded in persuading one new contribution out of a famous personality, he approached the legendary Miss Greenaway. He was told categorically that she never gave interviews and rarely appeared in public; and, when he consulted her publishers, a Routledge staff member advised against approaching Kate. 'We conduct all our business with her by correspondence – I have never seen her personally myself.' However, despite his earlier failures, Bok was sure he could crack the wall around Miss Greenaway. After all, he had once charmed Gladstone into consenting to write for him, by first offering to publish a series by his wife.

He went to Hampstead and knocked at Kate's door. It was opened by a hostile-looking woman, Kate's sister, who was obviously disturbed by this intrusion, as the family was still in mourning. 'Miss Greenaway is not at home,' she snapped, then tried to shut the door. 'But pardon me, has not Miss Greenaway returned? Is not that she?' he persisted, and when the woman turned to see, he placed his foot in the doorway and peered round its edge to watch a small, plainly dressed woman descend the stairs. He quickly stepped inside, before Kate's sister could close the door. He introduced himself, as he had done to Lewis Carroll, as a representative of the thousands of American children who admired her books. Without her glasses, Kate squinted disapprovingly, a little astonished at such impertinence. However, she could not be rude to an admirer, especially one who had come all the way from America to see her. There was something vaguely familiar about Bok, this thirty-one-year-old dapper gentleman with his well-cut clothes and courteous manner quite reminiscent of William Loftie at their first meeting. Whatever her reasons, Kate surprised her sister by inviting Bok into the garden, where, as he later recalled in his autobiography, they sat 'under the apple tree of Miss Greenaway's pictures. It was in full bloom, a veritable picture of spring loveliness.' There he set about charming her, talking of what he guessed were her favourite subjects – her flowers, books and, of course, the weather. Then a cat sauntered fearlessly over to inspect him. He stroked it, recognizing it from one of her books, and Kate noticeably warmed towards him. Only then did he sense that he was making headway. He seized the opportunity to describe his profession and to explain how he wanted Greenaway illustrations for his magazine; at this point, he remembered, 'Miss Greenaway conveyed the unmistakable impression that she had been trapped.' After luncheon in the garden, and more polite conversation, he returned to his proposal. She soon perceptibly thawed and he left with her promise that she would send one page of line illustrations – but only one page. However, the £30 a page serial rights he promised made her think again: it was as much as she charged for a finished watercolour landscape, which took many more hours to complete. She entered his name and address twice in her address book, and over the next two years, contrary to her original plan, she sent him several more drawings. It was, after all, easy money, earned from the most persistent and rewarding of her new patrons.[28]

At the end of April, following a few days rest at Rowfant, Kate had almost completely recovered from the sorrow of her mother's death. 'I think I am feeling stronger, but sometimes I do not feel very well, but of course it is rather a slow process, and it requires patience, which quality I don't possess,' she wrote to Maria Ponsonby on her return. 'I am at work again now – my ideas are coming back to me. I feel as if I'd been in the earth for the winter and was beginning to wake up.' The process was indeed slow, but she was determined to champion Ruskin's naturalism in her next works. She started on a new subject: a river scene using the blossom-filled view outside her studio for inspiration – a variation on her first disastrous riverbed studies for Ruskin. Clearly she had noticed that such nature studies were absent from the London galleries, and she intended to fill that gap.

But efforts to return to studio painting were abandoned by early summer, when friends again lured her into her beloved countryside. Then, at the end of July, Kate made a sudden return to Brantwood, and found Ruskin in complete seclusion, his days carefully guarded from intruders by Joan Severn. Although he was strong enough for occasional walks, his condition had considerably deteriorated, and he rarely spoke more than a few syllables. He was unable to write anything. His last letter (written the previous year to Susie Beever, then dying across the lake) had taken three tortured hours to write and consisted of eight short, almost illegible lines, pathetic in sentiment: 'I cannot think of you – except as cheerful and conquering all minor suffering – .' Kate had prepared herself for the worst, but on her arrival she was surprised to find Ruskin alert and responsive. After her return she described her amazement to Gerald Ponsonby: 'I found Mr. Ruskin so much better than I expected, of course not his old self, yet even at times there really seemed no difference – it has been great happiness – and the country there – as you know – is lovely beyond words.' She avoided embarrassing silences by keeping busy, taking brief excursions into the mountains, once visiting Wordsworth's home at nearby Grasmere, afterwards noting that Dove Cottage was being refurbished with period furniture ('protected by strings from the enthusiastic Americans'). Just before she left, Joan Severn gave her permission to dig in the Master's garden and she returned to London laden with precious cuttings and plants for her own garden. On arrival, she immediately wrote to thank Ruskin: 'I was so sorry to leave you – I am so sorry to have left – I feel too mournful to write today, yet long to say

The Locker dog, Dinah, August 1895, watercolour by Kate Greenaway.

just a few words to tell you what great happiness it has been to see you once more – and talk to you – I am so glad I have seen you.'[29]

The following week she left the uncomfortably close and warm summer weather in Hampstead for the bracing sea breezes at Cromer, where she walked the beach and completed Frederick Locker's book-plate. Instead of going back to London, she went south for her annual visit to the Ponsonbys at Bournemouth. She returned home via Lady Jeune's Berkshire home in early September ('lots to paint on the lonely downs'), her weeks of rushing about and sightseeing brought to an abrupt halt at the doorstep of a vacant house and studio as her brother was away on holiday in North Wales. 'I am desperately lonely here with no one but the dog,' she confessed to Maria Ponsonby, adding that even pampered Rover was little comfort. The 'faithful tyrant' often abandoned her for the Heath, returning at all hours for his specially prepared chop, cakes and sweets.[30]

By October, however, Kate forced herself to paint, only interrupting her work for short visits to the galleries. There hung works by members of the scandalous New English Art Club, who rejected the Royal Academy in favour of the more adventurous Impressionists. Their most effective member was Aubrey Beardsley, whose drawings horrified Kate; she once wrote to Maria Ponsonby, 'Tell Mr. Ponsonby I HATE Beardsley more than ever.' She could not admire the clarity of Beardsley's line when it was used to depict such shocking characters and stark, unnatural settings. Ironically, Beardsley had, as a boy, greatly admired Kate's work, and his first commission had been to copy Greenaway figures on menu cards. On another visit to a gallery, Kate studied some impressionistic children's portraits, which more than ever convinced her of the need for clarity in painting: to her the Impressionist haze clouded over what remained of good sense and true Beauty (in the Ruskinian sense). She returned home convinced that outline, the careful delineation of a model's features – the

181

Lucy Locket Lost her Pocket, watercolour exhibited at the Fine Art Society in 1894.

very tenets Ruskin had stressed in directing the Greenaway profile – had to be revived. The portrait exhibition had left her 'feeling a great deal of Funniness whenever I now visit an exhibition of Pictures'; and she intended to put things right.[31]

Reviving the once famous Greenaway profile, she made several pencil sketches and a painting of a six-month-old baby; this picture was successful enough to exhibit at the Royal Academy the following year. She also finished and posted her drawings to Edward Bok, with the accompanying letter: 'You must remember I only promised the one page of drawings.' She apologized that they were only brief ink sketches; they would certainly look better if printed in colour, although this had not been the original agreement. After due consideration, she had also decided that she might be able to find time to send more. 'If you care to have more I would do one when I could but I can't promise them at regular intervals or stated times.'[32] She stopped painting long enough to complete a second batch of drawings for Bok a short time later, and these, together with the first batch, were published in the March, April and Christmas issues of the following year. Her new almanack appeared in November; and although the *Athenaeum* acknowledged it, they failed to comment further. This is hardly surprising, for it was one of the thinnest of the almanack series, heavily padded at the back with postal information, the illustrations poorly printed and dwarfed by large margins. Kate attacked it for shoddiness, not at all pleased with Evans's assistants, who had produced the book (Evans was now too ill to work); and she determined that she would illustrate no more almanacks.

After the July visit to Brantwood, Kate had resolved to write longer, more detailed letters to Ruskin. She believed that these might entertain him and help to fill the idleness of his days, as well as to give her a chance to air her frustrations. She hated December, especially the dark mornings; but this year she had been slightly cheered by the arrival of her niece and nephew, Catherine and Eddie

Dadd, on Christmas holiday from their home in Plauen, Germany. They were the two bright spots in an otherwise gloomy Christmas, and Kate revelled in spoiling them. She planned a whirl of delights, day trips into London for the theatre, afterwards returning home for a children's party in their honour. Eddie delighted her by performing a barn dance, whirling round the huge studio with his sister, then singing nursery rhymes and 'Looby Loo'. Knowing Ruskin loved such things, Kate included them in her letters, but her descriptions suggest that beneath the laughter and holiday frolics lay a deep loneliness and depression at the passing of time. She noted with sadness that Eddie had changed, his 'little Correggio curls' gone for ever. When he left, she spent a gloomy New Year's Day, dreaming of tea with Ruskin; she then wrote to him: 'How much I wish things would not change so much – so soon – so often – I can never understand the *plan* of life at all, it is all so strange – try which way you will to think it out – it all seems of no use – yet you go on trying for this – for that – really for some mysterious end – you don't know.'[33]

There was little pleasure in Kate's life now, and, with little to look forward to, she decided that the fates had marked her to suffer. She slowly finished four large watercolours for exhibition; these were intended to have all the naturalistic qualities Ruskin would have approved. But only one, *Gleaners*

Gleaner theme sketched on a letter to Ruskin in preparation for the *Gleaners Going Home*.

Going Home, had in her estimation succeeded, 'the best – I fear you would say *of a bad lot*', she wrote to Ruskin. This was especially frustrating because she knew all too well what she wanted: 'but I always think they are going to be beautiful when I begin, then I generally get to hate them before they are done.' The *Gleaners* was indeed a sad painting, with four wistful Pre-Raphaelite-inspired maidens and six weary-looking Greenaway children, all tired after a day's gleaning in the fields, set against a murky sunset recalled from Cromer. It is easy to see why Kate attached so much importance to it, for it seemed to epitomize her present situation. The atmosphere was impossible to recreate – 'I can never make it look as I saw it one afternoon at Cromer, but my joy and enthusiasm was more delightful to myself than to the people who sat [for it].'[34] Figures that had once earned her fame in books now looked awkward in the natural settings of large paintings intended for the galleries. The *Gleaners* was not sold when it was exhibited at the Royal Institute, although the *Athenaeum* (16 March 1895) singled it out for its 'Stothardian theme, treated with much of Stothard's graceful spirit'.

Throughout the year Kate yearned for comfort and understanding. The rapid changes going on around her were depressing and she tried to insulate herself against further emotional upsets. Frederick Locker-Lampson's death on 30 May came as another great blow. 'I feel miserable – when the thought comes he is dead,' she told Ruskin.

In late October news came that Ruskin was well enough for her to visit Brantwood. She had been re-reading his letters, 'and I am ready sometimes to cry – sometimes to laugh'. However, the long-awaited visit proved frustrating. Ruskin was uncommunicative; if he spoke it was only to mumble some barely comprehensible word which he had decided was a favourite. This he repeated incessantly, until Joan Severn coaxed a more coherent response by speaking in their private baby talk. His eyesight was also a great deal worse and Joan had to read everything to him. This, Kate discovered, was of little use to her. She had hoped to receive at least slight nods of approval, after showing him her latest works. During the visit she tried to draw things she knew Ruskin would appreciate – a rock, a leaf, or his favourite flowers. He stared blankly over her shoulder; and, for the first time, she was unable to work in his presence. This failure seemed to be connected with a recurrence of her illness, and she was terrified now more than ever that another attack would finally cripple her facility to draw or paint. Only after she had returned to Hampstead did Kate find the courage to apologize for her inadequacies: 'I *am* sorry I can't draw when I am with you and can't do drawings you like now. One reason is I am never as strong as I was and I can't bear the strain. It is a considerable one to do a large pencil drawing of that sort. It wants to be so fresh and spontaneous – if it is rubbed out at all it is spoiled.' She had left Brantwood despondent, depressed and embarrassed by her weaknesses. She made a further pathetic confession to Ruskin some days later: 'It was worse leaving you this time than last – because you were so much your old self – and you were kind and gentle to me – . I shall all my life now think of those evenings.'[35] Sadly this was to be the last time she would ever see Ruskin.

Everything seemed uncertain, especially her painting, now that a recurrence of pain meant she could scarcely hold a brush. Obviously frightened by the attack, she did not know where to turn. When the pain eased, she thought more and more about safe, familiar illustration work; but she remained 'in a state of great perplexity'. The most distressing element, and one she had not anticipated, was that her illness had taken away her imaginative powers, as well as the desire to create larger, more challenging pictures. She now relied totally upon past skills, and churned out dull, uninspired copies of objects or scenes from nature, 'because I naturally do just what I see and do not think of the way to do it at all', she told Ruskin.[36] Her pencil drawings and watercolours became loose, the line indistinct, even sloppy. She even modified her harsh opinion of the Impressionists, thinking that theirs was a style that might hide poor draughtsmanship under an atmospheric haze. 'I have got to love the making of form by shade – the softness of it,' she wrote Ruskin. 'To be an impressionist opens a good wide space for leaving a good deal that is difficult to do *undone* – at least so it seems to me. It is so easy to begin, so difficult to finish.'[37] Later she attended a lecture by Roger Fry, and was puzzled by his belief that only

Kate Greenaway in 1895, from a photograph taken by Lily Evans.

'superior minds could like impressionism'. Slowly her new work drifted into a relaxed shoddiness that would have horrified Ruskin, who loathed the Impressionists; she still carefully defined the outlines of her figures, but now set them in vague landscapes.

These and other paintings were part of hurried preparations for a forthcoming exhibition. In spite of her illness and pain, she was determined to paint saleable pictures. By way of light relief, in December she prepared a new batch of Greenaway sketches, pen and ink children in the famous Greenaway style, which fulfilled her obligation to Edward Bok. 'I shall let you have another page I hope before long – It does not quite depend on me – You see how often you get them. I have other things often I must do – and I am working for another exhibition now,' she wrote to Bok, glad of the money such work would bring in. However, she still maintained a certain pride in her work and insisted that if he decided they were unsuitable or too shoddy, 'on no account are you to keep them.'[38] Bok was delighted, and Kate's drawings appeared in three separate issues the following year.

At the end of the disastrous year of 1895, Kate felt that only her painting could give meaning to her life. It was all she had left and she was determined to develop it before illness threatened to take even that away. With no one to please but herself, and her knowledge of what Ruskin would approve, she believed that this was the time to combat the disgusting tricks and 'funniness' of the moderns. At last she realized what Ruskin had so often tried to explain – how important it was to work with a purpose, to paint 'for all people who on earth do dwell'. And, inspired by his remarks to her, each day she entered her studio she felt a greater sense of purpose; that she alone was replacing what was sadly lost in the art world – the Beauty she and Ruskin had agreed was essential. She described her dedication to that goal in one of the verses inspired and written in this time of intense loneliness:

> *There are sometimes moments when I see*
> *A sort of divinity in it for me,*
> *To keep me separate and alone;*
> *To hold away and keep my heart*
> *All my work, set aside and apart,*
> *As if I were vowed away to Art.*[39]

9 The Fallen Star 1896–1901

Deserted, cast away, my work all done,
Who was a star that shone a little while,
But fallen and all its brightness gone –
A victim of this world's brief fickle smile.
Poor fool and vain, grieve not for what is lost,
Nor rend thy heart by counting up the cost.
                          KATE GREENAWAY

Kate's loneliness continued unabated throughout the winter of 1896, its short, dim days restricting her working hours, and forcing her to spend most of the time reading the books and periodicals recommended by her friends. She admired the novels of H.G. Wells, and she particularly enjoyed her friend Lady Ritchie's recently published memoirs. Remaining faithful to the Master's influence, she also read the French novels and plays he had recommended.

Winter's forced leisure gave her more time to write longer, descriptive letters to Ruskin. She resumed her habit of keeping a blank sheet of paper at her side, filling it with wandering thoughts, until she needed a break; then she would wrap up warmly and leave the empty house in search of a post-box. It was a change from brooding, and her letters indicate how much she enjoyed writing. She rambled on for pages, discussing the weather and her garden, freely confessing her likes and dislikes, trying at all times to conceal her feelings of solitude with descriptions of gallery visits and friends. She adopted a chatty, conversational tone, answering her own questions, obviously enjoying the game of guessing his reactions. 'If I were talking to you, you'd say NO to tease me – I know you would,' she assured him; in another she confessed, 'You might call these reflections of a dull mind.' Such monologues were a pitiful attempt to bridge what now seemed an insurmountable gap between them. She realised she had little hope of returning to Brantwood, that her letters were scrutinized by Joan Severn before they were read to Ruskin; this certainly influenced their content. No longer was Kate as intimate in expression or as frantic in her pleading; she kept her protests for undying love and affection to a minimum. But for all the bantering style, descriptions of the antics of her models, her determination to paint well, Kate's letters convey a sense of desperation. She describes her growing disappointment and disillusionment with her career; how she feels helpless in the struggle to make money; and her disgusted reaction to the rise of the 'New Era' artists.

The demise of the 'Old Era' was marked in Kate's mind by the death and funeral of one of its giants, Lord Leighton. Kate and Ruskin had long admired this Olympian of High Victorian classicism, whose pure classic figures stared aloofly into space in mythological themes painted to inspire rather than instruct. Here was true Beauty in every sense. As the President of the Royal Academy, Leighton was the pillar of artistic respectability, his stainless private as well as public reputation supported by a staunch belief in classical Beauty.

He was simply 'the most fortunate artist of our time', the *Athenaeum* eulogized. And so, in early February, Kate came out of her isolation to pay homage, with the rest of her colleagues, to this paragon; and she left the funeral service in St Paul's Cathedral awed and inspired. Later she wrote to Ruskin, 'I did not know him, I never talked to him – yet I am so sorry. He seemed always to me one of the few who cared for real Beauty. Now it is all something new – something startling, but if it is beautiful does not matter.' Easily impressed by pomp and grandeur, she found the funeral procession under the glittering dome, and the large numbers of famous people assembled, a breathtaking sight. 'I was so glad they were glad – to do him all that honour. Somehow it was nice to see all those other painters there.'[1]

Kate spent the next week enjoying herself in London, telling Ruskin, with a sense of guilt, that she was '. . . going about this week in a way unusual to me'. This included a visit to the children's play *Hansel and Gretel* with Lady Jeune and her daughters. Having accepted the play's grim plot, she studied each act in order to give Ruskin a full account; but the final scene, in which the witch is taken from the oven, a charred handful of bones, was too disturbing – 'such an object – still this part is rather awful.' Characteristically, she tried to find a deeper, hidden meaning in the simple story, but she decided that the Gothic qualities no longer appealed to her. She was reminded of a remark Ruskin had once made, that she was 'nature not gothic', and should not spend her time drawing witches and goblins. This seemed appropriate to her circumstances and she ended her letter: 'I feel this so often now as I like everything more and more natural. Once I used – to like unusual things. Now they interest me most if they are real – I don't like things that could not now happen, like the witch – I have a lingering regard for fairies – but I certainly have lost all taste for the absurd and distorted.'

Her need for more natural things made the quest to understand what heaven would be like a difficult task, and she decided that it would have to have apple blossom and blue skies. She was now spending more and more time reading Wordsworth, dwelling on his *Intimations of Immortality*, which reminded her of attempts to recall her childhood, the familiar happiness and joy of life in the country; it was 'as if I had known them in a former world'. Such feelings contrasted with her fading respect for Swinburne. She had recently been given his complete works, and after careful study she pronounced that she disliked his 'nastiness': 'I have never possessed the Swinburnes before – they are immense pleasure to me, such a pity he had not a nice mind. For he has such a clever one – gone astray and he might have been so wonderful, but the words he uses and the way he rhymes them – oh, it is beyond anything,' she wrote to Ruskin.[2]

Dazed and absent-minded, Kate failed to remember Ruskin's birthday in early February. One sleepless morning at half past three she jolted up in bed, suddenly remembering; she was overcome by remorse, ten days later sending a long, apologetic letter to explain that part of the reason for her oversight had been that she was engrossed in George du Maurier's novel *Peter Ibbetson*. She found the book a delightful change from the depressing Hardy and the curious, somewhat implausible H.G. Wells. Moreover, Du Maurier's romantic story of a man's reunion with a past love brought back memories, and she described the

Spring – a watercolour pair done under the influence of the classicists Leighton and
Poynter.

book accordingly to Ruskin, 'so wordly – such a beautiful idea – an exquisite
fancy'. She was influenced by her friendship with Du Maurier, her neighbour,
who occasionally visited her studio, and felt reassured by the fact that he was,
like Leighton and Millais, an 'Old Era' artist of the first rank.

Kate had retreated even further from the moderns and, although she had made
an attempt to understand it, Beardsley's work still annoyed her. In her opinion
his startling black and white graphics were grossly overrated. She yearned for
Ruskin to break his silence and reassure her: 'I wonder if you ever see any
illustrations of Aubrey Beardsley's and what do you think of them? I would like
to know.'[3] She was also disturbed by Beardsley's mastery of outline – the very
skill Ruskin had urged her to perfect. It seemed he had the ability to create figures
and evoke an atmosphere which she, and others, regarded as unwholesome and
decadent. Indeed, on Beardsley's death in 1898, the *Athenaeum* – that barometer
of respectability and good taste – described his work as 'the offspring of a

lubricious will unchastened by a healthy mind . . . invented in a darkened room when outside the sun was shining on a healthy and virtuous world'. This is what Kate felt as she found her work being passed over in favour of that of the moderns. She was conspicuously out of touch, isolated by her beliefs and thwarted in her attempts to find a way to regain her popularity – a popularity once earned by being perfectly in tune with current taste. 'A great many people are now what they call modern. When I state *my* likes and dislikes they tell me I am *not* modern, so I suppose I'm not – advanced. That is why, I suppose, I see some of the new pictures as looking so very funny,' she told Ruskin. She tried to counteract the impressionistic styles of her rivals by painting realistic portraits and landscapes derived from her careful study of the no longer fashionable Leighton, Millais, and Burne-Jones. 'Oh dear! I believe I shall ever think a face should look like a face, and a beautiful arm like a beautiful arm,' she wrote to Ruskin, while admitting, '– not that I can do it – the great pity I can't. Why, if I could, they should have *visions*.'

Kate could be quite honest about the cause of her shortcomings and admitted they were primarily due to her loneliness. It affected her desire to work, drained her of confidence, until at last she returned to tried and true nature studies. Hoping to avoid frustration, she sought simple, less demanding work in which she could escape her misery and still produce saleable pictures. 'Sometimes I almost wish I were shut up by myself with nothing to do but to paint – only I'm so dependent on people's affection,' she wrote to Ruskin after one successful day's work. 'I'm not lonely by myself but I want the people I like very much sometimes.' It was a desperate struggle to find her worth, dedicating each day to painting, fighting off the urge to abandon everything and seek companionship. In the past her popularity had given comfort enough to provide reassurance that people did want her work. But now that demand was gone, and with Ruskin far removed Kate yearned for someone who would understand her dilemma and be willing to listen to her. She found this new friend in a woman with all the youthfulness and frivolous spirit that had been drained from her own life.

Violet Dickinson is best known today for her later intimacy with young Virginia Stephen. Violet was at first glance a curious choice for the role of confidante: she was tall (six foot two) and graceless – Virginia Stephen (who later became Virginia Woolf) called her 'Kangaroo'. Violet's background was very different from Kate's: her father was a Somerset squire and her mother the third daughter of Lord Auckland. However, Violet had many of the qualities Kate admired and sought in her intimates. Her interests were bookbinding, music and literature; she liked social gatherings but, to Kate's delight, was free of social pretensions. She was openly frivolous, broadminded, always ready with a joke or a comment intended to make others laugh; and, most important of all, she was a spinster. At thirty-one, almost twenty years Kate's junior, Violet combined the youthfulness, independence and humour, that Kate had earlier found and loved in Lily Severn, with the warmth and understanding of an older, more mature woman.

Violet entered Kate's life at a critical moment, shortly after Kate had admitted feeling a need for such a free-spirited friend. This confession was made in response to reading the sensational – many thought scandalous – *Journal of Marie Bashkirtseff*, which in its introduction promised to be 'a book in the nude, breathing and palpitating with life'. It purported to be the true story of a nineteen-year-old adventuress and her private and public relationships with some of the most famous artistic personalities in England and on the Continent. 'I reveal myself completely, entirely,' the author assured her readers. This candour attracted Kate and once she had begun reading the book she could not put it down. Fascinated, she resorted to it like a naughty schoolgirl, shocked yet secretly enjoying the way the author shattered Victorian morality. Her criticism of the book, in a letter to Ruskin, is revealing. She pronounced the author of a 'common mind, odious – simply – but the book is wonderful in a way, so vivid'; and she continued, slipping up with her pronouns, 'and though you – or rather I – hate her you feel she must be clever'. Long after Kate had finished the book, and had been warned by her brother (who pronounced the whole thing unspeakably hateful) not to read the second volume, *Marie Bashkirtseff* still engrossed her. 'It is a study of supreme vanity, making yourself the centre of all things. It is queer to be ambitious in that way . . . Still her history does affect me, I keep thinking about her,' she wrote to Ruskin. 'She is so strange – so desperately worldly, and I think so cruel – because she was so vain.' But her common sense prevailed: 'I was so intensely interested – to get it done is to get back in natural life once more.'[4]

Violet Dickinson possessed distinct resemblances to Marie Bashkirtseff. With her long list of aristocratic friends, she was equally 'worldly'; and yet she was never cruel, vain or selfish. She and Kate became acquainted when Violet requested the loan of some Greenaway pictures for a charity exhibition she was organizing at Southwark in 1894. A brief correspondence ensued, followed by their meeting in London. There Kate appeared a sad, pathetic figure of the sort Violet loved to adopt; she set herself to console and charm the distraught and profoundly lonesome woman. Subsequently the two were frequently seen together in public, at evening suppers and private views. There, more often than not, they would cause a considerable stir. First, tall, gangling Violet would enter a room, her erect figure crowned by one of the huge flowered hats she loved. Behind her lurked the dowdy, always sombrely dressed Kate, dwarfed by and under the shadow of her friend. Violet offered jokes and amusing comments which would delight the assembled guests, since she was aware of her curious appearance and used it, poking fun at her prematurely grey hair and her plain face. Behind her jovial exterior lay what Quentin Bell called 'a breezy masculine assurance'. This undoubtedly helped to stabilize her intimacy with Kate. Not surprisingly, Kate jumped at the chance to talk about her problems to such an apparently understanding soul. She began to write long, affectionate letters to 'her Violet', using the words and the frank confessional tone once reserved for Ruskin, and even employing identical terms of endearment. She learned to joke about her appearance: 'We must get quite different views of things – you seeing over the tops – I always looking up to them.' Yet she felt uneasy. She feared that Violet might abandon her as Ruskin had done so cruelly in the past. It was a constant, inescapable fear, and it intensified as their relationship grew. Describing herself as 'this insignificant

A despondent Kate Greenaway in her studio tearoom, *c*.1895

me', she did not want to intrude on her friend's life; and yet she needed her as someone who could listen to her long tales of woe. A recurring one was 'I lead such a quiet life.' Violet assured her she would never abandon her, and she remained a faithful friend, although the letters passing between them seem to have stopped by mid-1898, after four years of intimacy. 'Don't begin to find me very dull – don't begin not to want me,' Kate pleaded in one typical letter to her friend. 'Yet you can't help it if you do. I suppose I am so slow and you are so quick.' The desperation that permeated this and other letters to Violet shows how much she still longed for affection: she needed someone to need and to return her love; and she felt that in Violet she had at least found someone who understood and appreciated her, despite her weaknesses and shortcomings.

All this raises a question as to the exact nature of their relationship. It has been suggested that Violet was capable of Lesbian relationships – for example in her intimacy with Virginia Stephen years later. There is no clear indication in Kate's letters of any consciousness of this element, though the letters are, it must be said, surprisingly candid about her needs and desires. It is certainly true that, after meeting Violet, Kate tried to change, to adopt some of her friend's high-spirited manners: 'I am such a reserved person. You tell everything to everybody and I can't,' she once began, obviously finding it painful to break a lifetime's habit of shyness. 'There's numbers of things I often long to say to you but I do not dare – and yet you are the one person in the world I'd like to talk about them with.' She wrote to Violet: 'I fear I like you when you look like a bad child in school – feeling you'd like to be naughty but not quite sure if your audience is going with you.'[5] Kate's address book charts her friend's every move, with nine separate entries, from Manchester Square to Longleat, Venice to Bergen. Presumably, on arrival at each of these places Violet would find a long letter from Kate.

Violet also exerted some influence over Kate's appearance. This can be traced as beginning from Kate's fiftieth birthday, when she began to reconsider her looks, the dowdiness that was so different from the bright-coloured dresses and outrageous hats that Violet enjoyed. From adolescence, and more so after her parents' deaths, Kate had worn dark colours, discarding these sombre outfits only when visiting Ruskin, who hated women dressed in black. Ruskin had taught her to admire tall, willowy women, but trying to emulate them was beyond her. It was only too obvious how far she fell short of his ideal. Violet, who was just as plain, if considerably taller, suggested to Kate the possibility of changing her style of dress. 'I was given quite the wrong sort of body to live in, I am sure,' Kate wrote to another friend. 'I ought to have been taller, slimmer, at any rate passably good-looking, so that my soul might have taken flights, my fancy have expanded.' To Violet she joked, 'If I were tall, I should make the lines of my backgrounds go quite different.' But she was growing more daring, even now. 'Now, if I make a lovely hat with artistic turns and twists in it, see what I look like! I see myself then as I see others in the trains and omnibuses with these things sticking over one eye. I say, "Ah, there goes me!" I do laugh often, as I look.'[6]

It has to be admitted that, according to photographs taken at this time, Kate's attempts to beautify herself in the current mode had little effect. She remained a haggard-looking, middle-aged woman, with a round, wrinkled face and dark rings under her once velvety brown eyes. Her mousy hair was greying, but she still insisted on pulling it carelessly back on the top of her head; and she had never changed the fringe she had adopted in childhood. Drawing her plans for a 'new look' in a letter to Violet, she confessed, 'I've got in a most dilapidated condition all my feathers standing on end and my skirts all anyhow – from various rains – I feel *so* untidy and need a thorough do up – now would be a good opportunity to come out startling – like I might – .' A London bookseller remembered her once coming into his shop: 'She came in . . . obviously without the least idea how plain and uninteresting she looked. It was only when she began to speak to me, and her face lighted up, that I realized that this was the famous artist about whom John Ruskin had been rapturous.'[7]

In March 1896 Kate's watercolour *Little Bo-Peep* was exhibited at the Royal Institute, and received the most generous review she ever had from the *Athenaeum*. The reviewer claimed that her little girl in an olive green dress, walking in a daisy-strewn, sunlit meadow was a model of watercolour technique: Kate Greenaway's 'firm yet delicate touch, her patience, and her love for pure colour and bright light ought to be imitated by all the ladies of our time who, venturing to call themselves artists, slur and daub paper and canvas as if neither she nor Mrs Allingham . . . were here to teach them better.' This model watercolour was priced at £25, while all around it hung pictures by colleagues priced from £100 to £250. Kate was uncertain about public reaction and had, as she always would from now on, underestimated herself.

The inescapable fact remained, she needed money. Despite last year's firm refusal to design another almanack, she realized that an almanack was the one fairly sure way of earning more money. So when a new publisher, J.M. Dent, (ironically Beardsley's first publisher) approached her about one, she reluctantly accepted the offer. A letter written in mid-April to Lady Dorothy Nevill makes it clear that Kate regarded work on the almanack as a necessary evil, and was toiling over the pages. 'I say toiling simply because I want to be getting on with other things, as it is important I should now if I am going to have any exhibition at all.'[8]

When the almanack was published in November, she was very dissatisfied with the 'commonplace' result. Altering the usual Greenaway formula, Dent had produced an almanack and diary combined in one volume, bound in a plain green cover with a gleaner figure embossed in gold in its centre. Kate felt that the larger format dwarfed her illustrations and the pages of obvious padding emphasized the difficulty she had in maintaining the quality of her work. 'When I try to do a thing like that I get nervous and think – and then it is all up,' she wrote to Violet in a letter accompanying a copy of the almanack.[9] To Kate's mind the almanack had failed, and it was the last she ever did. 'The next book I do I will totally design myself,' she insisted.

That winter she succumbed to an overwhelming urge to express herself in verse. Just before going to bed she would read from the works of her favourite poets. She longed to describe the loneliness that daily grew deeper, and the painful process of pondering over old feelings, especially the love she felt towards Ruskin, made her task even more difficult. 'But I'm going to try more than ever, and I'm going to try other things too if only I can keep well,' she promised Violet, describing herself as 'Solitary Hermit K.G.'. 'I do mean to try and do a little more in my life. I'm not content, for I have not yet *expressed myself*. It's such a queer feeling, that longing to express yourself and not finding a means or way – yet it goads you on and won't let you rest.'[10] Sharp, picturesque imagery had once come easily to her; but now, when a phrase seemed right, the more she thought about it, the more likely it would end up stifled by melancholy. She was quite aware of this handicap, but shrugged it off as the consequence of being 'a quarter Welsh'. The dark, brooding lament for what might have been was impossible to avoid. To Violet she sent the lines:

> *Across the lonely desert grand,*
> *Across the yellow rigid sand*
> *The lurid sunset filled the land*
> *With desolate despair . . .*

Her letter was accompanied by a sketch of herself, angry-faced and frustrated, hunched over her desk, at work on her poetry. These struggles often continued well into the night, when the darkness frightened, yet inspired her:

> *I lean from out my windows open space*
> *Upon the garden sleeping underneath*
> *Into the night the garden sleeps beneath . . .*
> *Between me and the moon do interlace.*
>
> *Is this the world I lived in yesterday*
> *When all the day was filled with light and sound*
> *How strange to think he laughed and talked away*
> *And now this night mysteriously profound.*
>
> *All round me is the silence of the night*
> *A bat flies and a night moth and a spider drops*
> *From leaf to leaf with a sound – so light*
> *It hardly stirs the darkness that emioraps* [sic]

Scent the warm air an exquisite delight
A kinship with God
And my soul grows nearer to its vision of a god
The strange sad night with mystery of stars
The large round yellow moon is rising slow and still
Into the myriad starred, strange sad night.[11]

Kate continued to describe her feelings in verse until the end of her life, filling hundreds of handwritten pages in four thick volumes. Many of these poems express a strong desire to probe deeper, beyond the simple, childish thoughts of her early books. She studied and tried to adopt the styles and language of masters: Tennyson, Shelley, Wordsworth, Emerson and the then popular, but now lesser known, Mrs Webster. She made a collection of their works, sometimes carefully clipped from periodicals and newspapers; and she also filled a notebook with brief lines and phrases borrowed from the masters.

1897 was another Jubilee year, celebrating the sixtieth anniversary of the Queen's accession, when militant women took the opportunity to bring before the public their struggles for equal rights, as citizens, workers and artists. To Kate's dismay she was singled out as an example of a successful woman artist; those exhibitions organized for women artists only, promoted by what Kate called the 'shrieking sisterhood', were in her opinion a disgrace. She flatly refused all appeals to appear or exhibit her work in that context. She believed that her fame had been won on her own merits and the fact that she was a woman was immaterial. The whole idea of women's rights and suffrage was an embarrassment, and in her letters to the Ponsonby's, Violet Dickinson and Ruskin, she was very decided about her views. She neither wanted the vote for herself nor believed other women should have it; for they 'would follow their feelings too much . . . and get up excitements over things best left alone.' She resented the militancy of women who threatened to 'crush MAN beneath their feet' and tried to build artistic reputations by flaunting their womanhood. 'They always feel they are not done justice to. I must say, I in my experience have not found it so. I have been fairly treated and I have never had any influence to help me,' she wrote confidently to Ruskin. With her 'great men' theory in mind, she concluded, 'it is generally the second rate ones who feel they should be the first if it were not for unfair treatment, and all the while it is want of enough talent . . . Not one of them can do a picture like a fine Leighton – yet they can't even look at him.'[12] 'Worm as I am, my friend,' she wrote to Violet Dickinson, 'oh what a worm they would think me if I dared write and say my true views, that having been fairly and justly treated by those odious men, that I would far rather exhibit my things with them and take my true place which must be lower than so many of theirs. For I fear we can only *hope* to do – what men *can* do. It is sad but I fear it is so. They *have* more ability.'[13]

Kate chose two recent watercolour portraits to exhibit at the Royal Institute in March: *Girl in Hat with Feather*, which the *Athenaeum* claimed 'would be irresistible if she had not painted the same sort of thing many times before'; and *Two Little Girls in a Garden*, described as 'ravishingly pretty, but it is "as before"'. The reviewer went on to point out: 'Nobody but Miss Greenaway could continue to attract the public for so many years, yet even her faithful public may end by getting tired of her quaintly clad girls and groups of children.'[14] After a review which cut so painfully near the bone, Kate was reluctant to send more works to the Royal Institute, and the two exhibited this year were in fact the last she consented to hang there. It was generally a bad year, especially 'for pictures to sell – everyone will spend their money on Jubilee things', she concluded. Moreover, she refused to send entries to the Brussels International Exhibition. Her Fine Art Society exhibitions had cleared her studio of her best, most representative pictures, and only the slight or the unfinished remained. The recent disappointment at the Royal Institute had removed what little confidence she had left and she wrote to the organizer of the British entries, Isidore Spielmann, 'I feel it really not fair to send those I now possess. I'm extremely sorry.'[15]

By April Kate was in a dilemma: she was unable to turn old sketches into saleable new pictures, yet she needed to find some way to earn her living. 'My mind is in a very perplexed state and I feel very depressed also,' she confessed to Maria Ponsonby. 'I seem not to do things well, and whatever I do falls so flat.' All the indications pointed to one disturbing fact: 'It is rather unhappy to feel that you have had your day. Yet if I had just enough money to live on I could be so very happy, painting just what I liked and no thought of profit . . . It's there comes the bother, but it's rather difficult to make enough money in a few years to last for your life. Yet now every one is so tired of things – that is what it comes to.' Ruskin received a similar pathetic letter: 'Every one wants something different so I will please myself now.'[16] But Kate still had to consider how to finance her self-indulgence, and as a first step she sold drawings to friends and their influential acquaintances, many of whom she had met through Lady Dorothy Nevill and Lady Jeune. Her address book is dotted with the names of wealthy possible patrons.

Lady Dorothy Nevill now occupied a prominent place among Kate's intimates, not only for her patronage (she had encouraged Leighton to admire Kate's work) and her large circle of influential friends, but also for her willingness to listen to Kate's worries. 'Miss Greenaway herself was the very incarnation of modest gentleness, and very far from being fitted to adopt these commercial methods by which alone her work might have received full pecuniary appreciation,' she concluded in her autobiography. Almost twenty years Kate's senior, with a personality unlike that of any of Kate's other friends, Dorothy Nevill seemed to understand Kate completely. The daughter of Horace Walpole, she had seen the giants of the Victorian age come and go, accepting with a rare degree of tolerance many of their quirks and follies; and, like Kate, she was saddened by the demise of the Victorian ideals of respectability and beauty.

Among others who cultivated Kate as a friend as well as an artist were Stuart Samuel and his family. Stuart Montague Samuel was a wealthy merchant banker and later a Member of Parliament, who lived in Berkeley Square with his beautiful wife – 'spring personified', Kate decided when they first met – and his two daughters. His first commissions were a watercolour portrait of his younger daughter, Vera and her book-plate, for which Kate charged the

Vera Evelyn Samuel. Watercolour by Kate Greenaway, commissioned by Stuart M. Samuel, of his daughter, 1896.

customary rates: £25 and £6 respectively. It had been arranged in a cautious, business-like manner, but as time passed – the portrait took two and a half years, the book-plate a year – she discovered that Stuart Samuel was more than a kind patron. He was genuinely interested in her work, the proud owner of her original drawings to *A Day in a Child's Life*, which he had framed and hung in his children's nursery. Anxious to add to his collection, during Vera's portrait sittings in Kate's studio he was allowed to look through her other pictures and was struck by some early processionals intended for Ruskin. He asked her to paint larger copies of these for his daughter's nursery, but Kate at first declined. She now found it almost impossible to copy anything, whether an old drawing, a painting or a reproduction; moreover, she did not want Samuel, still a relative stranger, to own copies of works intended for Ruskin and painted out of love for him. However, she needed the money and did not want to disappoint such an important patron, so she agreed to paint an entirely new processional scene of young Greenaway maidens dressed in flowing gowns, entwined by flower garlands.

However much Kate encouraged potential patrons to visit her studio, in doing so they interrupted her routine. She could not escape the sense that her privacy was being invaded. She was living in what Lady Jeune called the 'age of publicity', in which 'the struggle for everything – existence, fame, enjoyment – is keen and it is waged more keenly from year to year.'[17] This was not a time for the courtesy and rituals of the Victorian drawing room, or for a life of gentle ease and contemplation. Such changes in well-trodden ways made Kate feel

196

cornered and decidedly out of step with her neighbours; but, whenever possible, she insisted upon her old ways. 'I want to be left alone to live my life privately – like an English gentlewoman,' was her frequent response to requests for interviews. But, she could not control the flood of letters from editors hoping for an article, or at least a comment on a current problem. The legend of the recluse Miss Greenaway was still a challenge. She was asked ridiculous questions about the state of the world as she saw it (she was not generally concerned with newspaper events), how to find good servants, the best children's fashions. Some journalists deliberately treated her like a pheno-menon long out of fashion; a famous woman all but dead to her public. This especially angered her, and she wrote sharp letters in protest. Not every request was ignored, however. She co-operated with the distinguished art critic and journalist Gleeson White when he sought information about her book-plates for an article published in the *Studio* in 1897. It charted the rise of 'Children's Books and Illustrators', a general survey from the earliest to the present day, which placed Kate in the front rank (though, ironically, Lizzie Lawson, who had made her reputation by imitating the Greenaway style, was there too). But on the whole, Kate was not helpful. 'Every one seems possessed with the desire of writing articles upon me and sends me long lists of all I am to say,' she wrote in despair to Ruskin. 'Then America worries me to give drawings, to give dolls – and I have at last had to give up answering letters.' She decided the problem lay in her respectful nature: 'I'm very much afraid that I am too lenient a person – and people find it out – and impose on me accordingly – it is not a pleasant thought – ought I to be more stern?' she asked Ruskin. 'It *is* a tiresome world at times.'[18]

She could still recall with amazing clarity the details of her childhood, in particular the richly coloured and scented gardens and fields of Rolleston. These memories inspired many new paintings in which she sought to recapture the magic of deeply coloured and shaded flowers as she remembered them. On her visits to the galleries she discovered new delight in 'strong Rossetti colours' especially at the commemorative exhibitions staged to remind the public of the glories of their artistic past. These sparked off a childish response: 'Do you know I'm not grown up yet – it's funny – I'm not – . . . I grow to so many new things, so much new experience.'

The Royal Academy exhibition this year was a turning point; the *Athenaeum* used it to spread gloom over the art world, claiming that it was a testament to the death of true Beauty. The reviewer urged visitors to examine all the decidedly second-rate portraits, and concluded 'until this exhibition is thoroughly studied the public will not fully realize how much it has lost by the deaths of Leighton, Millais . . .'[19] At this time Kate was reading *Modern Painting*, written by the prophet of the modern movement, George Moore. The book attracted considerable attention with its extravagant claims that painters such as Whistler ranked with recognized old masters such as Velazquez. Daily, as Kate read on, she grew angrier and more upset. Moore asserted that works by revered artists such as Leighton and Millais could now quite easily be replaced, indeed eclipsed, by the so-called modern painters. She could only agree with the pencil notation of 'Shame' found at this point in the copy of the book she had borrowed, taking some comfort from the fact that someone else agreed with her. 'I feel my cheeks burn,' she wrote to Violet Dickinson. She found confirmation of her beliefs at an exhibition at the Guildhall. There examples of the work of the recognized masters of the Queen's sixty-year reign were hung side by side, in what seemed to many an elaborate eulogy to bygone standards. No less than six pictures by Millais were displayed near works by his Pre-Raphaelite colleagues Holman Hunt and Rossetti, as well as neoclassical pictures by Leighton and Alma-Tadema. It was a heart-warming experience for Kate to see her favourites again, and she was fired with enthusiasm and dedication. 'And what will this generation who run them down have to show?' she asked Ruskin. 'For them, *nothing* that I can see at present.' She had returned home confident, 'so much better for seeing them', and determined to continue working in the old manner. 'I'm quite sure there *is* no one in the whole world *can* love the old things more than I do,' she told Ruskin. 'Art is a queer thing and I think quite undefinable – it must be true – with an ideal of the most beautiful part of everything.'[20]

But this sense of security and faith in the past offered little when it came to making money. In late July Kate entertained a prospective American patron and his wife. They were delighted by her habit of strewing the studio with everything she had done – pencil sketches, finished and unfinished water-colours, ideas for new pictures. The husband gleefully enquired how much they were by the dozen, to which his wife added, 'Do you sell works on a wholesale basis?' Kate was horrified, but by now resigned to callous treatment by the philistine.

August was again spent at Cromer, where the rain and cold kept her confined indoors for a good deal of the time. However, her stay was enlivened by brief visits to some of Hannah Jane's fascinating neighbours. Among the staunch, wealthy local families, the Barclays, the Hoares, the Gurneys, there stood out a few who defied convention, like the elegant Cyril Flower, patron of Burne-Jones, who lived a perfect aesthete's life in a Lutyens-designed house, furnished in impeccable taste, at Overstrand. At Blickling there was Constance, Lady Lothian, a high-born dowager with an obsession for white. She proudly invited friends and acquaintances to visit her grounds inhabited by white cattle, white ponies, white pigeons and white peacocks. Kate was delighted with these curiosities and afterwards, in a letter to a friend in London, she noted seeing a fine collection of storks and kangaroos as well.

She returned home to an empty house, her brother being away for treatment in Switzerland. Johnnie was by this time a constant worry, with his sudden

3 Ovals: colour proofs to the *Language of Flowers*, 1884, showing Kate's struggles to incorporate nature study in tiny drawings. *Centre*: Poverty theme once used in *Language of Flowers*.
At foot: Original watercolour for 'P – Peeped in it', in *A Apple Pie*, 1886.

illnesses and crippling bouts of depression. Kate had often worried that her brother, too, might abandon her for some far-off clinic, leaving her to manage the house alone. This was an anxious time, at least until she received news from Switzerland that Johnnie was getting better and would be home soon. To her great relief, Johnnie returned in early October.

In January 1898, the Royal Academy put on a huge and surprisingly popular posthumous exhibition of Millais's work. The *Athenaeum* declared it 'the whole of the life's work of the best equipped artist that the English nation has produced', and urged its readers to attend. Kate was one of the large numbers who revelled in room after room of old favourites. Here, for example, was the renowned *Ophelia*, which she repeatedly claimed to be 'the greatest picture of modern times'. She hoped the tide in taste was changing, not least for the sake of her own forthcoming exhibition. She confessed to Ruskin: 'I fear the exhibition won't be in the least successful; there seems to me to be very few pictures sell now – or a person is popular just for a little time. And there's so much fad over art – .' She acknowledged that it was still the critics who could make or break a reputation: those ill-informed voices who attacked Leighton and Millais as antiquated with their 'so utterly ignorant' criticism. In truth, they were the very ones who had rocketed her to fame, and she was nervous about once again placing her future in their hands. ('They only want me to be always doing dressed up babies.') It was the public she wanted; the people who had once bought her books and would, she hoped, buy her paintings, despite what the critics said. And so, after a long-winded attack on the critics, she wrote to Ruskin that 'I wish people would care about what I do more now.'[21] And yet she lacked confidence in herself and her ability to create beautifully coloured pictures. A recent exhibition of Rossetti's work, with its admirable deep greens and maidens with flaming red hair, provoked greater feelings of inadequacy, the longing 'to do something nice – beautiful – like I feel'. She was frustrated by her technical shortcomings and often spent an entire day working on a minute detail before it came right. Infuriating as this was, it did prove a temporary release from worry. 'Even now, the moment I'm doing a new drawing the morning rushes by – I'm so happy, so interested, I only feel the tiredness when I can't go on because it is too late or too dark.'[22]

After two years of preparation and much altering of schedules, her long-awaited Fine Art Society exhibition opened in February. Despite all her efforts, it proved yet another disappointment. Of the 127 exhibits – original drawings for illustrations, watercolour landscapes and portraits – only about half were sold; total sales amounted to £1,024.1s., of which Kate's share was £645. The gallery had made valiant attempts to promote the show, with a sage green flag specially commissioned with the name 'Kate Greenaway' in large letters, to hang boldly outside the gallery and attract passers-by; and a second and important exhibition of mezzotints had been scheduled simultaneously, to attract the print collector audience. Unfortunately, both these efforts backfired

Little Miss Prim, a watercolour of Kate's landlady's daughter.

– the flag had to be sent back to correct a misspelling, and so was not available for the opening; the mezzotint exhibition was bought outright at the last minute, leaving an empty adjoining gallery. The private view fell on an especially cold day, with sleet and rain keeping away all but the most avid Greenaway admirers. Kate took her place in the hushed, gas-lit gallery and waited to receive her guests. Those who braved the weather turned out in a depressing trickle, in contrast to the crowds she expected. She nervously greeted them; they quickly looked at the pictures and left before the weather turned worse. Those that remained discussed Ruskin: 'It might have been your Private View – for everyone was talking about you and saying so many nice things of you,' she wrote to him later. The gallery itself had little to attract and hold the attention of the keenest Greenaway enthusiast, with fewer illustrations (the works that did sell well), and more of her recent paintings and experimental chalk studies. In despair, Kate wrote to Violet Dickinson, 'I've felt depressed about it and I hardly ever feel that unless there is a cause. It was so tiresome.' Three weeks later, when the empty adjacent gallery was filled with Helen Allingham's latest watercolours to outshine her feeble efforts, Kate concluded that the exhibition had been doomed from the start. It was now quite clear 'that my sort of drawing is not the drawing that is liked just now, and also that I am getting to be a thing of the past . . .'[23] In despair she tried to ignore her public image – 'a gentle, bespectacled middle-aged lady garbed in black' – and told Ruskin she was not yet ready to retire.

In August Kate as usual went to the Locker-Lampsons at Cromer, having refused an invitation to Brantwood ('I am obliged to do my work you see.') On one lazy Sunday, with her hostess away at church, Kate invited the children to a croquet match on the front lawn, in direct view of a rest home. The match went well until Hannah Jane arrived home, horrified that her children had broken the Sabbath by playing games. The game was stopped and the children were severely scolded, until Kate interrupted to accept full responsibility for the outrage. She thereupon stormed off to apologize to the incensed residents of the

Kate Greenaway in her studio, from a photograph taken by Mrs Miller.

rest home, making it clear that she did so out of respect for her hostess, and not from any personal religious conviction, for Kate found Hannah Jane's piety rather an embarrassment. However much her friend now pleaded with her to change her ways, to attend church, read the Bible, and live a Christian life, she obstinately refused. Heated arguments would ensue, as Hannah Jane pointed out the frightening consequences awaiting someone in Kate's situation. 'You can't sit on that sofa for five minutes without feeling steeped in sin,' she argued, to which Kate defiantly replied, 'I often sit on it, and I don't feel like that; if I did I should try hard not to do wrong things.' She clung fast to her belief in Beauty and nature as a religion. 'I have thought the same way ever since I have had the power to think at all. How is it possible that I should change? I know I shall not.' It was, however, a difficult dilemma, and when she returned home after her discussions at Cromer she tried to analyse her dislike of organized religion. She found that no provision had been made for celebrating the beauty and joy of the world around her.

> I never can, never shall see it is more religious to sit in a hot church trying to listen to a commonplace sermon than looking at a beautiful sky, or the waves coming in, and feeling that longing to be good and exultation in the beauty of things. How dreadful that sordid idea of God is with the mind getting more and more morbid and frightened. Why was the world made then? and everything so wonderful and beautiful?[24]

Her letters to Ruskin not only gave her a chance to express her thoughts on such things as art, religion and modern life (the motor car was 'so ugly . . . the whole thing looks maimed – but they are certain to become very general'; moving photographs she considered 'rather wonderful') but also brought the satisfaction of knowing that she alone had not forgotten the Master. 'Your letters (the only ones he at present has) he much enjoys,' wrote Joan Severn. 'How grateful I ever am for your untiring goodness to him,' she added, after learning how Kate planned to send drawings in a specially constructed wooden packing case, to be returned and refilled when necessary.[25] Kate remained stubbornly loyal to Ruskin, maintaining 'you were the only person I ever knew who cared so much as I care.'

Following a brief visit to Brantwood in October, Kate returned home determined to change her approach to painting. Her visits to the galleries demonstrated that portrait painting had now become popular with the public ('everyone has turned portrait painter'), and she decided to try her hand at it. The decision is not surprising; what is unusual and courageous is that she decided to abandon her skills as a watercolourist to take up painting in oils. Her reasoning was influenced by the enormous prices such pictures commanded, compared with the £25 watercolours she had been turning out by the dozen. Further, she was following in the footsteps of two respected colleagues, George du Maurier and Walter Crane, both of whom had tried (with little success) to break into the more respected, as well as more lucrative, profession of studio oil painting. She had had a brief grounding in the technique of oils at art school, and later, when influenced by the Master, had been warned against the smelly,

The Muff, an unfinished oil painting.

difficult medium. She realized that she was setting herself an arduous task. 'I don't at all like it. I don't feel near strong enough for the strain of it. I know what the children are like – quite unaccustomed to sitting still, and then to have to get a real likeness,' she complained to Ruskin.[26] And yet she was determined to succeed, giving up all other work until she did so. Locked away in her studio, alone except for fidgety models, her determination grew firmer, despite setbacks and minor catastrophes. She still could not copy old sketches on to canvas, or paint her models' faces. They almost always emerged as chalky pink smudges. The months went by, spent in mixing the unfamiliar thick paint, scraping canvases gone muddy, waiting for them to dry (normally three days) before beginning again. The process was infuriating to one accustomed to quick-drying, transparent watercolour, applied with delicate hair brushes, in contrast to the stiff bristles needed for oil. As she had expected, the fidgeting of her models was a serious problem, even after she installed a mirror over her head – an idea borrowed from Reynolds – so that her sitter could observe her progress.

After months of frustration over her 'awful beings in oil', late in March 1899 things began to brighten. One or two canvases of the large number stacked along the edge of the studio walls showed promise, and this made her confident enough to write to Ruskin, 'I'm going to emerge, I'm so interested but SO STUPID . . . But, as I said, I'm going to emerge – in the end – triumphant – ???? – but that appears to be a considerable long way off yet . . . Ah, well, I'm going to do lovely little girls and boys by and by. I *am*.'[27] Her confidence was partly due to the encouragement of her models: one of them climbed down from her chair to console Kate, looked at the smudged painting, and exclaimed, 'Oh, I don't think it's so bad!'

This was one of the reasons she chose children for models: they seemed intuitively to understand her, to want to raise her spirits when she was depressed. Most of her prospective models were chosen for their fair hair and blue eyes, or for being 'nice-looking and dark'. These seem vague qualifications, but Kate knew the standards she wanted, and her search, in schools, on walks or on trains, was always to fit the face to her ideal of childish beauty. Once in her studio she could be firm and uncompromising with those who proved too difficult. Others could and did melt her heart with their delightful remarks and unaffected behaviour. One simply refused to stand still: 'What can you do when she breaks out into Scottish reels and Highland flings in her rests?' But Kate put in a full working day, which often ended in her feeling prey to petty circumstances. After one trying session with a squirming model, she emerged a 'Victim – limp – worn – exhausted'. Another cheeky girl model deliberately set out to be annoying, calling her mother, who had accompanied her, by her Christian name, and joking about the cane they agreed she needed. 'I felt she was hardened in wickedness,' Kate decided afterwards. She could be just as outspoken in dealing with the less well-bred, like the love-struck young Ida. She spent her modelling sessions chattering about her undying love for 'Gus', which Kate constantly corrected to 'Augustus – it sounds less vulgar'.

Her oil painting had improved enough by late May for her to tell Ruskin how it had changed her whole outlook, the large canvases in particular showing her that size was important. 'You can't think how funny it is – but finding the power of oil-painting now, my curious mind is wishing to see, and seeing, all subjects large; it seems as if my long-ago and ever-constant wish – to paint a life-size hedge – might now be realized.'[28] Her visits to the galleries were not without incident. On one occasion, at the Exhibition of Home Art Industries at the Albert Hall, she was introduced to the Princess Louise. Nervous though she was, Kate remembered to curtsey, but as she rose all her loose change rolled out of her purse on to the floor, and she and the Princess scurried about trying to retrieve it. Humiliated at the time, but afterwards amused by the incident, Kate described it to Ruskin, concluding, 'Something always happens to me.'

She made a visit to the Tate Gallery which had recently been enlarged to house part of the Turner collection and, out of respect for Ruskin, she made a quick tour of those new rooms hung with the landscapes he had taught her to love. She returned home inspired by the realization that oil painting was a very permanent medium. This encouraged her, as she became aware that she might be creating pictures for posterity. She willingly returned to her self-imposed exile, shutting herself away from distractions, needless letter-writing and social visits. To Mrs Evans, neglected over the past few months, she wrote an apologetic letter, describing how she refused to be diverted from her work, which she believed was a considerable sacrifice, 'giving up a lot of time to practising, a year possibly, and making no money'.

Money was still a source of constant anxiety, and she was forced to consider various schemes to augment her income. The most significant of these was her

Christmas greeting sent to Ruskin in 1899.

autobiography, a task which she believed she could do well. 'A person must reveal himself most in that,' she had once said. The book she planned was to be an honest account of her life; her writing influenced by the books she had read and admired, including Ruskin's *Praeterita*, but avoiding the pitfalls in 'the horrid ones', such as Marie Bashkirtseff's *Journal*. She began haphazardly, jotting down memories and childhood impressions in the endpapers of an old sketchbook. She advertised in local papers for information about her forbears, hoping to fill the gaps in her family's history. As she alternated her writing with painting, the autobiography progressed slowly; she planned to have it hand-printed on fine paper. She took it with her on a visit to the Evans's new home at Ventnor, Isle of Wight, hoping to find time and quiet there to continue writing. Instead she spent the entire visit helping to decorate their house, and she returned home with only the childhood section completed; and there she stopped. The prospect of describing what lay ahead – her rise to fame, her love and respect for Ruskin and her present fall from public favour – may have seemed too daunting and painful. Her manuscript, about a hundred pages long, ends, appropriately enough, with a list of childhood fears, left unexplained.

She next turned her attention to old notebooks rediscovered while she was working on the autobiography. Here, assembled over the years, were pages of ambitious projects, ideas for books and paintings. She reconsidered her decision not to illustrate any more books. She had been incensed by the number of badly printed photo-engraved children's books now in the shops, that represented a shocking fall in standards from the clarity of line engraving, and the obvious care in design taken by Evans and his assistants. It was for this reason, coupled with the need to make money, that Kate again turned to book illustration. 'There are not any very good children's books about just now that I have seen. The rage for copying mine seems over, so I suppose some one will soon step to the front with something new,' she informed Ruskin.[29] She hoped to revive interest in her work before someone new came along. After all, there was now, twenty years on, a whole generation of children who had never known the original Greenaway books or the distinctive Greenaway style. In leafing through her adolescent proverbs she considered having a select number printed with new illustrations, and ticked in pencil those most appropriate. Her selection from the maxims – which had once been intended to guide a developing woman's life – is significant. On page after page she ticked those that best describe her discontent: 'Grief pent up, will burst the heart'; 'You gazed at the moon and fell into the gutter'. Others hint that she saw a glimmer of hope for her future: 'When lands are gone and money spent. Then learning is most excellent.'[30] But the books she planned were not as ambitious as they might have been. She relied rather heavily upon the commercial instincts of publishers. Recalling one of Caldecott's successes, she planned a book of Greenaway children printed in sepia; only hers were to be printed as 'very, very delicate outlines like old fashion plates'. There was a plan for a tiny book (two inches by three) of nursery rhymes, made appealing with 'a band of pretty coloured elastic round the back' of the spine; also a plan for 'a big book of Modern children', printed in strong outline and colour; as she described it, 'a very large book for very little children'. The most curious idea was what she called 'a book pencil', intended as a large pencil with faint, slightly coloured figures printed along its edge, the whole thing deceptively labelled a book. While none of these ideas went beyond the notebook planning stage, several more practical schemes reached preliminary pencil sketches. Favourites were a shilling edition of Blake's *Songs of Innocence*, and *The Book of Girls* which she mentioned several times in one notebook. Twelve preliminary sketches also survive for Hans Andersen's *The Snow Queen* and *What the Moon Saw* (four sketches), as well as for a small book titled *Baby's Debut* (fourteen sketches) and a volume of *Nursery Rhymes* (twenty-two sketches). She even worked diligently on a 'rather fantastic' drawing of three girls' souls,' who left this earth and found a better country.'

But when Kate approached publishers with her ideas it soon became clear that she would have to look elsewhere. Some editors showed an interest in some projects, rejected others; but in almost every case she was unable to get a definite promise of publication. She was horrified to receive an offer for twenty precious drawings at thirty shillings each: this upsetting turn of events was in dire contrast to the time publishers clamoured for Greenaway books and proposed new projects to her. It certainly damaged Kate's confidence. Not for long, however, for by now she was used to disappointments; they only made her look elsewhere. Deciding that the one thing she had not yet fully developed or exploited was her literary skill, she began writing and revising old stories, some based upon her dog Rover and his adventures, others mythical celebrations of spring. In late December she felt impelled by a strong desire to express herself as a playwright. She wrote to Ruskin, 'What do you think it is doing – Trying to write a play in the midst of all this bother! . . . Of course it won't be good or of any use – only I must do it!'[31]

On 20 January 1900 Ruskin died, following a sudden attack of influenza. At first Kate was stunned. The entry in her diary is short, giving no hint of her feelings. She was equally calm and reserved to her brother and her friends, showing little of the despair that was building up inside her. She had received the news not from Joan Severn, as she had always expected, but from Stuart Samuel, who had read it in the Sunday papers. Learning about such a monumental loss at third hand only added to the feeling of unreality; and Kate at first refused to believe it. Only after she received Joan Severn's letter the following day could she begin to comprehend it. The day after, a second letter arrived from Brantwood, with details of the circumstances of the death: that it had been unexpected, but mercifully painless. In the first of three replies, Kate, still dazed, wrote; 'I can hardly believe it but I cannot be grateful enough that since death must come – that it came painlessly – and he deserved no pain – .' Her second letter, written two days later, emphasized the sacrifices that still needed to be made. She understood Joan's fearsome task of answering the hordes of letters, especially now, with her servants ill; and she begged her not to worry about answering her's right away. She noted that she had made an effort to find violets at Covent Garden, which she sent as a reminder of their tea-times together. Joan loyally placed them on the grave near her own wreath of red roses. Then the decision to hold the service and burial at Coniston aroused an outcry among Ruskin's admirers, who insisted that the burial should have been at Westminster Abbey; Kate, too, was surprised by Joan's decision and had 'never thought it would be anywhere else' but the Abbey. As it turned out, two services were held simultaneously, one at Coniston church, the other at Westminster Abbey. On that day, the shock of Ruskin's death gave way to an outpouring of Kate's despair. At last realizing the loss, she sent a third letter to Joan, written just after the funeral. This was a pathetic attempt to explain the feelings she had kept bottled up inside her for so long.

> One feels all one can say is of no use – nothing is but time – and it is merciful – that is – I knew I should feel it – but I did not know that I should feel it like I do – but nearly every morning and evening writing little bits of my letter – I am so bitterly sorry that the last two years have been such different ones to me, that I had so little to draw for him or write properly. I might have done so much more – but I was always hoping things would get better and I would have more leisure – but you see it is a necessity I do my work. I am so dreadfully sorry when I feel I might have given him more pleasure – .

She yearned to make amends for her selfish neglect over the past few months, and proposed designing his tomb, 'all girls and children and angels – with flowers growing at the top. He would like it. I wish I could do it later on', she added; but the problems and illnesses which followed during the next few months left this poignant plan unfulfilled.[32]

Friends and acquaintances offered the solicitude and sympathy Kate needed. One of the most effective of these was Marion H. Spielmann, editor of the *Magazine of Art* and an enthusiastic disciple of Ruskin – he wrote the first memorial tribute to the Master, published in 1900. Immediately following Ruskin's death, he and Kate renewed and strengthened their friendship, as together they lamented the loss of the great man. Then, as an influential art critic who had championed the work of Millais and Watts, Spielmann became a

Joan (Mrs Arthur) Severn, from a portrait by Joseph Severn.

valued adviser and confidant. Aware that Kate's reputation needed reappraisal, he proposed a series of articles for his magazine, to be entitled 'The Later Work of Kate Greenaway', in which he planned to publish reproductions of her recent portraits in the hope of attracting a wider audience for her work. Kate willingly agreed in principle, and she lent him new drawings and paintings to illustrate the articles. On one occasion, during a visit to her studio, she thought enough of their friendship to give him a drawing, which she nervously signed 'Kate Spielmann'. Nevertheless, she refused to let him disturb her daily work routine. When she received a request for pictures to be exhibited at the Paris International Exhibition she refused that as well; although it would have been an opportunity to repeat her success of eleven years earlier, and she must have realized this. But she had neither the successful older works (most of which had been sold at the Fine Art Society) nor the time to interrupt her oil portraits to paint pictures representative of her old style. Her oil work was certainly not yet good enough to be shown in public.

1900 was also the year Frederick Warne purchased from his old business partner and now rival publisher, George Routledge, the rights to reissue selected Greenaway books. This was presumably an attempt to fill the need for well printed and tastefully produced books at a time when the *Athenaeum* was reviewing with obvious disgust what they called the 'stupidity and gaudiness' of most new children's books. In addition, Macmillan offered Kate a new commission, *The April Baby's Book of Tunes*, written by one of her favourite authors, the Countess von Arnim, author of *Elizabeth and her German Garden*. It was her enjoyment of the *Elizabeth* book, which she had once recommended to Ruskin, that influenced Kate's acceptance of the proposal. After three years away from illustrating, she found it particularly difficult to complete the work on time. Bouts of winter illnesses had weakened her, and forced her to work more slowly than usual. She wrote pathetic apologies to the author, reassuring her that she was working as fast as she could. At last, a few weeks before her deadline, she completed the drawings, and the book appeared in early December. Those of the author's friends who had known the original 'April Babies' marvelled at the way Kate had caught their likeness (she had not worked from photographs). The *Athenaeum* too believed it was 'Miss Greenaway . . . at her best', although the reviewer felt that the absence of the familiar sharply drawn profiles prevented the book's being a complete success: '. . . she has not drawn them with quite all the delicacy and finish which distinguish her earlier efforts.' This weakness can in fact be traced to the printing; it was the clarity of the wood-engraved line which had been lost, since this was the first time a Greenaway book was printed by chromolithography, although the process had earlier been used to reproduce her greeting cards.

Kate had endured a depressing struggle throughout the spring and summer, in order to complete *The April Baby's Book of Tunes*. Immersed in mourning and despair over Ruskin's death, she was very susceptible to illness. She and her brother both suffered attacks of influenza. Following this, sharp pains caught her unawares, attacking her chest so severely that she was unable to lift a pen or brush. She was afraid of the dark and refused to go into her dark studio at night, confining herself to her sitting room below, where she idly shuffled through pages of half-finished verses. A glimmer of hope came one day in the form of loud cheering down the street: her neighbours were celebrating the march to Pretoria that they mistakenly believed would end the terrible Boer war. Briefly infected with their enthusiasm, Kate took up her pen and sketched a Greenaway child waving a Union Jack, inscribed it 'Marching Onwards to Pretoria to Fight for Queen Victoria', and sent it to Dolly Locker-Lampson. But for the most part everything about her seemed silent, dark, and gloomy; even her reading was of little comfort. She found unnatural and depressing passages in Thomas Hardy's *The Woodlanders*, and in her usual stubborn way she refused to read on, or indeed to read any more Hardy. What little pleasure she had came from daydreaming about the past, especially of Rolleston, with its apple blossoms and its primroses. 'This is what it is, you see, to have gone through life with an enchanted land ever beside you – yet how much it has been!'[33]

She could not forget Ruskin's part in that 'enchanted land', and even in death his influence remained as strong as ever. In her verses she eulogized and fantasized the Master's role in her life.

> *Ah – you are far away – and I am here*
> *Compelled by fates unkind control*
> *No more can our hands meet – nor our eyes look*
> *Each into each – to learn the other's soul.*
>
> *We two were to each – so very . . . dear*
> *Must read now in – a separate book*
> *Your voice speaks – I can't hear a word*
> *Or see the page on which you look.*

I cannot watch your lips move – and half know
What – the halfspoken word is going to be
You cannot anymore – divine my smile
And lightly smile and answer back to me.

The straight road – has turned cross – the finger points
The finger points – this way you turn – that other way I go
And both those paths – lead to engulphing [sic] sea
Down into deeps – of overpowering woe.

Your fingers stretch – in vain – in vain
Mine – are not there to meet their touch
They only grasp the vacant air
                              much . . .[34]

Significantly perhaps, she left the last line unfinished.

In several verses it seems that she looked upon death as a welcome release from her present despair over money, the future and her loneliness.

Yes, I will follow when you go through that door
Whence no one, any more
Comes back or looks again
Ah no – no – all is vain
But only call and I will come to thee.[35]

And so by June 1900 Kate's life revolved solely around her memories of the past. Joan Severn had by then sorted through Ruskin's papers, burnt his love letters to Rose La Touche, and was helping in the preparation of a library edition of his works. Searching through his papers, Joan had found all the letters Kate had written to Ruskin since 1887, and she asked if she could use some of them in the biographical section. She felt, however, that a certain amount of editing would be necessary to avoid any misconstruction being put upon their relationship. She was especially conscious of the need for caution because she had been worried by hearing that some of Ruskin's 'pets' were selling his affectionate letters to them; this could give rise to any number of misconceptions about his emotional life. Now that Ruskin was dead, Kate desperately wanted her name associated with his in whatever way possible. She replied to Joan that she had all Ruskin's letters to her, 'one for nearly every day for three years'. Her own letters to the Master might be placed in two categories: the frantic love letters of the 1880s, which only Joan should read, as 'there might be things in some one would feel perhaps better not published'; and the descriptive, calm, comforting letters of the 1890s: 'In the later letters, I think, there is nothing I should object to anyone reading.' And yet she preferred the early ones, which Joan had by now destroyed; she noted that Ruskin had admired her skill in writing love letters, reminding Joan that he had once told her they 'ought to exist as long as the most beautiful of my drawings should – because they were also beautiful'. She was still deeply moved by what she called 'the affection ['friendship' crossed out] between us', and proud of her small place in his life. 'I feel so honoured by it, that I can only feel honoured by my name ever to appear near his.'[36]

The illnesses she described to friends as colds, influenza or rheumatism continued throughout the year. June was the only month when she did not need to send for the doctor; and yet Kate preferred not to reveal the real cause of her illnesses to anyone. The medical report on her death certificate reveals that in November 1899 she had been told by her doctor that she had breast cancer, and would have to have an operation. Kate delayed entering hospital for nearly eight months, placing all her hopes in the medicine she had been prescribed. She was worried enough to cancel a long-anticipated visit to the Samuel family at Cromer in May, her letter saying she would be unable to come because 'I never felt so ill before.' Confined to the house, and too ill to work, she grew restless. During an unusually cold June, when she ordered roaring fires 'to make us feel more cheerful', her health surprisingly improved, although her spirits remained low, 'for I've not seen a picture or been anywhere now', she wrote to Maria Ponsonby. Determined to have her own way, she ended the letter, 'I'm going out in the rain for a walk.'[37] The pain returned in July, and at last Kate reluctantly agreed to enter hospital for the required and much-delayed operation. The prospect certainly horrified her: she had once written to Dolly Locker-Lampson, 'I am a real downright coward when I go to the dentist.' Somehow she endured the rushed preparations, had the operation, and afterwards was given the dreadful news that even her doctor had not expected. The cancer had spread throughout her chest – the cause of the recent pains and colds – and her life was seriously endangered.

The shock stunned her and made her unable to think about what little time there was left. She sought comfort at Newhaven Court ('I want the sea and change'), where she stayed under Hannah Jane Locker-Lampson's care from mid-August to early September. There, even after walks on the beach, followed by hot seawater baths, the pain returned, bringing with it the inescapable reality. Before she left, she signed the guest book:

> When I am dead, and all of you stand round
> And look upon me, my soul flown away
> Into a new existence – far from the sound
> Of this world's noise, and this world's night and day . . .

She completed the verse on her return to London:

> No more the inexplicable soul in this strange mortal body
> This world and it in severance eternal:
> No more my presence here shall it embody,
> No more shall take its place in time diurnal –
>
> What beauteous land may I be wandering in
> While you stand gazing at what once was I?
> Why, I may be to gold harps listening
> And plucking flowers of Immortality –
>   Why, Heavens blue skies may shine above my head
>   While you stand there – and say that I am dead![38]

212

Catherine Dadd, Eddie's sister, used in an early periodical illustration.

Back in Hampstead, and suffering from what she still called a 'bad cold', she described to Maria Ponsonby her condition after the operation: 'I soon get tired and my arm keeps very stiff. However I suppose it is to be expected for a time.'[39] To add to her worry, her brother also nursed an injured arm, which failed to heal properly and was still kept in a sling after a fall a year earlier. Each month the doctor called to see what progress they had both made. While Johnnie's arm gradually improved, Kate's condition grew worse. News of her illness and the need for money to pay the doctor worried her friends. Lady Dorothy Nevill wrote to suggest buying a drawing, but Kate refused, although she was touched by the gesture. Her need for money did not allow her to forget her friends, and she insisted that if Lady Dorothy wanted a drawing she would love 'to GIVE YOU anything you like – drawings are the only things I have to give my friends'. She did stress that, providing her health improved, she might accept new portrait commissions if Lady Dorothy could find them. Her letter ended, 'Dear Lady Dorothy, I do feel you so kind and I send you much love,' as if it were her last chance to thank her friend.[40]

Such gestures only made Kate feel more guilty as she fretted that her illness made her neglect her friends and her work. 'I seem to have been ill all the year,' she wrote to Mrs Marion Spielmann, with whom she had become close before the operation. 'I had a long illness all the autumn which I am not yet recovered from – and then colds so bad they have been illnesses . . . I have seen no one hardly and done so little work. I'm so sorry when I don't work. For the time so soon goes and I always have so much I want to do.'[41] Mrs Spielmann had asked her to illustrate a book of stories she had previously published in *Little Folks*, and it was this that worried Kate. She did not want to go back on her promise to supply drawings, and eventually she sent two rather inappropriate pencil studies. These were obviously derived from her children's portrait work, the

Study from Life being a large sketch of her nephew Eddie Dadd. Unfortunately, she had neither the strength nor the will to illustrate properly Mrs Spielmann's story of 'Ronald's Clock', itself a splendid fantasy about a boy's adventures while shut away in the base of a magic grandfather clock that projected him through time. It was published with Kate's pencil drawings, alongside other stories illustrated by some of the rising young illustrators, such as Arthur Rackham, Jessie King and Phil May. Marion Spielmann's introduction to the book makes it clear that her works were included as a tribute rather than for their worth. When it was published in 1902, Spielmann honoured her by writing of 'how our dear Kate Greenaway showed her sympathy with childhood, in whose service she passed her life . . . they were among the last drawings she ever made.'

The months of suffering, from what she still insisted were only colds and muscular pains, seemed odd to her friends, but Kate still refused to explain the exact cause of her pain. Later accounts by relatives bear out that she never confessed her breast cancer to anyone. Her favourite nephew, Eddie Dadd, for example, remembered, and still insisted years after her death, that his Aunt Kate had died following an illness incurred after being struck on the head by a case while travelling. Only in her letters to Joan Severn, whom she still looked upon as one of her closest friends, was she more forthcoming about her pain and suffering. On the anniversary of Ruskin's birthday she wrote to Joan, describing her life spent under the shadow of certain death. She had been given a complicated and time-consuming medical routine, and this made life 'so difficult to me of late years'. But not even Joan was told about the breast cancer. At last, however, Kate had realized the seriousness of her condition, and she followed the doctor's instructions to the letter. 'As it is I take everything I can. Medicine, 9 times a day; beef tea, 8 times; port wine, champagne, brandy and soda, eggs and milk. I'm all day at it. Can I do more? Am I not a victim?'[42] This prescription, with its frequent doses of alcohol, was obviously designed to alleviate the pain; the nourishment she needed consisted only of eggs, milk and beef tea. And yet her spirits were somewhat restored by the spring, when she went to see Helen Allingham's exhibition of water colours of 'English Country Life and Venice' at the Fine Art Society, and spoke briefly to her old friend. Helen later recalled their meeting: 'I thought she looked fairly well, and seemed so, though she spoke of having felt tired sometimes. But she said nothing of the serious illness of the year before.'[43]

The medicine, alcohol and liquid nourishment were taken religiously each day, and Kate gradually rallied enough for brief spring and summer outings. In April she spent a fortnight at Freshwater, Isle of Wight; in June she admired the irises growing along the water at Kew Gardens, and she later described the memorable day to Dorothy Nevill, promising at the same time to get her friend's china dishes on another excursion into London 'the first afternoon I can get to the shop'.[44] Matters seemed to be improving enough for her to think about work, and there was talk of a Greenaway dressmaking business, an idea often previously discussed with her sister Fanny. She mentioned schemes for modelling processionals in bas-relief, as her friend Caldecott had once done so successfully; and there was a plan to illustrate a children's Christmas paper in colour. Longmans proposed that she should illustrate a series of elementary readers, but Kate knew that such work demanded more time than she had left to her. A few months later she was offered the editorship of a children's magazine, but this too was refused, on the grounds that she hadn't the proper qualifications or the strength for such a long-range project.

In July the agonizing pain returned, as a result of the cancer's spreading from the area of the operation scar towards the spine. She decided that, before things got worse, she would return to Cromer to be among friends. 'I've been very ill – acute muscular rheumatism – horribly painful,' she wrote to Mrs Samuel from Cromer.[45] On her return to London the pain increased, and with it the excruciation of being unable to sleep. Helen Allingham knocked at her door one day, but was politely turned away by the maid, who told her that Kate was in no condition to receive visitors. Having been kept in the dark for so long, Joan Severn wrote; begging for news. All she wanted was a postcard saying Kate was well and prospering; and she added 'I am unceasing in gratitude for all you were to him [Ruskin] – of all friends in late years – you were the chief comforter with your goodness and sweet letters.'[46]

Heartening as this was, Kate had neither the strength nor the will to write back. Daily she hovered closer to death; the cancer spread to her lungs, making breathing difficult; her strength deteriorated and she lost weight; then it became almost impossible to move, her fight for breath turning into a struggle for survival. Outside, during the last few days, one of the thickest fogs in years swirled and dropped over Hampstead, bringing life to a temporary standstill. Shops were forced to close and people stayed indoors. Inside 39 Frognal, at nine o'clock on the evening of 6 November 1901, the light that for fifty-five years had shone from the 'curious Greenaway woman' was finally extinguished.[47]

To some it seemed a pathetic end to a sad, and in many ways unfulfilled, life. Others felt it in a way appropriate that one so dedicated to the Victorian age should die the year it came to an official close. Newspapers noted the loss of a singular individual, who had given innocent pleasure to countless homes and families. 'It is a little thing to be good in this life – to get a happy one after,' she had once written to Ruskin. Admirers and colleagues sent flowers, including a large wreath presented by the artist Lawrence Alma-Tadema and his painter wife on behalf of the members of his profession. The ribbon read: 'In grateful memory of a beautiful art, from fellow workers'. On 12 November, in the rain and wind, the flower-covered coffin was taken by road to Woking, where, according to Kate's wishes, she was cremated – an unusual practice for the time. On the following day, Kate's ashes were placed in Hampstead cemetery in the family plot, next to her mother and her beloved father. The ceremony was conducted with all the solemnity and concern for privacy she would have wanted. 'One who thus lived shunning at all times publicity, may well have deserved a funeral as studiously simple and private as that,' claimed a local newspaper.[48] Kate's grave remains neglected, in spring obscured by the blossoming fruit trees she loved, the headstone inscribed with her own verse:

> *Heaven's blue skies may shine above my head,*
> *While you stand there – and say that I am dead!*

Epilogue

Johnnie Greenaway found the weeks following his sister's funeral especially trying, particularly the sorting out of all Kate's things, deciding what was important and what could be thrown away. Kate had not made a will, so her estate, sworn at over £6,000, or a net value of nearly £3,000, went to her brother by intestacy. Johnnie wanted to do what he believed his sister would have wished, and he gave all Kate's furniture and personal items to his sisters. He also set aside the most personal items as mementoes for Kate's closest friends. In a letter to Joan Severn, in which he described the clearing out process as 'a sort of nightmare time', he assured her that he had not forgotten her role in comforting Kate up to the end. He had vainly searched through the studio for Kate's cup and saucer to send to her, but failing this (he concluded that the servants must have broken it), he sent Joan some of Kate's needlework.[1]

The studio proved the greatest problem. Johnnie spent days looking through the piles of unfinished drawings, smeared oil paintings, and what remained of her book illustrations after the Fine Art Society sales. In an attempt to clear up the mess, and to re-establish Kate's reputation in the galleries, he planned a posthumous exhibition of her studio works at the Fine Art Society. Marcus Huish was again given the task of organizing the event, and Marion Spielmann wrote the catalogue and advised on the exhibits that appeared early in 1902. Every effort had been made to produce an impressive display. In the middle of the gallery stood an imposing glass case filled with Kate's illustrated letters to Ruskin, with tiny paper shutters placed over what one critic guessed were sections 'too intimate and particular, no doubt, for the vulgar eye'. These had been loaned by Joan Severn, as had six of her own Greenaway watercolours to help pad out the sparse walls. In the catalogue Spielmann's eloquent essay emphasized the merits of Kate's entire artistic career, but necessarily dwelt most lengthily on her fame as a book illustrator.

At the private view Johnnie approached Spielmann on the subject of Kate's biography. After a brief discussion, Spielmann agreed to write it. The subject was forgotten for several months, during which time Johnnie sold the Frognal house, which he found much too large for himself alone, and moved to a riverside flat at Chertsey. Eventually, he reminded Spielmann of his promise, and the work began. There were difficulties, however. Spielmann had, quite understandably, requested access to all Kate's correspondence, and, as a keen disciple of Ruskin, placed particular emphasis on the letters between Kate and Ruskin. It was on this point that problems arose. Johnnie asked for Joan Severn's advice on the treatment of the Ruskin correspondence. He knew only too well that Joan had firm views on anything concerning her beloved cousin's memory and reputation. In her reply, Joan stressed that the relationship between Kate and Ruskin should be handled with utmost caution, ideally by someone who had known and understood them both. Earlier she had told another friend that it would be best 'to let the world think it was only an

216

ordinary affectionate friendship – and suppress the idea it meant anything else', and she now re-emphasized this.[2] She took on the task of censoring each of Ruskin's letters to Kate before Spielmann was allowed access to them, pencilling out those sections he was not to be allowed to quote, and this made it almost impossible for Spielmann to piece together Ruskin's role in his subject's life. He decided that all he could do was print in full, almost always without editorial comment, those letters or brief passages which Joan allowed him to use. The resulting biography is a scrappy, disjointed book, at times thoroughly confusing in its lack of chronology or interpretation. When it was published, in 1905, after nearly three years in preparation, Johnnie Greenaway and his family and friends were deeply disappointed. For 300 pages Spielmann rambled on, interspersing his text with ink sketches and elaborate colour plates (the printing of which had been supervised by Edmund Evans, who died as the book was being printed). Every effort had been made to produce an appealing tribute: the endpapers were printed from colour blocks given by the wallpaper manufacturer who had once delighted Kate with his sanitary nursery wallpapers based on her almanack designs. Although a limited edition of the biography (which had an original Greenaway pencil sketch inserted), was authorized by Johnnie Greenaway, he and his family never liked Spielmann's book.

Meanwhile Kate's friends prepared their own tributes. Austin Dobson continued his relentless efforts to champion the Greenaway style, writing articles for the *Art Journal* and later supplying Kate's entry in the *Dictionary of National Biography*. Eighteen friends and admirers, including Walter Crane, Arthur Liberty and his wife, Lady Jeune, Lady Maria Ponsonby, Lady Dorothy Nevill, Marion Spielmann and Hannah Jane Locker-Lampson organized a Greenaway memorial fund. Appeals were placed in newspapers and popular magazines, promising that a Greenaway memento would be sent for each donation received. Eventually nearly a thousand pounds was collected, which, after expenses, was used to endow a cot at the Great Ormond Street Children's Hospital, London. In 1903 there was an unveiling of a bronze plaque designed by Mrs Liberty. It was hoped that further memorial cots might be endowed throughout the country, and the campaign for funds continued; but, unfortunately, the response was too small.

The Kate Greenaway Memorial plaque.

Greenaway designs adapted for wall murals based on the seasons spring and autumn. From the American periodical, *The Craftsmen* (February, 1905).

Left: Kate Greenaway inspired smocked dress, from Liberty's *Catalogue of Art Fabrics and Personal Speciality* – 'Artistic Dress for Children' (1887). *Below*: 'Freda', a Greenaway dress offered by Liberty's from their 1905 colour catalogue.

Nevertheless, despite the efforts of her staunch admirers and tributes in the press, Kate's artistic reputation in England barely survived the twenty years following her death, although she fared better on the Continent and in America. European journalists wrote enthusiastic articles trying in vain to analyse her work, and to establish her importance for a new generation of aspiring young illustrators. The Germans compared her work favourably with that of their own caricaturists, and some still believed her talent was the outcome of German descent. (The legend had long circulated there that she had been born in Düsseldorf, where a street, Grüne Weg, held the key to her name, and that her father had only later emigrated to England and anglicized it to Greenaway.) Perhaps more to the point was the fact that Kate's favourite model, Eddie Dadd, now lived and worked in Germany. Forever proud of his connection with his famous Aunt Katie, he used his reputation as the 'Greenaway boy' in her books to help him enjoy German society, always flattered by being associated with Kate. He treasured his role in her life, and, according to his daughter years later, was constantly referring to her in instructing his own children.

In fashion-conscious France, Kate's books had spawned a dress style called *Greenawayisme*. The contemporary painter Jules Breton refused to dress his children in anything but Greenaway costumes, which he claimed were 'dignes d'embellir les chefs-d'oeuvre du bon Dieu!' Kate's obituary in the *Times* noted that 'Miss Greenaway's success in France was, indeed, immense; and it is safe to say that without her M. Boutet de Monvel and his school would never have existed.' The French flocked to the Paris branch of Liberty's to buy Greenaway gowns for themselves and their children, and the fashion vogue continued well into the 1920s.[3]

Perhaps more importantly in terms of the present-day interest in Kate's work, the American critics floundered for adjectives to describe what was lost by her death. They could only conclude that there were certain permanent qualities in her drawings, the outlines were 'Flaxman-like', drawn with the 'affectionateness of Stothard, the soul of William Blake'. Long articles summarizing her work appeared in New York periodicals, and friends and associates, such as Oliver Locker-Lampson, were persuaded to record their impressions of the woman behind the Greenaway legend.

For all this, even in America the large orders usually received for Greenaway books gradually decreased; the sales of even her most popular books dwindling to a few hundred.[4] But with the failure of the Greenaway books to attract a public among children and parents, came the rise of a new audience − the indefatigable Greenaway collector. Almost as quickly as Kate's books went out of print, they were sought out and snapped up by keen book collectors willing to pay exorbitant prices. There is a favourite story among Greenaway collectors of President Theodore Roosevelt's formidable daughter, Mrs Alice Longworth, on a special trip to London, storming into a famous bookshop and demanding all the Greenaway books in stock. Ignoring the high prices, she bought them all, paying for them with a handful of notes she pulled from her Dolly Varden handbag. Almost inevitably, as the market for Greenaway originals, paintings, drawings and sketches rose, a plethora of Greenaway forgeries entered the London galleries, some originating from a workshop started up in the early part

Mr John Greenaway, Kate's brother, from a photograph taken in 1931, seven years before his death.

of this century by a group of enterprising copyists; although, it seems they were not entirely competent, for they churned out obvious imitations, drawn in a brown ink Kate seldom used.[5]

This misrepresentation deeply upset Johnnie Greenaway, as he solemnly tried to preserve his sister's reputation. In his flat at The Orchard, Chertsey, he had become something of a legend himself, as the keeper of the Greenaway secrets, which he willingly revealed to his guests when they arrived to study the shrine he had constructed in his study. All along the walls hung Kate's carefully framed drawings, below them the books she had created and those she had been given by Ruskin. When asked for the loan of a Greenaway original for some memorial exhibition, he generally consented, but not without learning exactly how the works were to be presented, and checking on whether the organizers had followed his precise hanging instructions. By the late 1920s, arrangements were made to present his entire collection of original drawings, proofs, cards and paintings to the Hampstead local library, and the librarian wrote a twenty-seven-page catalogue to the collection. Johnnie was so pleased with this succinct tribute to his sister's memory that he had several extra copies printed, gave them to friends and admirers, and claimed that this was the book he and his family preferred to the Spielmann biography. He continued his efforts on Kate's behalf until his death in 1938.

During the 1920s, publishers awoke to the interest in Kate's work among collectors, and elaborate volumes were produced, designed to appeal to the Greenaway connoisseur. For example, in 1921 a compilation of watercolours originally sent to Ruskin was produced as a lavish art book, with hand-tipped colour plates printed on fine paper. The introduction was reverential: 'One may venture to prophesy that long after the present craze for the works of the Cubists and Vorticists has been forgotten, interest in Kate Greenaway's drawings . . . will continue to survive.'[6] A series of Greenaway almanacks, based upon Kate's previously published almanack designs, was launched between 1924 and 1929. This was Frederick Warne's attempt not only to revive Kate's work (the firm had been reissuing selected Greenaway books from 1900), but also to cash in on the remarkable success of Kate's heir apparent as nursery illustrator, Beatrix Potter. The huge popularity of her *Peter Rabbit* had indicated that there was a market for meticulous watercolours in the Greenaway vein. Moreover, when Beatrix Potter was asked by Warne's to prepare her own *Peter Rabbit Almanack*, she understandably turned to Kate's almanack series for inspiration.[7]

In 1946, the centenary of Kate's birth, the Greenaway legend was given a new impetus. Articles and tribute books, all relying heavily on Spielmann's book, boosted interest in Kate's work. By then Greenaway collecting had become a cult, with articles in American antique magazines recording the variant bindings of her books, the number of Greenaway buttons, silver tea services, christening sets, or the discovery of a new china Greenaway doll complete with several changes of costume. It was an ironic about-face, this preserving of Kate's reputation by the very objects of ephemera that had once vitiated her originality and reputation. In 1955 the Kate Greenaway Medal was established, to be awarded to the most distinguished annual contribution by a British illustrator of children's books. Interest grew during the 1960s; her house in Frognal was bought by the local council in 1961. It was given a commemorative plaque, and, although today it is broken into flats, it still retains much of its original appearance. The tall studio window looms over what is now a crowded neighbourhood filled with mansions leading up to Greenaway Gardens. A Kate Greenaway nursery school was established in Islington, and a Kate Greenaway children's library was named in nearby Hackney.

Today the Greenaway legend continues to thrive. Interest in original Greenaway material brought to the London sale rooms means that a good drawing or watercolour will fetch prices undreamed of at the end of her life, and first edition books are so expensive that only the most ardent collector can afford them. Certain Greenaway books are still in print and are sold widely, while Greenaway paintings on greeting cards are extremely popular. The most sophisticated of twentieth-century tastes, it seems, can still be captivated by the unexpected charm of a simple, escapist view of life. To lose ourselves in one of Kate's brick-walled, carefully clipped gardens, to escape our problems by projecting ourselves back in time, remains an alluring prospect.

Notes

CHAPTER 1

1. *The Brothers Dalziel* (London, 1901), p. 8.
2. There is a considerable amount of discrepancy in Cavendish Street house numbers: Spielmann and Layard give it as 1 Cavendish Street; the Hoxton rate books (1845–6) give 39; the Greenaway family papers 21.
3. John Greenaway's engraved book work included: *A Treasury of Pleasure Rhymes for Children* (1850), illustrated by J. Absolon and Harrison Weir; Robert Bloomfield's *Farmer's Boy*, and *Cat and Dog* (both 1858), engraved with A.L. Mason; *Favourite English Ballads* (1859); J. Cundall's *Poetry of Nature* (1861), with 24 engravings after Harrison Weir; *Three Hundred Aesop's Fables* (1867); *Tuppy, or the Autobiography of a Donkey* (1868); S. Trimmer's *History of the Robins* (1869), engraved after Harrison Weir; and *Trottie's Storybook* (1878), after Harrison Weir.
4. Spielmann and Layard, *Kate Greenaway* (London, 1905), p. 216.
5. Spielmann and Layard, *Kate Greenaway*, pp. 17–18.
6. Spielmann and Layard, *Kate Greenaway*, p. 235.
7. Spielmann and Layard, *Kate Greenaway*, p. 35.
8. Spielmann and Layard, *Kate Greenaway*, p. 36.

CHAPTER 2

1. Spielmann and Layard, *Kate Greenaway*, p. 245.
2. Spielmann and Layard, *Kate Greenaway*, p. 246.
3. Spielmann and Layard, *Kate Greenaway*, p. 41.
4. Spielmann and Layard, *Kate Greenaway*, p. 237.
5. Spielmann and Layard, *Kate Greenaway*, p. 26.
6. Spielmann and Layard, *Kate Greenaway*, p. 16.
7. M.V. Hughes, *A London Child of the 1870s* (Oxford, 1977), p. 62.
8. Lady Butler, *An Autobiography* (London, 1922), pp. 34, 50.
9. *Art Journal*, 1870, p. 91. The ceremony, held in February, was for student work completed during the twelve months preceding April 1869.
10. W.S. Spanton, *An Art Student and his Teachers in the Sixties* (London, 1927), p. 16.
11. Spanton, *An Art Student*, p. 30.

CHAPTER 3

1. Spielmann and Layard, *Kate Greenaway*, p. 16.
2. Spielmann and Layard, *Kate Greenaway*, p. 52.
3. Spielmann and Layard, *Kate Greenaway*, p. 57.
4. Spielmann and Layard, *Kate Greenaway*, p. 70.
5. Michael Hutchins, *Yours Pictorially* ((London, 1976), p. 32.
6. Hutchins, *Yours Pictorially*, p. 32.
7. Ruari McLean, *The Reminiscences of Edmund Evans* (London, 1967), p. 61.
8. Austin Dobson, Introduction to Frederick Locker, *London Lyrics* (London, 1904 ed.), pp. xxi–xxii.
9. Letter of 16 December 1878, Berg Collection, New York Public Library.
10. Letter of 24 December 1878, Berg Collection.
11. Letter of 18 February 1879, Berg Collection.
12. Hutchins, *Yours Pictorially*, p. 32.
13. Hutchins, *Yours Pictorially*, p. 224.
14. McLean, *Edmund Evans*, p. 66.
15. Spielmann and Layard, *Kate Greenaway*, p. 80.
16. Spielmann and Layard, *Kate Greenaway*, p. 71.

CHAPTER 4

1. Spielmann and Layard, *Kate Greenaway*, pp. 80–81.
2. Spielmann and Layard, *Kate Greenaway*, p. 85.
3. Spielmann and Layard, *Kate Greenaway*, p. 81.
4. Spielmann and Layard, *Kate Greenaway*, pp. 109–10.
5. Spielmann and Layard, *Kate Greenaway*, pp. 82–3.
6. Spielmann and Layard, *Kate Greenaway*, p. 223.
7. Letter of 15 January 1880, Pierpont Morgan Library, New York.
8. R.H. Wilenski, *John Ruskin* (London, 1933), p. 72; see also Mary Anderson de Navarro, *A Few More Memories* (London, 1936), p. 23.
9. Undated letter (December 1873), Pierpont Morgan Library.
10. Wilenski, *Ruskin*, p. 172.
11. Wilenski, *Ruskin*, p. 275.
12. Joan Evans, *John Ruskin* (London, 1954), p. 321
13. Wilenski, *Ruskin*, p. 277.
14. Arthur Severn, *The Professor* (London, 1967), p. 94.
15. Henrietta Corkran, *Celebrities and I* (London, 1902), pp. 259–60.
16. Spielmann and Layard, *Kate Greenaway*, pp. 48, 60.
17. Letter of 12 November 1880, Free Library of Philadelphia.
18. Spielmann and Layard, *Kate Greenaway*, p. 91.

19. Spielmann and Layard, *Kate Greenaway*, pp. 84–5.

20. Spielmann and Layard, *Kate Greenaway*, p. 87. She was not far wrong. Publishers issued *The Ruskin Birthday Book* (1883), *The Birthday Book of Art and Artists* (1884), and *The Robert Browning Birthday Book* (1886).

21. Spielmann and Layard, *Kate Greenaway*, p. 84.

22. Spielmann and Layard, *Kate Greenaway*, pp. 86–7.

23. Spielmann and Layard, *Kate Greenaway*, p. 84.

24. Spielmann and Layard, *Kate Greenaway*, p. 93.

25. Spielmann and Layard, *Kate Greenaway*, p. 92.

26. Spielmann and Layard, *Kate Greenaway*, p. 95.

27. Spielmann and Layard, *Kate Greenaway*, p. 95.

28. Spielmann and Layard, *Kate Greenaway*, p. 98.

29. Spielmann and Layard, *Kate Greenaway*, pp. 104–5.

30. Spielmann and Layard, *Kate Greenaway*, p. 105.

31. Letter of 26 March 1882, Free Library of Philadelphia.

32. Spielmann and Layard, *Kate Greenaway*, pp. 89–90.

33. Spielmann and Layard, *Kate Greenaway*, p. 91.

34. Letter of 21 December 1882, Berg Collection.

35. Telegram of 24 December 1882, Berg Collection.

36. Letter of 25 December 1882, Pierpont Morgan Library.

37. Spielmann and Layard, *Kate Greenaway*, p. 110.

38. Spielmann and Layard, *Kate Greenaway*, p. 210.

39. Letter of 16 January 1884, Pierpont Morgan Library.

CHAPTER 5

1. Letter of 18 February 1883, Pierpont Morgan Library.

2. Cheque dated 24 January 1883, Berg Collection.

3. Sheila Birkenhead, *Illustrious Friends* (London, 1965), p. 296.

4. Thomas Wise (ed.), *Letters from John Ruskin to Ernest Chesneau* (London, 1894), p. 42.

5. Letter of 8 March 1883, Pittsburgh.

6. Anne Ritchie, *Records of Tennyson, Ruskin and Browning* (London, 1892), p. 69.

7. Spielmann and Layard, *Kate Greenaway*, pp. 15, 113.

8. Wise, *Letters from Ruskin*, p. 43.

9. Helen Viljoen (ed.), *The Brantwood Diary of John Ruskin* (London, 1971), pp. 315–20.

10. Spielmann and Layard, *Kate Greenaway*, p. 15.

11. Letter of 17 May 1883, Pierpont Morgan Library.

12. Spielmann and Layard, *Kate Greenaway*, p. 89.

13. Augustine Birrell, *Frederick Locker-Lampson* (London, 1920), pp. 106–7.

14. Letter of 20 May 1883, Pierpont Morgan Library.

15. Margaret Spence (ed.), *Dearest Mamma Talbot* (London, 1966), p. 118.

16. Letter of 7 June 1883, Pierpont Morgan Library.

17. Letter of 15 June 1883, Pierpont Morgan Library.

18. Letter of 22 June 1883, Pierpont Morgan Library.

19. Letters of 1, 4 July 1883, Pierpont Morgan Library.

20. Letter of 5 July 1883, Pierpont Morgan Library.

21. Letter of 10 July 1883, Pierpont Morgan Library.

22. Letter of 26 July 1883, Pierpont Morgan Library.

23. Letter of 29 July 1883, Pierpont Morgan Library.

24. Letter of 2 August 1883, Pierpont Morgan Library.

25. Letter of 5 August 1883, Pierpont Morgan Library.

26. Letter of 7 August 1883, Pierpont Morgan Library.

27. Letters of 2, 6 September 1883, Pierpont Morgan Library.

28. Letter of 10 September 1883, Pierpont Morgan Library.

29. Letter of 25 September 1883, Pierpont Morgan Library.

30. Letter of 1 October 1883, Pierpont Morgan Library.

31. Spielmann and Layard, *Kate Greenaway*, p. 113.

32. Letter of 10 October 1883, Pierpont Morgan Library.

33. Letters of 14, 16 October 1883, Pierpont Morgan Library.

34. Letter of 25 October 1883, Pierpont Morgan Library.

35. Letter of 4 November 1883, Pierpont Morgan Library.

36. Letter of 6 November 1883, Pierpont Morgan Library.

37. Letter of 23 November, telegram of 24 November 1883, Pierpont Morgan Library.

38. Spielmann and Layard, *Kate Greenaway*, pp. 90–91.

39. Letter of 2 December 1883, Pierpont Morgan Library.

40. Letter of 10 December 1883, Pierpont Morgan Library.

41. Letters of 12, 24 December 1883, Pierpont Morgan Library.

42. Letter of 26 December 1883, Pierpont Morgan Library.
43. Spielmann and Layard, *Kate Greenaway*, p. 121.
44. Letter of 7 January 1884, Pierpont Morgan Library.
45. Letter of 11 January 1884, Pierpont Morgan Library.
46. Letter of 18 January 1884, Pierpont Morgan Library.
47. Letters of 20, 23 January 1884, Pierpont Morgan Library.
48. Letter of 23 January 1884, Pierpont Morgan Library.
49. Letter of 8 February 1884, Pierpont Morgan Library.
50. Letter of 26 February 1884, Pierpont Morgan Library.
51. Letters of 5, 8 March 1884, Pierpont Morgan Library.
52. Letter of 18 March 1884, Pierpont Morgan Library.
53. Leslie Linder (ed.), *Journal of Beatrix Potter* (London, 1966), p. 70.
54. Letter of 15 March 1884, Pierpont Morgan Library.
55. Ralph Nevill, *The Reminiscences of Lady Dorothy Nevill* (London, 1906), p. 247.
56. Letter to the author, 15 January 1972.
57. Unpublished verse, De Grummond Collection.
58. Letter of 25 March 1884, Pierpont Morgan Library.
59. Letter of 31 March 1884, Pierpont Morgan Library.
60. Letter of 17 April 1884, Pierpont Morgan Library.
61. Letter of 20 April 1884, Pierpont Morgan Library.
62. Letters of 25, 29 April 1884, Pierpont Morgan Library.
63. Letter of 14 May 1884, Pierpont Morgan Library.
64. Letters of 16, 18 May 1884, Pierpont Morgan Library.
65. Letter of 22 May 1884, Pierpont Morgan Library.
66. Nevill, *Reminiscences*, p. 246.
67. Letter of 4 June 1884, Pierpont Morgan Library.
68. Letter of 5 June 1884, Pierpont Morgan Library.
69. Letter of 6 June 1884, Pierpont Morgan Library.
70. Undated letter, Berg Collection.
71. Letter of 27 June 1884, Pierpont Morgan Library.
72. Letter of 1 July 1884, Pierpont Morgan Library.
73. Letters of 6, 16, 28 August 1884, Pierpont Morgan Library.
74. Letters of 2, 9 September 1884, Pierpont Morgan Library.
75. Letter of 12 September 1884, Pierpont Morgan Library.
76. Letters of 8, 9 October 1884, Pierpont Morgan Library.
77. Spielmann and Layard, *Kate Greenaway*, p. 128.
78. Letters of 1, 21 December 1884, Pierpont Morgan Library.
79. Spielmann and Layard, *Kate Greenaway*, p. 141.
80. Letter of 31 December 1884, Pierpont Morgan Library.

CHAPTER 6

1. Letter of 4 January 1885, Pierpont Morgan Library.
2. Letter of 6 January 1885, Pierpont Morgan Library.
3. Letter of 7 January 1885, Pierpont Morgan Library.
4. Letter of 15 January 1885, Pierpont Morgan Library.
5. Letter of 16 January 1885, Pierpont Morgan Library.
6. Letter of 19 January 1885, Pierpont Morgan Library.
7. Letter of 20 January 1885, Pierpont Morgan Library.
8. Letter of 29 January 1885, Pierpont Morgan Library.
9. Letter of 6 February 1885, Pierpont Morgan Library.
10. Letter of 8 February 1885, Pierpont Morgan Library.
11. Letter of 15 February 1885, Pierpont Morgan Library.
12. Letter of 29 April 1885, Detroit Public Library.
13. Letter of 29 April 1885, Detroit Public Library.
14. *Hampstead Annual*, 1906–7, p. 101.
15. Spielmann and Layard, *Kate Greenaway*, p. 144.
16. Letter of 8 March 1885, Pierpont Morgan Library.
17. Letter of 17 March 1885, Pierpont Morgan Library.
18. Letter of 25 March 1885, Pierpont Morgan Library.
19. Letter of 27 March 1885, Pierpont Morgan Library.
20. Letter of 1 April 1885, Pierpont Morgan Library.

21. Undated letter (April 1885), Detroit Public Library.
22. Letter of 11 April 1885, Pierpont Morgan Library.
23. Letter of 14 April 1885, Pierpont Morgan Library.
24. Joan Evans and John Whitehouse (eds.) *The Diaries of John Ruskin* (Oxford, 1959), vol. III, pp. 1105–7.
25. Letter of 26 April 1885, Pierpont Morgan Library.
26. Telegram of 30 April 1885, Pierpont Morgan Library; Spielmann and Layard, *Kate Greenaway*, p. 147.
27. Letters of 4, 11 May 1885, Pierpont Morgan Library.
28. Letter of 13 May 1885, Pierpont Morgan Library.
29. Letter of 26 May 1885, Pierpont Morgan Library. Spielmann and Layard, *Kate Greenaway*, pp. 150–1.
30. Telegram of 27 May 1885, Pierpont Morgan Library. Diary entry of 29 May 1885, Evans and Whitehouse, *Ruskin Diaries*, p. 1111.
31. Letter of 13 June 1885, Pierpont Morgan Library.
32. Letter of 21 June 1885, Pierpont Morgan Library.
33. Letter of 22 June 1885, Pierpont Morgan Library.
34. Letters of 3, 5, 6 July 1885, Pierpont Morgan Library.
35. Letter of 8 July 1885, Pierpont Morgan Library.
36. Letter of autumn 1885, Pittsburgh.
37. Letter of 2 December 1885, Pittsburgh; Spence, *Dearest Mamma Talbot*, p. 137.
38. Letter of 1 January 1886, Pierpont Morgan Library; letter of 2 January 1886, Pittsburgh.
39. Letter of 3 January 1886, Pierpont Morgan Library; letter of 8 January 1886, Pittsburgh.
40. Letters of 22, 27 January 1886, Pierpont Morgan Library.
41. Letter of 10 February 1886, Pierpont Morgan Library.
42. Letters of 12, 15 February 1886, Pierpont Morgan Library.
43. Spielmann and Layard, *Kate Greenaway*, p. 70.
44. *Praeterita*, vol. I, p. 430.
45. Letters of 21, 23 February 1886, Pierpont Morgan Library.
46. *Praeterita*, vol. I, p. 422.
47. Letter of 19 March 1886, Pierpont Morgan Library.
48. Letter of 30 March 1886, Pierpont Morgan Library.
49. Letter of 6 April 1886, Pierpont Morgan Library.
50. Letter of 15 April 1886, Pierpont Morgan Library.
51. Letter of 18 April 1886, Pierpont Morgan Library.
52. Letter of 20 April 1886, Pierpont Morgan Library.
53. Letter of 27 April 1886, Pierpont Morgan Library.
54. Spielmann and Layard, *Kate Greenaway*, p. 206.
55. Letter of 14 June 1886, Pierpont Morgan Library.
56. Letter of 7 May 1886, Pierpont Morgan Library.
57. Letter of 1 June 1886, Pierpont Morgan Library.
58. Letter of 27 May 1886, Pierpont Morgan Library.
59. Letter of 8 June 1886, Pierpont Morgan Library.
60. Letter of 14 June 1886, Pierpont Morgan Library.
61. Letter of 20 June 1886, Pierpont Morgan Library.
62. Letters of 2, 3 July 1886, Pierpont Morgan Library.
63. Letter of 28 June 1886, Pittsburgh.
64. Letter of 24 August 1886, Pierpont Morgan Library.
65. See for example, letters of 27 August and 7 September 1886, Pierpont Morgan Library.
66. Letters of 20, 21 September 1886, Pierpont Morgan Library.
67. Spielmann and Layard, *Kate Greenaway*, p. 156.
68. Letter of 12 November 1886, Pierpont Morgan Library.
69. Letter of 14 November 1886, Pierpont Morgan Library.
70. Letter of 28 November 1886, Pierpont Morgan Library.
71. Letter of 14 December 1886, Pierpont Morgan Library.
72. Letter of 27 December 1886, Pierpont Morgan Library.

CHAPTER 7

1. Letters of 2, 3 January 1887, Pierpont Morgan Library.
2. Letter of 4 January 1887, Pierpont Morgan Library.
3. Telegram of 1 February 1887, Pierpont Morgan Library.

4. Letter of 27 February 1887, Pierpont Morgan Library.
5. Letter *c.* 1885 from Robert Browning, Berg Collection.
6. Letter of 5 March 1887, Pierpont Morgan Library.
7. See letter of 8 March 1887, Pierpont Morgan Library.
8. Spielmann and Layard, *Kate Greenaway*, pp. 168–9.
9. Letter of 5 April 1887, Pierpont Morgan Library.
10. Letter of 6 April 1887, Pierpont Morgan Library.
11. Letter of 12 April 1887, Pierpont Morgan Library.
12. See letter of 13 April 1887, Pierpont Morgan Library.
13. Viljoen, *Brantwood Diary*, pp. 450–1.
14. Telegram of 16 April, letter of 21 April 1887, Pierpont Morgan Library.
15. Letters of 22 April and 5 May 1887, Pierpont Morgan Library.
16. McLean, *Edmund Evans*, p. 63.
17. Letter of 23 June 1887, Pierpont Morgan Library.
18. Letter of 25 June 1887, Pierpont Morgan Library.
19. Letter of 5 July 1887, Pittsburgh; Spielmann and Layard, *Kate Greenaway*, p. 165.
20. Letters of 5, 8, 14 January 1888, Pierpont Morgan Library.
21. Letter of 15 January 1888, Pierpont Morgan Library.
22. Letter of 16 January 1888, Pierpont Morgan Library.
23. Letter of 22 January 1888, Pierpont Morgan Library.
24. Letter of 27 January 1888, Pierpont Morgan Library.
25. Letter of 18 February 1888, Private Collection.
26. Letter of 23 February 1888, Pierpont Morgan Library.
27. Letter of 24 February 1888, Private Collection.
28. Letter of 28 February 1888, Pierpont Morgan Library.
29. Letter of 7 March 1888, John Rylands Library, Manchester.
30. Letter dated March 1888, John Rylands Library.
31. Letter of 10 March 1888, Pierpont Morgan Library.
32. See letter of 8 November 1887, Free Library of Philadelphia.

33. Spielmann and Layard, *Kate Greenaway*, p. 173.
34. Spielmann and Layard, *Kate Greenaway*, pp. 160–1.
35. William Allingham's *Diary* (London, 1907), pp. 352–3.
36. Spielmann and Layard, *Kate Greenaway*, p. 172.
37. Letter of 24 November 1888, Private Collection.
38. Spielmann and Layard, *Kate Greenaway*, p. 166.
39. Letter of 1 May 1889, Pierpont Morgan Library.
40. Letter of 12 May 1889, Pierpont Morgan Library.
41. Spielmann and Layard, *Kate Greenaway*, p. 173.
42. Letter of 15 November 1889, Ruskin Galleries, Bembridge, Isle of Wight.
43. Letter of 20 November 1889, Ruskin Galleries.
44. Letter of 20 November 1889, Ruskin Galleries; letter of 28 November 1889, Berg Collection.

CHAPTER 8

1. Letter of 8 January 1890, Ruskin Galleries.
2. Letter of 14 January 1890, Ruskin Galleries; letter of 17 March 1890, Pittsburgh.
3. Letter of 16 January 1890, Ruskin Galleries.
4. Spielmann and Layard, *Kate Greenaway*, p. 258.
5. Letter of 22 January 1890, Ruskin Galleries.
6. Letter of 27 January 1890, Ruskin Galleries.
7. Letter of 1 February 1890, Ruskin Galleries.
8. See letter of 7 March 1890, Ruskin Galleries.
9. Spielmann and Layard, *Kate Greenaway*, p. 173.
10. Spielmann and Layard, *Kate Greenaway*, pp. 173–4.
11. Letter of 2 January 1891, De Grummond Collection.
12. Lionel Robinson, catalogue of Fine Art Society exhibition, 1891.
13. M.H. Spielmann and Walter Jerrold, *Hugh Thomson* (London, 1931), pp. 65–6.
14. Letter of 29 November 1891, Private Collection.
15. Letter of 21 August 1892, Ruskin Galleries.
16. Letter of 12 September 1892, Ruskin Galleries.
17. Spielmann and Layard, *Kate Greenaway*, p. 92.
18. Letter of 7 November 1892, Ruskin Galleries.
19. Letters of 23, 31 December 1892, Ruskin Galleries.
20. Letter of 25 January 1893, Ruskin Galleries.
21. Letter of 2 February 1893, Ruskin Galleries.
22. Letter of 7 February 1893, Ruskin Galleries.
23. Letter of 19 March 1893, Ruskin Galleries.
24. Letter of 9 April 1893, Ruskin Galleries.
25. Spielmann and Layard, *Kate Greenaway*, pp. 182–3.

26. Letters of 10, 13 February 1894, Boston Public Library.
27. Letter of 16 March 1894, De Grummond Collection; letter of 31 January 1894, Pittsburgh.
28. Edward Bok, *An Autobiography* (London, 1921), p. 200.
29. Spielmann and Layard, *Kate Greenaway*, pp. 186–7; letter of 7 August 1894, Pittsburgh.
30. Letter of 8 September 1894, Pierpont Morgan Library.
31. Letters of 16, 21 October 1894, Detroit Public Library.
32. Letter of 28 November 1894, Free Library of Philadelphia.
33. Spielmann and Layard, *Kate Greenaway*, p. 196.
34. Spielmann and Layard, *Kate Greenaway*, p. 197; letter of 2 November 1897, Pittsburgh.
35. Spielmann and Layard, *Kate Greenaway*, p. 198; letter of 31 October 1897, Pittsburgh.
36. Spielmann and Layard, *Kate Greenaway*, pp. 197–8.
37. Spielmann and Layard, *Kate Greenaway*, pp. 198–9.
38. Letter of 8 December 1895, Free Library of Philadelphia.
39. De Grummond Collection.

CHAPTER 9

1. Spielmann and Layard, *Kate Greenaway*, p. 203.
2. Letter of 1 February 1896, Ruskin Galleries.
3. Spielmann and Layard, *Kate Greenaway*, p. 205.
4. See Mathilde Blind (ed.) *The Journal of Marie Bashkirtseff* (London 1890); Spielmann and Layard, *Kate Greenaway*, p. 188; letter of Christmas 1894, Pittsburgh.
5. Spielmann and Layard, *Kate Greenaway*, p. 189; letter of 1 December 1896, Pittsburgh.
6. Spielmann and Layard, *Kate Greenaway*, p. 208.
7. Letter of 21 September 1896, Pittsburgh; W.T. Spence, *Forty Years in my Bookshop* (London 1923), p. 17.
8. Ralph Nevill (ed.), *Life and Letters of Lady Dorothy Nevill* (London, 1919), p. 204.
9. Spielmann and Layard, *Kate Greenaway*, p. 213.
10. Spielmann and Layard, *Kate Greenaway*, p. 253.
11. De Grummond Collection.
12. Spielmann and Layard, *Kate Greenaway*, p. 213.
13. Spielmann and Layard, *Kate Greenaway*, p. 214.
14. *Athenaeum*, 20 March 1897, p. 384.
15. Letter of 6 March 1897, Victoria and Albert Museum.
16. Spielmann and Layard, *Kate Greenaway*, p. 212.
17. Lady St Helier, *Lesser Questions* (London, 1894), pp. 9–10.
18. Spielmann and Layard, *Kate Greenaway*, pp. 211–12; letter of 11 May 1896, Pittsburgh.
19. *Athenaeum*, 1 May 1897, p. 581.
20. Spielmann and Layard, *Kate Greenaway*, pp. 219–20; letter of 4 October 1896, Pittsburgh.
21. Spielmann and Layard, *Kate Greenaway*, pp. 228–9.
22. Spielmann and Layard, *Kate Greenaway*, p. 229.
23. Spielmann and Layard, *Kate Greenaway*, p. 226.
24. Spielmann and Layard, *Kate Greenaway*, pp. 234–5.
25. Spielmann and Layard, *Kate Greenaway*, p. 166.
26. Spielmann and Layard, *Kate Greenaway*, pp. 239–40.
27. Spielmann and Layard, *Kate Greenaway*, pp. 240–1.
28. Spielmann and Layard, *Kate Greenaway*, p. 242.
29. Spielmann and Layard, *Kate Greenaway*, p. 245.
30. Greenaway papers, Private collection.
31. Spielmann and Layard, *Kate Greenaway*, p. 248.
32. Viljoen, *Brantwood Diary*, pp. 452–4.
33. Spielmann and Layard, *Kate Greenaway*, p. 240.
34. De Grummond Collection.
35. De Grummond Collection.
36. Spielmann and Layard, *Kate Greenaway*, p.x.
37. Letter of 24 June 1900, Boston Public Library.
38. Entry dated 15 August–2 September 1900, Private collection; Spielmann and Layard, *Kate Greenaway*, p. 254.
39. Letter of 1 November 1900, Boston Public Library.
40. Nevill, *Life and Letters*, p. 205.
41. Spielmann and Layard, *Kate Greenaway*, p. 250.
42. Spielmann and Layard, *Kate Greenaway*, p. 251.
43. Spielmann and Layard, *Kate Greenaway*, p. 174.
44. Letter of 6 June 1901, Detroit Public Library.
45. Spielmann and Layard, *Kate Greenaway*, p. 252.
46. Letter of 25 October 1901, Pierpont Morgan Library.
47. Death certificate; I am grateful for medical advice supplied by Dr Jerry Wood and Dr W. Coltart.
48. *Hampstead and Highgate Express*, 16 November 1901.

EPILOGUE

1. Letter of 8 May 1902, Ruskin Galleries.
2. Letter of 24 July 1902, Houghton Library, Harvard.
3. See Alison Adburgham, *Liberty's* (London, 1975).

4. See Routledge Papers, British Library.
5. See M. Heseltine, P. Wilson and A. MacDonald (editors), *Art at Auction* (London, 1970–1).

6. H.M. Cundall, Introduction to *Kate Greenaway Pictures* (London, 1921), p. 11.
7. Leslie Linder, *A History of the Writings of Beatrix Potter* (London, 1971), p. 254.

Appendix

ILLUSTRATED BOOKS

This list of books illustrated wholly or in part by Kate Greenaway was compiled from the following sources, which appear in abbreviated form after the dates, to indicate obvious discrepancies in publication dates; brackets indicate approximations.

(BM)   British Museum
(NU)   National Union Catalogue
(VA)   Victoria and Albert Museum
(S)   Sotheby's sale catalogues
(D)   Detroit Public Library catalogue (Detroit, 1977)
(H)   Brian Holme, *The Kate Greenaway Book* (London, 1976)
(BR)   Book reviews announcing publication in contemporary periodicals
(A)   Contemporary advertisements
(E)   Rodney Engen, *Kate Greenaway* (London, 1976)
(EE)   Ruari McLean, *The Reminiscences of Edmund Evans* (London, 1967)

1867 (E)
INFANT AMUSEMENTS, OR HOW TO MAKE A NURSERY HAPPY by William Henry Giles Kingston, with a frontispiece in black and white by Kate Greenaway. London: Griffith and Farran.

1870 (H) 1871 (S)
AUNT LOUISA'S NURSERY FAVOURITE: DIAMONDS AND TOADS from a series of London Toybooks, with six unsigned colour lithographs after watercolour drawings by Kate Greenaway, printed by Kronheim. London: Frederick Warne and Company.

1870 (H) 1871 (BM) (BR)
MY SCHOOL DAYS IN PARIS by Margaret S. Jeune, with illustrations by Kate Greenaway. London: Griffith and Farran. (New edition, 1881.)

1870 (BR)
[1871] (H)
MADAME D'AULNOY'S FAIRY TALES: (1) THE FAIR ONE WITH GOLDEN LOCKS; (2) THE BABES IN THE WOOD; (3) TOM THUMB; (4) BLUEBEARD; (5) PUSS IN BOOTS; (6) THE BLUE BIRD; (7) THE WHITE CAT; (8) HOP O' MY THUMB; (9) RED RIDING HOOD, each story issued separately and illustrated from watercolour drawings by Kate Greenaway. Edinburgh: Gall and Inglis.

1872 (VA)
A CHILD'S INFLUENCE, or KATHLEEN AND HER GREAT UNCLE by Lisa Lockyer, with three full-page black and white plates by Kate Greenaway, engraved by John Greenaway. London: Griffith and Farran.

1873 (BR)
1874 (BM)
THE CHILDREN OF THE PARSONAGE by Aunt Cae (H.C. Selous), with four full-page illustrations by Kate Greenaway, engraved by John Greenaway. London: Griffith and Farran. (Second edition, 1875.)

1874 (H)
1875 (BM)
FAIRY GIFTS, OR A WALLET OF WONDERS by Kathleen Knox, with four full-page illustrations and seven small woodcuts by Kate Greenaway, engraved by John Greenaway. London: Griffith and Farran; New York: E.P. Dutton and Company. (Reissued, 1,000 copies in 1880; 5,000 copies in 1882.)

[1875] (H)
THE FAIRY SPINNER by Miranda Hill, with four black and white illustrations, colour title page and frontispiece by Kate Greenaway. London: Marcus Ward and Company. (New editions, *c.* 1880 (S), also 1885.)

[1875] (H)
A CRUISE IN THE ACORN by Alice Jerrold, with six mounted colour lithograph illustrations in colours and gold by Kate Greenaway; also issued as greeting cards. London: Marcus Ward and Company.

[1875] (H)
TURNASIDE COTTAGE by Mary Senior Clark, with coloured frontispiece, title page and four full-page black and white illustrations by Kate Greenaway. London: Marcus Ward and Company.

[1875] (H)
CHILDREN'S SONGS with pictures and music, plates in colour and sepia by Kate Greenaway. London: Marcus Ward and Company.

1875 (BR)
MELCOMB MANOR: A FAMILY CHRONICLE by Frederick Scarlett Potter, with six full-page colour lithograph illustrations in colour and gold by Kate Greenaway; first issued as greeting cards. London: Marcus Ward and Company.

1875 (H)
PUCK AND BLOSSOM, A FAIRY TALE by Rosa Mulholland, with six mounted colour lithograph illustrations by Kate Greenaway; also issued as greeting cards. London: Marcus Ward and Company.

[1875] (D)
A CALENDAR OF THE SEASONS FOR 1876, the first of a series of calendars (cf. 1876, 1880, 1881 entries), consisting of two cardboard sheets, folded in a booklet of eight pages with four coloured illustrations of the seasons, differing for each year, followed by text, information on holidays, postage, etc. Illustrations by Kate Greenaway. London: Marcus Ward and Company.

1875 (BR) 1876 (BM)
SEVEN BIRTHDAYS OR THE CHILDREN OF FORTUNE, A FAIRY CHRONICLE by Kathleen Knox, with illustrations by Kate Greenaway. London: Griffith and Farran.

[1876] (D)
A CALENDAR OF THE SEASONS FOR 1877 with four illustrations by Kate Greenaway in colours and gold. London: Marcus Ward and Company. (The illustrations were later used in Flowers and Fancies, 1883.) (cf. 1875 entry.)

1876 (BM)
THE QUIVER OF LOVE: A COLLECTION OF VALENTINES ANCIENT AND MODERN edited by Rev. W.J. Loftie, with plates by Walter Crane and four full-page colour lithograph illustrations in colour and gold by Kate Greenaway. Also issued as 4 greeting cards. A revised edition in 1880 contained different plates. London: Marcus Ward and Company. (An additional revised edition, Flowers and Fancies, was issued in 1883.) (cf. 1883 entry.)

1876 (S) 1877 (H)
TOM SEVEN YEARS OLD by H. Rutherford Russell, with four full-page black and white illustrations by Kate Greenaway. London: Marcus Ward and Company.

1876 (BR) 1877 (BM)
STARLIGHT STORIES TOLD TO BRIGHT EYES AND LISTENING EARS by Fanny Lablache, with four full-page black and white illustrations by Kate Greenaway, engraved by John Greenaway. London: Griffith and Farran.

1877 (EE) 1878 (VA) [1878] (S) [1879] (BM) 1879 (BR)
UNDER THE WINDOW with coloured pictures and rhymes for children by Kate Greenaway, engraved and printed by Edmund Evans. London: George Routledge; New York: McLoughlin Bros. (undated pirated American edition). (Reissued, London, New York: Frederick Warne, 1900.)

AM FENSTER In Bildern und Versen von Kate Greenaway, der Deutsche text von Käthe Freiligrath-Kröker. München: Theodor Ströfer (1880 German edition).

LA LANTERNE MAGIQUE par J. Levoisin avec les dessins de Kate Greenaway. Paris: Librairie Hachette et Cie (undated French edition). Both the German and the French editions were engraved and printed by Edmund Evans. (First edition dark green border, lighter green background, reversed in subsequent editions.)

1878 (E)
POOR NELLY by Mrs Bonavia Hunt, with numerous illustrations by Kate Greenaway. London: Cassell, Petter, Galpin (from the story serialized in Little Folks, 1877).

1878 (BM)
TOPO: A TALE ABOUT ENGLISH CHILDREN IN ITALY

by G.E. Brunefille (Lady Colin Campbell), with 44 black and white illustrations by Kate Greenaway. London: Marcus Ward and Company. (Second edition, 1880.)

1879 (BM)
HEARTSEASE, OR THE BROTHER'S WIFE by Charlotte M. Yonge, with three full-page black and white illustrations by Kate Greenaway, engraved by Swain. London: Macmillan and Company. (Several other editions until 1901.)

1879 (BM)
THE HEIR OF REDCLYFFE by Charlotte M. Yonge, with four full-page black and white illustrations by Kate Greenaway, engraved by Swain. London: Macmillan and Company. (Several other editions until 1901.)

1879 (E)
AMATEUR THEATRICALS by Walter Herries Pollock, with three illustrations by Kate Greenaway. London: Macmillan and Company. (From Rev. W. Loftie's 'Art at Home' series.)

1879 (E)
TROT'S JOURNEY pictures, rhymes and stories, with over sixty woodcut illustrations by Kate Greenaway. New York: R. Worthington. (Originally published in *Little Folks*, January 1879.)

c. 1879 (E)
TOYLAND, TROT'S JOURNEY, AND OTHER POEMS AND STORIES with illustrations by Kate Greenaway. New York: R. Worthington.

1879 (E) [1879] (BM)
THE LITTLE FOLKS PAINTING BOOK with a series of 107 outline engravings for watercolour painting by Kate Greenaway, with verses and stories by George Weatherly. London, Paris and New York: Cassell, Petter, Galpin.

[1879] (D)
WOODLAND ROMANCES; OR FABLES AND FANCIES by C.L. Mateaux, with Greenaway illustrations for 'The Buried Seeds' (pp. 18–19), duplicated in *The Little Folks Painting Book*, 1879.

[1879] (E)
THE LITTLE FOLKS NATURE PAINTING BOOK with the headpiece and a few figures by Kate Greenaway, stories and verses by George Weatherly. London, Paris and New York: Cassell, Petter, Galpin.

[1879] (E)
A FAVOURITE ALBUM OF FUN AND FANCY with four illustrations by Kate Greenaway to the allegory 'Kribs and the Wonderful Bird'. London, Paris and New York: Cassell, Petter, Galpin.

[1879] (E) 1879 (D)
THREE BROWN BOYS AND OTHER HAPPY CHILDREN by Ellen Haile, with illustrations by Kate Greenaway and others. London, Paris and New York: Cassell, Petter, Galpin.

1880 (H) (D)
THE TWO GRAY GIRLS AND THEIR OPPOSITE NEIGHBOURS by Ellen Haile, with black and white illustrations by Kate Greenaway, M.E. Edwards and others. London, Paris and New York: Cassell, Petter, Galpin.

1880 (EE) [1880] (BM)
KATE GREENAWAY'S BIRTHDAY BOOK FOR CHILDREN with 382 illustrations, 12 plates in colour, printed by Edmund Evans. London: George Routledge. (Reissued, London, New York: Frederick Warne, 1900.)

LE PETIT LIVRE DES SOUVENIRS. Paris: Librairie Hachette (French edition, 1882).

KATE GREENAWAY'S GEBURTSTAGBUCH FÜR KINDER mit 382 illustrations gezeichnet von Kate Greenaway. München: Theodor Ströfer (undated German edition).

[1880] (D)
THE LITTLE FOLK'S OUT AND ABOUT BOOK by Chatty Cheerful (William Martin). Illustrations signed 'KG', pp. 39, 87, unsigned p. 50. London, Paris and New York: Cassell and Company.

[1880] (S)
SONGS FOR THE NURSERY edited by Robert Ellice, with black and white illustrations by Kate Greenaway and others. London: W. Mack; New York: E.P. Dutton.

[1880] (E)
THE OLD FARM GATE, Stories in Prose and Verse for Little People with 25 full-page illustrations by Kate Greenaway, M.E. Edwards and Miriam Kerns. London: George Routledge.

[1880] (S)
THE ILLUSTRATED CHILDREN'S BIRTHDAY BOOK written in part and edited by F.E. Weatherly,

with 12 colour plates by Kate Greenaway and others. London: W. Mack. (Also undated edition, London: Ernest Nister (S).)

[1880] (D)
A CALENDAR OF THE SEASONS FOR 1881 with four illustrations by Kate Greenaway. London: Marcus Ward and Company. (cf. 1875 entry.)

1880 (E)
FREDDIE'S LETTER: STORIES FOR LITTLE PEOPLE with a frontispiece by Kate Greenaway and designs by others. London: George Routledge.

1881 (S)
ROUTLEDGE'S CATALOGUE OF NEW CHRISTMAS BOOKS with six colour illustrations by Kate Greenaway and others. London: George Routledge.

1881 (E)
THE LIBRARY by Andrew Lang, with a chapter on English illustrated books by Austin Dobson, including illustrations by Kate Greenaway. London: Macmillan and Company.

1881 (BM)
LONDON LYRICS poems by Frederick Locker (new edition), frontispiece by Randolph Caldecott, tailpiece 'Little Dinky' by Kate Greenaway. London: Chiswick Press; New York: White, Stokes and Allen. (1886 edition with Locker's book-plate in red in the title page.)

1881 (EE)
A DAY IN A CHILD'S LIFE with music by Myles B. Foster and colour illustrations by Kate Greenaway. London: George Routledge. (Reissued, London, New York: Frederick Warne, 1900.) (1887 edition with variant binding two children on log, surrounded by a rose wreath.)

1881 (EE) [1881] (BM)
MOTHER GOOSE OR THE OLD NURSERY RHYMES with illustrations by Kate Greenaway. London: George Routledge.

SCENES FAMILIERES avec les dessins en couleur de Kate Greenaway. Paris: Librairie Hachette (undated French edition).

[1881] (S)
A CALENDAR OF THE SEASONS FOR 1882 with four colour illustrations by Kate Greenaway. London: Marcus Ward and Company. (cf. 1875 entry.)

[1882] (NU)
ART HOURS Painting Book No. 1 with 12 plates after Kate Greenaway. New York: McLoughlin Bros.

[1882] (NU)
STEPS TO ART Painting Book No. 2 with 12 plates after Kate Greenaway. New York: McLoughlin Bros.

[1882] (BM)
HAPPY LITTLE PEOPLE by Olive Patch, with three illustrations by Kate Greenaway and others. New York: Cassell and Company.

1882 (S) 1883 (EE) [1883] (BM)
LITTLE ANN AND OTHER POEMS by Jane and Ann Taylor, illustrated by Kate Greenaway. London: George Routledge. (Reissued, London, New York: Frederick Warne, 1900.)

POEMES ENFANTINS PAR JANE ET ANN TAYLOR traduction libre de J. Girardin. Paris: Librairie Hachette (1883 French edition).

THE PROUD GIRL and other pictures and rhymes for children after Kate Greenaway (presumably adapted from *Little Ann*). New York: McLoughlin Bros. (undated (NU)).

[1882] (BM)
ALMANACK FOR 1883 illustrated by Kate Greenaway. London: George Routledge. (Republished with new text as *Almanack for 1924*, London, New York: Frederick Warne.) (Undated French edition, Paris: Librairie Hachette.)

1883 (E)
KATE GREENAWAY'S CALENDAR FOR 1884 with coloured illustrations on four separate cards. London: George Routledge.

1883 (BM) 1882 (D)
FLOWERS AND FANCIES, VALENTINES ANCIENT AND MODERN by B. M. Montgomerie Ranking and Thomas K. Tully, with four full-page colour illustrations by Kate Greenaway, adapted from the *Calendar of the Seasons for 1876*. London: Marcus Ward and Company.

1883 (S)
JINGLES AND JOYS FOR WEE GIRLS AND BOYS by Mary D. Brine, with 18 illustrations by Kate Greenaway and others. New York: Cassell and Company.

[1883] (BM) 1882 (D)
TALES FROM THE EDDA by Helen Zimmern, with
two full-page illustrations by Kate Greenaway
and others. London: W. Swan Sonnenschein and
Company (her name incorrectly placed on the
third illustration, page 127).

[1883] (BM)
ALMANACK FOR 1884 illustrated by Kate
Greenaway. London: George Routledge (two
editions: one with printed card cover; the
second with gold embossed figure, title on white
card cover). (Undated French edition, Paris:
Librairie Hachette.)

1883–4 (E)
FORS CLAVIGERA by John Ruskin: Letters to the
Workmen and Labourers of Great Britain: Letter
the 91st, September 1883 (one illustration);
Letter the 93rd, Christmas 1883 (one
illustration); Letter the 94th, 31st December
1883 (headpiece and tailpiece); Letter the 95th,
October, 1884 (headpiece); Letter the 96th,
Christmas 1884 (full-page frontispiece). London
and Orpington: George Allen.

[1884] (E)
KATE GREENAWAY'S CAROLS issued as four
pictorial cards with coloured figures, borders
and music. London: George Routledge. (Also
edition with greeting in French.)

1884 (VA)
[1884] (BM)
A PAINTING BOOK by Kate Greenaway, with
outline engravings from her various works.
London: George Routledge. (Reissued as *Kate
Greenaway's Painting Book*, London, New York:
Frederick Warne, 1900.)

MALBUCH FÜR DAS KLEINE VOLK ÜBERSETZT VON
FANNY STOCKHAUSEN. München: Theodor Ströfer
(undated German edition).

1884 (EE) [1884] (BM)
THE LANGUAGE OF FLOWERS illustrated by Kate
Greenaway. London: George Routledge.
(Reissued, London and New York: Frederick
Warne, 1900.)

LE LANGAGE DES FLEURS. Paris: Librairie Hachette,
c. 1884. (French edition with new selection of
French poems on flowers and plants instead of
the original English poems.)

[1884] (BM)
ALMANACK FOR 1885 illustrated by Kate
Greenaway. London: George Routledge.
(Undated French edition, Paris: Librairie
Hachette.)

[1884] (S)
A SUMMER AT AUNT HELEN'S with 13 illustrations
by Kate Greenaway and others, frontispiece and
three small early Greenaway wood engravings
(dating from 1870s); story bound with TOMMY
DODD, illustrated by 21 black and white wood
engravings, four possibly by Kate Greenaway,
the remaining 17 by T. Pym (Clara Creed) in the
Greenaway manner. New York: Dodd, Mead,
and Company.

[1884] (S)
BABY'S BIRTHDAY BOOK with coloured
frontispiece, numerous coloured illustrations
from cards and early books by Kate Greenaway,
with others by colleagues. London: Marcus
Ward and Company.

1884 (BR) (S) 1885 (BM) (D)
THE ENGLISH SPELLING BOOK by William Mavor,
illustrated by Kate Greenaway. London: George
Routledge. (Reissued, London, New York:
Frederick Warne, 1902.)

1885 (BM)
DAME WIGGINS OF LEE AND HER SEVEN
WONDERFUL CATS by a lady of ninety, with four
additional verses by John Ruskin and four new
illustrations by Kate Greenaway. London and
Orpington: George Allen. Also rare larger
(quarto) edition, 1885 (S). (Sixth edition, 1913.)

1885 (EE)
MARIGOLD GARDEN with pictures and rhymes by
Kate Greenaway. London: George Routledge.
(Reissued, London, New York: Frederick Warne,
1900.)

1885 (E)
KATE GREENAWAY'S ALBUM with 192 coloured
illustrations, with gold borders, printed by
Edmund Evans. London: George Routledge. (One
of the rarest Greenaway books: only eight copies
were printed; the book was never published.)

[1885] (BM)
KATE GREENAWAY'S ALPHABET with each letter a
coloured illustration by Kate Greenaway.
London: George Routledge. (A reissue of the
individual letters in *The English Spelling Book*.)

[1885] (BM)
ALMANACK FOR 1886 illustrated by Kate
Greenaway. London: George Routledge.
(Undated French edition, Paris: Librairie
Hachette.)

1886 (EE) [1886] (BM)
A APPLE PIE with illustrations by Kate
Greenaway, engraved and printed by Edmund
Evans. London: George Routledge. (Reissued,
London, New York: Frederick Warne, 1900.)

[1886] (BM)
THE QUEEN OF THE PIRATE ISLE by Bret Harte,
illustrated by Kate Greenaway, engraved and
printed by Edmund Evans. London: Chatto and
Windus. (Only a few copies were sent for the
American edition, Boston, New York: Houghton
Mifflin and Company, 1887.) (Reissued, London,
New York: Frederick Warne, 1900, 1931, 1955.)
(First edition with gilt edges, subsequent
reprints with yellow edges.)

[1886] (A)
RHYMES FOR THE YOUNG FOLK by William
Allingham with two illustrations by Kate
Greenaway, others by Helen Allingham, Caroline
Paterson (Mrs Sutton Sharpe) and Harry Furniss.
London, Paris, New York, Melbourne: Cassell
and Company. (Later edition ROBIN REDBREAST
AND OTHER VERSES (1941) with Kate's *Bubbles* as
frontispiece, published New York: Macmillan.)

[1886] (BM)
ALMANACK FOR 1887 illustrated by Kate
Greenaway. London: George Routledge.
(Undated French edition, Paris: Librairie
Hachette.) (Reissued with new text as
ALMANACK FOR 1925, London, New York:
Frederick Warne.)

1887 (BM) (D)
QUEEN VICTORIA'S JUBILEE GARLAND with four
full-page gold and colour illustrations by Kate
Greenaway to mark fiftieth anniversary of
Victoria's accession. London: George Routledge.
(A booklet comprising previously published
processional illustrations.)

[1887] (BM)
ALMANACK FOR 1888 illustrated by Kate
Greenaway. London: George Routledge. (Undated
French edition, Paris: Librairie Hachette.)

1888 (D)
ORIENT LINE GUIDE Chapters for Travellers by

Sea and Land rewritten third edition by W.J.
Loftie, with half-title drawing of 14 black and
white outlined children carrying flowers and
fruit by Kate Greenaway. London: Sampson,
Low, Marston, Searle and Rivington. (Revised
fourth edition, also with Greenaway drawing,
1890.)

1888 (E) (D)
AROUND THE HOUSE stories and poems, with
black and white frontispiece, sepia illustrations
by Kate Greenaway taken from *Little Folks*:
'Chatterbox Hall'. New York: Worthington and
Company.

[1888] (BM)
ALMANACK FOR 1889 illustrated by Kate
Greenaway. London: George Routledge. (The
designs were borrowed from the letters of *Kate
Greenaway's Alphabet*, 1885.) (Undated French
edition, Paris: Librairie Hachette.)

[1888] (D) [1889] (BM)
THE PIED PIPER OF HAMELIN by Robert Browning,
with 35 colour illustrations by Kate Greenaway.
London: George Routledge. (Reissued, London,
New York: Frederick Warne, 1903.)

L'HOMME A LA FLUTE interprétation de J.
Girardin, illustrations de Kate Greenaway. Paris:
Librairie Hachette (1889 French edition).

[1889] (BM)
KATE GREENAWAY'S BOOK OF GAMES with 24 full-
page colour illustrations by Kate Greenaway,
engraved and printed by Edmund Evans.
London: George Routledge. (Reissued, London,
New York: Frederick Warne, 1927.)

JEUX ET PASSE-TEMPS avec illustrations d'après
Kate Greenaway. Paris: Librairie Hachette, [1890]
(S) (French edition).

[1889] (BM)
THE ROYAL PROGRESS OF KING PEPITO by Beatrice
F. Cresswell, illustrated by Kate Greenaway,
engraved and printed by Edmund Evans.
London, Brighton: The Society for Promoting
Christian Knowledge. (American edition, New
York: E. and J.B. Young and Company.)

[1889] (BM)
ALMANACK FOR 1890 with illustrations by Kate
Greenaway. London: George Routledge.
(Undated French edition, Paris: Librairie
Hachette.)

[1890] (BM)
KATE GREENAWAY'S ALMANACK 1891 with
illustrations by Kate Greenaway. London:
George Routledge. (This edition marked the new
title wording.) (Undated French edition, Paris:
Librairie Hachette.)

[1891] (BM)
KATE GREENAWAY'S ALMANACK 1892 with
illustrations by Kate Greenaway. London:
George Routledge. (Undated French edition,
Paris: Librairie Hachette.)

[1892] (BM)
KATE GREENAWAY'S ALMANACK 1893 with
illustrations by Kate Greenaway. London:
George Routledge. (Undated French edition,
Paris: Librairie Hachette.)

[1893] (BM)
KATE GREENAWAY'S ALMANACK 1894 with
illustrations by Kate Greenaway from *The
English Spelling Book*, 1885. London: George
Routledge. (Undated French edition, Paris:
Librairie Hachette.)

[1894] (BM)
KATE GREENAWAY'S ALMANACK 1895 with
illustrations by Kate Greenaway. London:
George Routledge. (Reissued with new text as
ALMANACK FOR 1928, London, New York:
Frederick Warne.) (Undated French edition,
Paris: Librairie Hachette.)

1896 (E)
KATE GREENAWAY'S CALENDAR FOR 1897 with
coloured figures of childhood, youth, and old
age. London: George Routledge. (The
illustrations are similar to those of *Kate
Greenaway's Carols, c.* 1884.)

1896 (S)
KATE GREENAWAY'S ALMANACK AND DIARY FOR
1897. London: J.M. Dent and Company.
(Reissued with new text as KATE GREENAWAY'S
ALMANACK AND DIARY FOR 1929, London, New
York: Frederick Warne.)

1898 (E)
KATE GREENAWAY'S CALENDAR FOR 1899. London:
George Routledge.

1900 (BM)
THE APRIL BABY'S BOOK OF TUNES WITH THE
STORY OF HOW THEY CAME TO BE WRITTEN by
Countess von Arnim (M. A. B. Russell),

illustrated with 16 colour lithographed plates
including six full-page by Kate Greenaway.
London: Macmillan and Company. (American
edition, New York: Macmillan, 1900.)

Posthumous publications

1901 (BM)
LONDON AFTERNOONS by W.J. Loftie, with a
drawing by Kate Greenaway from one of the
Cottonian Manuscripts, depicting an effigy of
Abbot John of Berkhampstead, originally drawn
for the Society for the Promotion of Christian
Knowledge, published for the first time,
London: Cassell and Company. (American
edition, New York: Brentanos (1902) (D)).

1903 (BM)
LITTLEDOM CASTLE AND OTHER TALES by Mrs
M.H. Spielmann, illustrated by Arthur Rackham
Hugh Thomson, Harry Furniss, Kate Greenaway
and others. London: George Routledge (with
Kate Greenaway's two drawings to 'Ronald's
Clock').

1908 (BM)
DE LIBRIS Prose and Verse by Austin Dobson,
with illustrations by Kate Greenaway, Hugh
Thomson and others. London: Macmillan and
Company. (Second edition, 1911.)

Index

Kate Greenaway's Family Tree

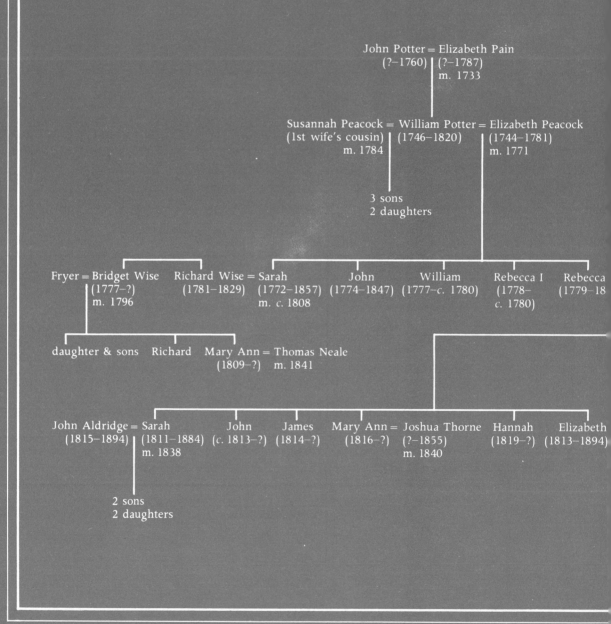

John Potter = Elizabeth Pain
(?–1760) (?–1787)
m. 1733

Susannah Peacock = William Potter = Elizabeth Peacock
(1st wife's cousin) (1746–1820) (1744–1781)
m. 1784 m. 1771

3 sons
2 daughters

Fryer = Bridget Wise   Richard Wise = Sarah   John   William   Rebecca I   Rebecca
(1777–?)   (1781–1829) (1772–1857) (1774–1847) (1777–c. 1780) (1778–   (1779–18
m. 1796   m. c. 1808   c. 1780)

daughter & sons   Richard   Mary Ann = Thomas Neale
(1809–?)   m. 1841

John Aldridge = Sarah   John   James   Mary Ann = Joshua Thorne   Hannah   Elizabeth
(1815–1894) (1811–1884) (c. 1813–?) (1814–?) (1816–?) (?–1855)   (1819–?) (1813–1894)
m. 1838   m. 1840

2 sons
2 daughters